The give and take of writing

scribes, literacy and everyday life

Jane Mace

niace
promoting adult learning

Published by the National Institute of Adult Continuing Education
(England and Wales)

21 De Montfort Street
Leicester
LE1 7GE

Company registration no. 2603322
Charity registration no. 1002775

First published 2002

promoting adult learning

NIACE, the National Institute of Continuing Adult Education,
has a broad remit to promote lifelong opportunities for adults.
NIACE works to develop increased participation in education
and training. It aims to do this for those who do not have
easy access because of class, gender, age, race, language
and culture, learning difficulties or disabilities, or
insufficient financial resources.

Cataloguing in Publication Data
A CIP record of this title is available from the British Library

ISBN 1 86201 124 9

Cover design by Brooke Calverley
Designed and typeset by Boldface, London
Printed and bound in Great Britain by Alden Press, Oxford

To Anissa
whose smiling starfish hands
made the proofreading possible

Acknowledgements

The subject of this book has stimulated many conversations that have been immensely enjoyable. Among those to whom I owe particular thanks, both for their own interest and for their help in connecting me with others, are: Jacqui Armour, David Barton, Sue Gardener, Andy Gilroy, Mary Hamilton, Walter Hemingway, Jess Killick, Ruth Lesirge, Monica Lucero, Sally Malin, Jess Mace, Tara McArthur, Sharon Miller, Caroline Nursey, Frances Rock, Kate Tomlinson, Cath de Veuve, Anita Wilson, Berhane Woldegabriel, Mary Wolfe and Meta Zimmeck. South Bank University Library, the Poetry Library, London and the Fawcett Library have all been good places to search and find. More than any previous book I have written, this one has been enriched by the generosity of the internet, which I hope is fully acknowledged in the references. For comments on drafts, thanks to Pat Gauge of City of London Citizens' Advice Bureau, Jess Killick, Juliet Merrifield, Kate Tomlinson and three anonymous editorial readers. To Virman Man of NIACE publications I repeat: there is nothing so motivating to a writer as to be given an ISBN a year before publication. Thank you.

About the author

Jane Mace is a founding member of the Research and Practice in Adult Literacy Network and a trustee of the World University Service (UK). She began teaching in adult literacy in 1971 and was co-founder of the 'Write First Time' collective that published writing by adult literacy students from 1975–85. Now a grandmother, she is the author of a number of books and continues to teach and research in the field of adult literacy studies (currently at South Bank University, London).

Other titles of interest by the same author:

Working with Words: Literacy beyond school (Writers and Readers, 1979)

Talking about Literacy: Principles and practice of adult literacy education (Routledge, 1992)

Playing with Time: Mothers and the meaning of literacy (UCL Press, 1998)

Contents

PART THREE: It takes two to collaborate

Introduction

This book takes a new look at an old story: the story of scribes. Ever since writing began, they have been there. Seen as a professional, the scribe's status has ranged from lowly labourer to learned priest; seen as a role, the scribe is part of a relationship which many of us engage in on an almost daily basis. When I take down a phone message that you want to leave for my colleague, my son, or anyone else, I am acting as a scribe for you. I am writing down a version of your words; we are both involved.

Yet this collaborative way of writing is not the kind usually mentioned in debates about literacy standards or government reports on basic skills. Nor, for that matter, is it always acknowledged in the authorship of literary works. 'Achievement', in the terms understood by the funding structures of education, is about individual achievement. Authorship, more often than not, is constructed as the work of one person. Rewards are given to single people, whether for improvement in their standards of education or for perceived brilliance in the written word. All this behaviour masks what is often the collaboration of one person with another, the inspirations and influences which two or more people can give each other. In published writing, we try to show something of this through the conventions of acknowledgements and bibliography. In all the many other ways that writing occurs in everyday life, it is how things are, so ordinary, that we barely notice it.

The way that 'being literate' is usually understood is this. Individually, on their own, a person can read and write. If they cannot – in those societies that see themselves as literate – they are odd. It takes a highly literate person to question this, as the writer Hans Magnus Enzensberger did at a gathering when he was being awarded a literary prize. 'Is the written word dispensable?' he asked, and went on:

> That is the question. Whoever poses it has to talk about illiteracy. The matter has one small catch however. The illiterate is never present when he [sic] is being discussed. He simply does not turn up, does not take any notice of our assertions, he remains silent.

Those are the words of a writer and a poet, speaking on the occasion of being awarded a prize for his writing. In the speech, he went on to argue against himself, asking 'why a writer of all people wants to take the side of those who cannot read?'. His answer was that 'it was the illiterate who invented literature', that without the great oral traditions of prose and poetry that pre-dated writing by centuries, literature, as we know it, could never have happened.[1]

Extracts from this speech, given in 1985, appeared in a journal that I came upon some 5 years after he had given it. It was not till several years later that I had the opportunity to listen to the voice of the speaker, reading his own poetry,[2] by which time challenges to the 'great divide' theory of literate/illiterate were coming from other quarters.[3] Reading the text of the speech reminded me of the first encounters I had had with people who had made the choice to become 'students' of literacy in the programme for which I worked in the early 1970s. That was a time when the Right to Read campaign was setting up its stall in Britain; a time when journalists were hungry to find interview material for feature articles on the new sensation. For that reason, it was also a time when it seemed important to find literacy learners to talk firsthand about their experiences.[4] Twenty years later, it still seemed necessary to be arguing for more of the 'authentic voices' of literacy learners themselves.[5] Later still, with my colleague Mary Wolfe, I began to consider another angle on the same issue: the way that fiction and fact may mutually reinforce each other and perpetuate a stereotype of 'the illiterate': how the person who writes the newspaper article may (the week before) have been to see a film, and the chair of a government committee may (the previous evening) have been reading a novel. Our search, into both film and fiction, was to collect examples of how a 'deficit model' of someone short of perfect reading and writing skills might be expressing itself. From our first findings, we suggested three groups of images present in what we had found: that of the *prisoner*, the *dumb animal* and the *outsider*.[6]

By way of illustration, Mary's commentary on the American film *Stanley and Iris* is worth summarising here, for in this film (as she sees it) the main character Stanley (played by Robert de Niro) combines all three sets of images: he is trapped, effectively speechless, and excluded.[8] The story is a rags-to-riches romance, with literacy as the key to a happy ending. Stanley and Iris (Jane Fonda) both work in the same factory. When his boss finds out he cannot read and write, Stanley gets the sack. The scene shows Stanley as humiliated and unresisting. In the next scene we see him, mop and bucket in hand, washing the graffiti off the walls of public toilet – the only job he could get. In Iris's kitchen, later, Iris puts him through his phonic paces, and, in a miraculously short time, teaches him to read. Soon after that, Stanley achieves affluence and the film ends with him driving them both off in his car to a new home in the city.[9]

Because of the work we did together I have watched a video of that film several times. Reading the way in which Mary described and analysed detailed moments in it reminded me of how it may take more than one re-reading of what often goes past our conscious minds at speed for us to notice what sinks in at an unconscious level as a set of assumptions. I had seen more than once, for instance, the scene of Stanley cleaning graffiti, and registered that we were supposed to be recognising him as having sunk very low indeed. Yet even after all that reviewing, it was not until Mary pointed this out in her paper that I caught its full metaphoric weight: the image of a man who (we have been told) is unable to read even the lowest level of literature, being shown as only fit to erase it.

To return to Enzensberger. After expressing a certain envy for the 'cunning, ingenuity, tenacity and fine ear' of 'the illiterate', he went on to recognise the progress which the campaigns for state education in Europe had achieved and to restate his passion for literature. Despite all those achievements (or possibly because of them), he concluded that there still remained a problem; namely, that 'behind the figure of the illiterate, the figure of the subhuman is already emerging.'[10] Fortunately, a growing number of studies undertaken in the 1980s and 1990s were beginning to be published to expose this 'problem', some of which had become grouped under the banner of 'The New Literacy Studies'.[11] There is also an unknown number of unpublished research studies undertaken by adult literacy teachers (or practitioners) in the unpublished form of MA theses or project reports. Some of these, in the UK at least, have seen the light of day in the publication of a national network of researcher-practitioners.[12]

Now that (at last) a national Research and Development Centre has been established for this field of work in the UK[13] we may look forward to a shift in popular understandings of what literacy means. Nevertheless it will take time. It takes a while for academic research to become ordinary conversation. It will also take a longer while before stereotypes are finally supplanted by a set of ideas that takes for granted how literacy is always a social matter.

It is from within that set of ideas that the argument of this book has grown, which can be summarised as follows:

- moments of illiteracy are a common experience;
- in many spheres of everyday life all kinds of people turn to others to act as our scribes; and
- scribing is part of a 'give and take' pattern of social behaviour.

Like all simplicities, these assertions compress a wonderfully rich complexity, some glimpse of which I hope the book reveals. Two experiences had led me to want to think about them, both in countries strange to me and both leading me back to look again at how people read and write in my own country, and elsewhere.

In 1998, when I was working with a team of others to evaluate a programme of literacy education with women in North Sudan, I met a street scribe at work outside a courthouse.[14] From the meetings we had already had in the villages, we knew that this man at his table in the street represented only one kind of scribing which went on, alongside the less public work in communities that occurs between people every time there is a letter to be read or written. He, and other such figures, sitting all day long beneath the shade of the trees, were professionals: I knew their job to be one of the oldest in the world and it was the first time I had spoken with one. In interview with my colleagues, the man told of the prices he charged for different kinds of letters, which ranged from requests for Zakat (alms) from the destitute, asking for medicine or food, to complaints to the district attorney (land disputes, grazing rights, alimony). Another such scribe, sitting outside the post office in an adjacent street, said he had been doing this job for 35 years, writing between four and ten letters a day. In his view, 'even university graduates cannot write a proper application to the judiciary'.[15]

Two years later, I was invited to give a workshop to community development workers in Nepal on *language experience* and its potential for community publishing work. Our discussions were intended to help them think how they could extend the way they already produced local newsletters and magazines to include the non-literate people in the villages where they worked. These colleagues were not literacy educators, but community workers, many of them volunteers. Their approach had been that of a journalist: to interview a villager and then write up the interview. The thought that they could read back what they had written and ask the interviewee to check it for them, maybe even amend it; that they might copy it out in legible writing and read it again, more slowly, so that their interviewee might read it out after them; that they might then even encourage the interviewee to try and read it out unaided, and later maybe enable them to copy it out themselves – all this was what we talked about. These ideas were received enthusiastically; after 3 days of work we arrived at the term 'community literacy scribes' for what they would be doing. As one said later, 'helping them to read just one sentence of their own is making a change.'.[16]

Scribes such as those outside the post offices in Sudan have been around a long time, but the role of scribe, such as the one we discussed in the workshop in Nepal, is one that you or I take on in any number of situations. Scribing means writing down the words of another person and checking, one way or another, that the version written down is the one they agree to. At the start of this introduction, I suggested that taking a phone message is a kind of scribing (it entails some kind of checking back with the caller that the message we have written is the one they want us to pass on). This is just one variation, of course, sometimes the scribal task is about accurate copying. Another time it is more about writing something more or less from scratch, on the basis of what the other person wants to say. When it comes to scribing for a group, there is a distilling to be done; several people have spoken, several things said, and the scribe's job is to produce a selective version of many voices. Since (I suggest) it goes on all the time, we barely notice it. However since, also, there remains an idea that people who are properly literate do all their literacy work unaided, it became a project for me to seek out examples of how it happens.

The book opens with a section on *Problems of the imagination*. This begins with a discussion on the way that representation of illiterates in fiction and film may filter into policy writing and government thinking. The second chapter then looks at the role of scribes, the different kinds of status they have occupied in different societies and some of the ways in which scribing features in social and cultural life. This is a deliberately transnational (and transhistorical) section, providing a backdrop for the more local focus in the third chapter, where we consider the key scribal activity of letter writing – based mainly on interview material gathered from various settings in metropolitan London.

The second section, *Scribes and situations*, shows how scribes and scribing have operated in three arenas: offices, religion and the law; or to put it in more dynamic terms: clerical work, religious life and the legal system. From a mix of autobiography, fiction and history, there emerge pictures of different ways at different times that scribes and authors give and take power over the making of a text – as secretaries, as guardians of religious law, as copyists, as the takers (or makers) of statements, or as advocates. There are clearly different power relations at work in different settings, but always the scribal role is primarily to act as a conduit for the words of another.

Literacy (as I suggested earlier) is best seen as a relative matter. This helps us understand how in certain situations, some individuals are perceived as better or more expressive in their writing than others. The third section, *It takes two to collaborate*, first looks at the scribe's experience of scribing, noting that while they are putting their own literacy at the service of another, far from being mere technicians they may feel disturbed by the texts they have to produce, scornful of their authors or wearied by the process. The following chapter looks at situations from literature and film when the poetic writer is turned to for amorous purposes, with consequent tensions between the roles of 'muse' and 'secretary'. From there, we move on to consider accounts of how scribing is used as a means not only to find written expression but also to enable the author (as a student of literacy, seeking to 'improve' their skills) to become their own scribe. With accounts from four different adult literacy teachers, the reader is invited to notice the variety of purposes for which such an approach is being used as a teaching method. As much as a discussion about methods and issues for teachers themselves, my hope is that this chapter will illuminate and even demystify something of what goes on in a basic skills classroom.

The last section of the book, *Postscripts*, contains three themes that seem to me to persist in the phenomenon of scribing:

- the tension between individual and group;
- the issue of authorship;
- the transition from thought to utterance.

My discussion on these is not a deeply theoretical analysis, rather, like the book as a whole, it is intended to be a suggestive commentary on what seems to me to be an intriguing area of human life.

1 Enzensberger, 1987, p96.
2 Enzensberger, 1997, reading at Kings Lynn poetry festival, Norfolk, UK, 1998.
3 Street, 1991, p10.
4 One result of which was the first book I wrote, Mace, 1979.
5 Mace, 1992, pp3–22.
6 Mace and Wolfe, 1994.
7 Ritt, 1989.
8 Stanley tells Iris that the inventions in his shed are like the drawings on the walls of a prison cell; later, he asks, 'Am I a human being if I can't write?'; and describes himself as the ultimate outsider – a 'skid row bum'.
9 Wolfe, 1996.
10 Enzensberger, 1987, p101.
11 For a useful summary, see Gee, 2000.
12 The Research and Practice in Adult Literacy network has published a regular bulletin of reports and articles since 1985: www.literacy.lancs.ac.uk/rapal/rapal.htm.
13 The Research and Development Centre for literacy and basic skills was launched in January 2002. See www.dfes.readwriteplus.
14 I went with Richard Brooks, then Projects Officer with World University Service (UK). For more information about this organisation, see their website: www.wusuk.org.
15 From an interview with Richard Brooks and colleagues, quoted in the evaluation report of the Literacy Training Development programme 1996–99, Women's Education Programme, Gedaref, Sudan (WUS(UK)), 1999.
16 The Community Literacy Project Nepal is a programme that makes strategies for literacy learning known to local community development organisations so that they can increase the participation of non-literate people. Their website is: www.eddev.org/hosted/clpn.

PART ONE

Problems of the imagination

CHAPTER ONE

The literate mistake

H ow do literate people imagine illiteracy? For those of us with 'text bound minds'[1] how do we overcome the limits of our own imaginations and conceive of life where we would no longer read and write? Since it is the literate who write research reports, policy papers and newspaper articles about the matter, this is an important question to consider. It becomes even more important when such writing is about something else altogether, and includes casual assumptions that illiteracy is bad and dangerous. The following example of such assumptions comes from an article about jury service:

> One of the juries I sat on contained someone who could not read the oath. After three attempts she was gently told by the judge to repeat the words after the court official. *Maybe she had a great understanding of human nature. But if I was the defendant or a witness, I would be a lot more confident if I knew the trial was being heard by a jury that was literate. Particularly as the tricky word in question was 'verdict'.*[2] (My italics.)

What's wrong with the emphasised section? Well, I think it is in the sarcastic use of 'maybe'. It is sarcastic because, from the rest of the paragraph, it is clear that Rosie Millard (who wrote this) does not really think 'maybe' at all. This juror would not have a great understanding of human nature. How could she? She could not read the oath aloud! For Millard, it is so obvious it is not even worth dwelling on. Her next paragraph moves to her main theme, which is the finding of a recent report that juries are 'unrepresentative' of the population. She takes it for granted that her readers will agree with her. We too would worry, surely, if we were on trial by a jury one or more of whom could not read aloud the word 'verdict' from the text of the oath?

If anyone was at fault, it was the court official. Every juror should be offered the choice of repeating the unfamiliar words of the oath after someone who is familiar with them. Reading aloud to a room full of strangers is bad enough if you already are at ease with yourself and with speaking publicly. You do not have to be unable to read at all to have difficulty with reading in those circumstances. Implicit in what Rosie Millard says are two assumptions. The first is that literacy means being able to read aloud an unfamiliar text, alone and unaided, and that any 'literate' person would always be able to do this. The second, more worrying assumption, is that literate people have a 'greater' under-standing of human nature than those who cannot read and write by themselves in public circumstances.

The whole thing took me back more than 20 years to a discussion in an adult literacy class I taught, provoked by one of the students, a woman called Mel, of her recent experience as a juror. Mel knew at first hand the experience of having to be 'sworn in' as a juror, and her anxiety at having to do it. She also knew a great deal about the sleepless nights she went through during the 4 weeks of the trial, after which her jury had to arrive at a judgement. To have to read out the oath had been nerve-racking. Much more onerous to her, however, had been the responsibility of weighing up the evidence. She took the job seriously. Together, we compiled an account of her experiences with which to advise others – about what to expect, and how to deal with the oath-reading. For this piece of work I had been Mel's scribe – and also her pupil for, at the time, I had never been called to jury service and everything she described was news to me. I typed out her text, we duplicated and circulated it around several literacy classes, as material for reading and discussion. (Later, inspired by the whole conversation, I also wrote some guidelines on being a juror for the same readership.)[3] As I read Rosie Millard, I remembered Mel.

I stress 'alone' and 'by themselves' in Millard's assumptions because this is the stress that much of the culture which she and I live in puts on the idea of literacy. It is an assumption that the literate person is able to read and write entirely *without help*. At the time of writing this, a new national test for adult literacy achievement is being piloted in the UK. There are guidelines to teachers on how adult literacy students should do it. They should do it *without cheating*.[4] This extreme emphasis on individual skills is in stark contrast to the way people actually work – well described in the pictures of 'literacy practices' in a community in the North of England that David Barton and Mary Hamilton have painted. These authors are not only literate, they are bookishly literate; they are both Professors and have chosen to earn their living by reading and writing. Yet (as their book makes clear) they have also chosen to spend years listening to and learning from other people who do not. They took time to observe and record, and as a result of an enormously detailed study they concluded that literacy is something far more than a private act that you and I do on our own. It is a whole lot of different things, all of them to do with relationships between people. Literacy is best understood, they say, 'as a communal resource, rather than simply a set of skills located in individuals'.[5] I find that a helpful idea. I hope some of the material in this book will add to it.

To go back to my original question. How do literate people imagine illiterates? In the following section, *The addict's tale*, I first suggest the idea of a literacy addict, with the fears of deprivation and withdrawal that go with addiction. Next I pick out three extremes in how the very literate writer may portray illiterate people (or those who 'lack basic skills'): as *Blindfolded*, *Abnormal* and *Secretive*. The chapter ends with two *Alternatives* in which illiterate individuals are portrayed as more successful and wiser than their literate observers.

The addict's tale

Bookish people worry at the thought of not having anything to read; we rarely go anywhere without things with which to write. The idea of being stuck on a train or in a waiting room without even an out-of-date magazine to browse through is alarming. You might think such people are the least qualified to write about illiteracy, yet governments continue to recruit them to do so. The result (which is hardly surprising) is that there is much said about the limited lives of illiterate people and very little, outside the world of academic research, that shows illiteracy as different, rather than wrong. There is a simple reason for this; it has to do with fear. Illiteracy provokes fear in us. We are frightened at the idea of becoming or having to be illiterate. Life, we feel, would be awful.

The public line on literacy is that it is a matter of entitlement. Policies and campaigns are promoted on the idea of literacy as a right. This is how the argument goes. It is an unjust and unfair world that allows adult populations to be without the choices that literacy gives in a literate world. All men and women in the world should have the right to be able to read and write in their own language. This argument is fine, and I profoundly agree with it. The problem it creates, however, is that in promoting literacy as good, it implies that its opposite is bad. A whole mass of work has been done that challenges this, but it has not yet been made sufficiently popular to shift what we might call the 'dominant discourse' about illiteracy.[6] In this chapter some of the ways that this discourse gets expressed are considered. All the studies that have been done have begun to shift the idea of literacy as an absolute. More needs doing to recognise how relative a matter *illiteracy* is too.

Literate people define ourselves as people who are able, at any given moment, to write or to read what we want. Of course, we find some things harder to read or write than others, but we actually read and write routinely for a lot of the day, every day, in the middle of doing other things. For some of us, this has almost the feeling of an addiction; the prospect of being deprived of our literacy is as it might be for an addict to be deprived of their drug:

> I can't imagine the void that would open for me if I suddenly became unable to read. I read for pleasure, of course – novels, articles, biographies, crosswords – and for information of all kinds. I also read because I have to. I have no choice. Reading is a compulsion, an obsession. Why else would I read the headline in someone else's newspaper again and again? Why read such things as 'Way In', 'Way Out', 'Push', 'Pull', on doors I've been through a thousand times? Why read all the notices in the waiting room and then read them again? I just can't ignore print. I have to read it wherever I see it. And I'm very glad I'm able to.[7]

This writer is describing reading only, with no reference to writing. She is someone who sees herself as a reader, a person who finds enjoyment in all sorts of reading. But she is honest enough to suggest that it goes further than this. She reads all the time. 'I have no choice', she says. She cannot avoid it; in fact, she cannot resist it.[8]

You may see this as an exaggeration. But if, like me, you have had experience of training people in literacy awareness, you too may feel that, even if this idea of addiction is not widely true, there remains something that follows from it. Literacy addicts who are unaware of how much they depend on literacy also tend to forget that they have their own moments of illiteracy. It is this forgetfulness that leads them to portray illiteracy (or the 'lack of basic skills') as an unfortunate affliction that other people have. Believing themselves to be fully literate all the time, they are astonished at those other people who apparently are not. The astonishment arises because, indeed, just as they have cast themselves as fully literate, all the time, they have perceived (or been led to perceive) these other people as *illiterate all the time, in all situations.* (Thus did Rosie Millard see the juror, not as someone with what could be a temporary failure of nerve, but as a person wholly without both literacy skills and, what is worse, without moral understanding.) Thus portrayed, those other people, living in the midst of an apparently literate society, provoke a kind of fear that, in its mild form, is expressed as concern. The forgetful literacy addict worries about these people. She or he thinks how *awful* it must be not to be able to read and write and feels appalled at the idea that it might be difficult, let alone impossible, to do so. 'How do they *manage?*' is the question. Every adult literacy teacher has been asked it: in conversation with friends or relatives trying to imagine who these people might be, unable to conceive of 'managing' daily life without the routines of literacy.

For the literacy addicts among us, it is not just hard to think of a day in which we neither read nor write something. We are struck with the feeling of how *deprived* we would feel if we could not pick up a paper and idly turn the pages, picking up the gist of this report, the sense of that headline, the meaning of those captions; how *lacking* our lives would be if we could not lose our present preoccupations in the course of turning the pages of a novel that invites us into those of other, fictional people; and how *disadvantaged* we would be if we could not write our own letters in our own way.

As David Barton has shown us, these associations are relatively new. From a close inspection of 20 dictionaries published in the nineteenth and early twentieth centuries, he found that the word 'illiterate' is an older word than 'literate'. He also found that, for most of its history, it seems to have had a more neutral meaning than today, even, on occasion, a positive one. In 1865 there was a concern that if the army were to introduce 'intellectual tests' it would risk excluding from its ranks:

> the dashing *illiterates* whose stout hearts and strong thews and sinews made it what it was under the Duke.[9] (My italics.)

What fine and jovial men these sound! How bold and strong-thewed! Far from being expected to pity or despise them, the reader is invited to rejoice in the very idea of these excellent specimens of manhood. Today, the word 'illiterate' seems a poor sad thing by comparison. It is a negative word. To call someone illiterate is to accuse them of ignorance and stupidity. Polite society prefers to stick with 'deprivation' or 'disadvantage' as associated ideas, rather than rough words such as these. Nevertheless variations on all these ideas find expression, from time to time, in reports of the latest literacy statistics, or in representations of illiterate people in documentary or fictional film and print. They are also ideas that become hitched to the wagon of entitlement every time another literacy campaign is launched.

Blindfolded

No matter whether in Russia in the 20s, in Nicaragua, Afghanistan or India – symbols which repeatedly express the hope for a better world are the light and the sun…To create a contrast, these posters often show the illiterate person in darkness as a person who can hardly see. Such a representation may carry a pathological image of illiteracy and negate the richness of oral culture.[10]

As part of its activities to promote the idea of an International Literacy Year, UNESCO put together what must have been an extraordinary exhibition of posters collected from many countries round the world. These had originally been posters designed to encourage and motivate illiterate people to participate in education programmes. In the catalogue published to accompany the exhibition, one of the striking themes to be found was this: that illiteracy means being in the dark, and literacy is a means to come to the light. 'Illiteracy is ignorance and darkness. Let us learn how to read!' is the caption of a poster from Afghanistan, showing a blind man reaching out towards a text framed in bright yellow daggers of light. The image on the poster from the Philippines shows a child whose eyes are covered in a bandage and wrists bound with a rope. Here, the caption reads: 'What chance does he have?'. An Ethiopian poster, dated 1979–80, shows a line drawing of a blindfolded man with one foot on a cliff and the other about to step into a chasm, with the words 'Illiteracy means walking in darkness'. Its inspiration is suggested in a poster from Russia in the 1920s showing a man in profile, one foot on, the other foot off the cliff, a thick blindfold tied above his bearded chin: 'An illiterate is a blind man. He has to face failure and unhappiness everywhere' are the words below.[11] A gentler version of the same idea appears in an undated poster from Ecuador showing a girl, her blindfold head tilted to one side as she looks down on a sheet of white paper showing the first three letters of the alphabet. Behind her is a boy, apparently untying the blindfold. The caption reads: *'Amar es...Alfabetizar'* [To love is...to make literate].[12]

At least three of these pictures carry the 'pathological image' of someone unable to read and write. Those from the Philippines, Ethiopia and Russia are clear: the illiterate is a person who is imprisoned and in danger. From nineteenth century Britain, here is another such image:

> It must be a strange state to be like Jo! To shuffle through the streets, unfamiliar with the shapes, and in utter darkness as to the meaning, of those mysterious symbols, so abundant over the shops, and at the corners of streets, and on the doors, and in the windows! To see people read, and to see people write, and to see the postmen deliver letters, and not to have the least idea of all that language – to be, to every scrap of it, stone blind and dumb! It must be very puzzling to see the good company going to the churches on Sundays, with their books in their hands, and to think (for perhaps Jo *does* think, at odd times) what does it all mean, and if it means anything to anybody, how comes it that it means nothing to me? To be hustled, and jostled, and moved on; and really to feel that it would appear to be perfectly true that I have no business, here, or there, or anywhere; and yet to be perplexed by the consideration that I *am* here somehow, too, and everybody overlooked me until I became the creature that I am![13]

These are the words of a very literate man, constructing for his readers the portrait of an utterly illiterate boy. The writer is a person who not only wrote for a living, but read for it as well. The author, Charles Dickens, earned good money from his public readings. He must have written this passage sometime early in 1853. Reading it over a century later, three elements in it feel familiar to the way that illiteracy is seen today. There is the idea of illiteracy as *strange*; there is the link between illiteracy and *blindness* or *living in the dark*; and there is the idea of the illiterate as *intellectually simple*. Dickens adds an extra dimension to Jo, as a key character in the structure of his novel: this is an innocent in the midst of corruption. His role is to be the unwitting witness to the unravelling of the central drama; his death scene has been referred to as one of the most affecting in all Dickens' writing. Jo's illiteracy is central to his innocence; for in this novel, the uses to which literacy are put – in an interminable court case, in excessive missionary zeal and in blackmail – are destructive and immoral.

Jo is in 'utter darkness' as to the words in the street and on the doors or in the windows; no less dark is the shop kept by Krook, the second illiterate protagonist in *Bleak House*. A master of the gloomy and the menacing, Dickens' description of Krook's rag and bottle shop is one of his best. Krook himself famously died of spontaneous combustion, just when he was working on a blackmail plot with letters between his recently-deceased lodger and a certain lady – letters that he himself could not read, but could still put a price on. With his own motives always suspect, Krook's only effort to learn to read and write displays a characteristic suspicion of other people's. Dickens shows him explaining this to Mr Jarndyce (referred to here as the narrator's guardian):

> 'What are you doing here?' asked my guardian 'Trying to learn myself to read and write,' said Krook. 'And how do you get on?' 'Slow. Bad,' returned the old man, impatiently. 'It's hard at my time of life.' 'It would be easier to be taught by someone,' said my guardian. 'Aye, but they might teach me wrong!' returned the old man with a wonderfully suspicious flash of his eye. 'I don't know what I may have lost, by not being learned afore. I wouldn't like to lose anything by being learned wrong now.'[14]

Jo, in his innocent darkness and Krook in his more malevolent gloom both stand as contrasts to the main narrative engine of this novel: the huge machine of legal bureaucracy (about which there will be more in Chapter 6).

Abnormal

There is beautiful writing also in *The Reader*, a novel written more than a century after Dickens wrote his. When read in English, it is the work of two people: the author, Bernard Schlink, and his English translator, Carol Brown Janeway:

> I leaned quietly against the doorpost and watched her. She let her eyes drift over the bookshelves that filled the walls, as if she were

reading a text. Then she went to a shelf, raised her right index finger chest high and ran it slowly along the backs of the books, moved to the next shelf, ran it finger further along, from one spine to the next, pacing off the whole room. She stopped at the window, looked out into the darkness, at the reflection of the bookshelves and at her own.[15]

The watcher is Michael, a 15-year-old boy, by this time already the lover of the watched: Hanna, a woman some 20 years older than him. The narrator is Michael, looking back on the scene with 30 years' hindsight, recalling it with knowledge he did not have that long time before when, infatuated with the woman he was watching, he stood leaning against the doorpost. The man looks back at the boy looking at the woman looking at herself. Yet despite (or was it because of?) the intensity of his gaze, the boy at that time did not see, as the man now does, the true identity of this woman. That summer of their secret meetings, Michael and Hanna met almost daily and made passionate love at every meeting. In exchange for the induction into erotic desire that she gave him, he read to her – at her request – from some of the books he carried to and from his school studies. Given his youth, their liaison had to be carried out in secret. Later, among his friends by the swimming pool, he sees her walking towards him and has to pretend he does not know her. The end of their affair is nigh. Next day he cannot find her either at her flat or at her workplace. She has left town. (The reason I want to summarise the rest of the plot here is because we find a slice of it, taken out of its context, cited at the beginning of an influential government report arguing for a strategy to improve the nation's level of 'basic skills'. So stay with me.)

The next time Michael sees Hanna, years later, she is in court on war crime charges. As a university law student, Michael is among a group who were observing the trial and he recognises her. As a one-time concentration-camp guard in occupied Poland, she has been charged, along with others, with having cold-bloodedly allowed the death by fire of several hundred women locked up in a church as it burned down. For Michael to see his former lover in dock on such a horrific charge is deeply shocking. What redeems her, in his eyes, is the realisation (which he only comes to half way through this trial) that Hanna is illiterate. Schlink's device is to make Hanna indict herself, rather than reveal her illiteracy. She admits to having written an official report on the church fire, which she could not have written. It is this admission that persuades the jury that she was the most guilty of those on trial. Only Michael realises the true story. On a solitary walk in the woods one Sunday morning 'Hanna's secret became clear' to him. It did not come 'like a bolt from the blue' but was something that had been 'growing inside me, to be recognised and accepted'.[16] Hanna, he realises, could not read or write. Suddenly that explained everything about her. Getting him to do all the reading and writing on a bicycle trip they had taken. Losing 'control' at the hotel when she had found a note he had left and knew he would assume she could read it and feared exposure. Not wanting to be promoted at work, and now, in court, saying she had written a report rather than be found out again. Always, as Schlink would have it, Hanna is driven by shame and by guilt; the secret fact of her illiteracy must at all costs, at the cost of an 18-year prison sentence, be kept secret.

In the third part of the novel, some years into Hanna's sentence, Michael renews contact with his former lover, and begins another kind of 'reading' to her, echoing the readings in bed all those years before. This time he tape-records himself reading classic works of literature. For 4 years he receives no reply from Hanna; then, suddenly, comes a note: 'Kid, the last story was especially nice. Thank you. Hanna.'[17] Michael is overcome with emotion:

> I read the note and was filled with joy and jubilation. 'She can write, she can write!' In these years I had read everything I could lay my hands on to do with illiteracy. I knew about the helplessness in everyday activities, finding one's way or finding an address or choosing a meal in a restaurant, about how illiterates anxiously stick to prescribed patterns and familiar routines, about how much energy it takes to conceal one's ability to read and write, energy lost to actual living. Illiteracy is dependence. By finding the courage to learn to read and write, Hanna had advanced from dependence to independence, a step towards liberation.[18]

On the day before she is due to leave prison he visits her, having volunteered to help her rehabilitation on release. The next day he returns; Hanna has hanged herself. It is then that the prison governor tells him how important his tapes had been for Hanna. It had been by following the text of his reading on books borrowed from the prison library that she had become literate.

Michael, then, makes two discoveries about Hanna's literacy, years after their affair is over. The first (revealed to him as he walks and thinks in the wood) is of her illiteracy. The second (provided by Hanna herself in the form of her note) is of her newly-achieved literacy. What she has of his literacy is his voice reading to her: hour after hour, year after year, these tapes of Michael's voice reading works of literature (and sometimes his own work, too), just as he had done years before during their love affair. In contrast, Michael never writes back to her – for after this first short note, Hanna begins to write to Michael regularly. So, in a sense, she is twice exposed to him; while he, once past his boyish infatuation, remains closed to her. Meanwhile, outside Michael's powers of imagination is the world she inhabited before he entered it; how she had negotiated all kinds of literacy moments without his help, how she had lived and worked in the world with other ways of reading and writing than the kind he knew about. Schlink strains credibility in having Hanna subject herself to this prison sentence in the first place; like Michael, the reader is expected to swallow this without question. (Eighteen years in prison so that no one might know she found it hard to read and write?)

Back to the government report. On page 3 of what has become known as *The Moser Report*, the chair of the group that produced the text writes this, by way of a preface:

> We are at pains in the Report to show how serious the consequences of poor or limited basic skills are for society, for the economy, and – always at the forefront of our thinking – for families and individuals. At their most severe, the handicaps for the individual can be devastating. I can't put this better than by quoting from the remarkable recent novel by Bernhard Schlink *The Reader* (1998).[19]

At this point, he quotes the passage you have just read: 'I read the note and was filled with joy and jubilation…'. Published in 1999, the Moser Report's full title is *A Fresh Start: Improving literacy and numeracy*. It was the result of less than 6 months' work by a group set up at the instruction of the then Secretary of State for Education, David Blunkett. Its geographical remit was confined to England. Briefing papers submitted to it included research carried out 2 or 3 years earlier for the Basic Skills Agency – of which Sir Claus Moser was then Chair. The Report regretted what it saw to be an unacceptably high level of poor basic skills in the English population (20% were found to be having 'problems') and its recommendations for a strategic response were quickly followed by the setting up of a new Unit within the Department for Education and Science (as it was then known) and the production of a new framework for the training and professionalisation of basic skills' teachers. In short, the publication of the Moser group's recommendations carried some weight among government policy circles. So it is worth noting how its main (but by no means sole) author chose to introduce it. Of all possible texts on the subject of literacy which he could have picked, he chose an extract from a fictional account of a literate man's discovery of the literacy achievement of his former lover, a woman characterised as previously lacking, not merely basic skills, but common morality, as well.

Anyone among the Report's readers who had not read the novel would have no way of knowing how Schlink had represented Hanna's arrival at literacy, to which Sally Johnson and Frank Finlay, among others, offer a fierce critique. As they tell us, Schlink himself made it quite clear, in an interview after the book was published, that illiteracy was a metaphor he chose to use to convey the connection between public and private guilt. Hanna's illiteracy, as he saw it, was a metaphor for post-war German secrecy about the holocaust and for those who had 'forgotten their moral alphabet during the war.'[20] Johnson and Finlay argue that Schlink's portrait of Hanna as a total illiterate is implausible. (In order to have kept her job so long as a tram conductor, they point out, there must have been times when she would have had to manage some reading.) More seriously, they charge him with having equated an inability to read and write with what they call *moral illiteracy*. First published in 1995, *The Reader* has sold several hundred thousand copies in Germany, been translated into 25 languages, received numerous prizes and, in February 1999, was chosen as the Oprah Winfrey book of the month. This is a book that has gone far and wide. It shows a creature who is all animal lust and no human feeling, whose punishment is to discover both literacy and literature in jail. It is the illiterate as morally abnormal.

To read *The Moser Report* in its entirety, you could be forgiven for thinking that literacy learners themselves were incapable of providing their own evidence. Dozens of individuals and organisations are listed in the appendices as having been consulted; among them four focus groups with adults in basic skills programmes; yet only four individuals are (anonymously and briefly) quoted.[21] Instead, the report opens with a fictional character reporting the 'joy' he felt at the 'liberation' of his ex-lover being able to write to him. Michael, a lawyer, is assumed to be fully and permanently literate himself: the novel's readers are clear about this, because he reads so much to Hanna, and because we know that to get qualified as a lawyer you have to do an awful lot of reading and writing. Hanna, locked up in prison, is being 'liberated' by his literacy; a liberation which somehow leaves her feeling so far plunged into despair that she must take her life on the day she is due to be actually released from prison.

It is an odd and jarring piece to have quoted in the government report. With the context of the novel around it, the message could easily be read as the opposite from that which Sir Claus intended. Literacy is oppressive; it is about a legal system run by lawyers like Michael, whose pleasure at causing and controlling a 'liberation' for Hanna is entirely self-absorbed. The connection between this character and Sir Claus himself is that both men take it for granted that they themselves are literate, both discover the 'consequences of poor or limited basic skills' and both set about rescuing the people they see as suffering from them.

The voice is a dramatic instrument. Hearing words spoken gives none of the warning you can have when you see them written. One Monday evening in March 2000, radio listeners heard a deep, authoritative male voice tell us this:

> Some seven million adults in Britain have serious problems reading and doing number...I'm aware that these people have very very limited lives. They find it very difficult to get jobs. They find it difficult to fill out forms. *They can't lead a normal life, like you and me.*[22] (My italics.)

The voice was that of Sir Claus or rather, as he has later become, Baron Moser of Regents Park in the London Borough of Camden (his life peerage was awarded in 2001) – a man whose list of honours fills several lines in *Who's Who*, including Chairing the Royal Opera House, Covent Garden, acting as Chancellor for Keele University, and frequenting the prestigious Garrick Club in London. This is plainly not someone who finds it difficult to get jobs or to fill out forms. But is it someone who is capable of judging what a 'normal life' might feel like? He sees the 'abnormality' of someone who may have reading and numeracy difficulties (writing is mentioned only as the business of 'filling out forms') to be a fact. It is actually nothing of the sort, but another example, I suggest, of the literate's problem of the imagination. Given the status of the speaker, it was a particularly alarming one to hear that evening.

Secretive

Hanna lived the truth of her illiteracy as a secret. The first words of that radio programme included the phrases: '…a secret society a million strong' and 'the fact of widespread illiteracy'. The programme's title was announced: *The Great British Secret*. In the 1970s, when the British 'Right to Read' campaign was launched, there was a lot of press coverage, and one of the words that kept coming up in headlines and journalistic copy was the word 'secrecy'. From all the hundreds, maybe thousands of human interest stories, feature articles and interviews that were featured in those years, the language which was common was that of shame and concealment – and the consequent 'bravery' of those people who had taken the step of 'coming forward for help'. Those were the days when much of the education on offer for an adult education student of literacy was still organised as individual, private tuition – an arrangement designed partly to give personal attention, but mainly to protect people's perceived sense of embarrassment. A growing number of adult education teachers and their students began to challenge this,[23] the teaching strategy adopted changed to the more usual (and now seen to be more effective) form of a class or group. In the years since then, adult basic education (ABE) has come out of the closet, with decades of funding and development. Yet, after all those years of change and development, Radio 4 on a Monday evening in March 2000 was capable of entitling a documentary programme on adult literacy policy as *The Great British Secret*.

The programme went on. We listened to a woman called Dawn, who lives on a council estate in Sheffield, talk of how she had not been able to read and write when she left school, and how glad she was that, at the time when she had taken her driving test, they had not yet brought in the requirement to write. The commentator intoned: 'For years, Dawn kept her embarrassing secret to herself.'

The blurb on the back of Ruth Rendell's *A Judgement in Stone* has this from the *Daily Express* reviewer: 'It will be an amazing achievement if she ever writes a better book'. Ruth Rendell, also (since 1986) known as Barbara Vine, was already publishing regularly when *A Judgement in Stone* appeared in 1977, and since then has published over 40 more novels. Although this one was subsequently republished (and anthologised in the 1993 *Ruth Rendell Omnibus* published by Arrow), I think it unlikely that it is her best, and it is certainly not among those for which she is best known. (The television serialisation of some of the 18

'Wexford' novels was probably enough to make these scoop that prize.) There are two reasons why it merits consideration here. First, it is the story of an illiterate woman who killed a family *because they discovered the secret of her illiteracy*.

At first, that was all I could see in this book: a ghastly stereotype of the worst kind, showing illiteracy to be the same thing as inhumanity. It is that, and – who knows? – the book may very well have been among the influences on Rosie Millard's view of illiterate jurors. But there is another reason to look at this book. By no means all the author's sympathy falls on the family who are murdered. When I read the book a second time, I found that the victims, as well as the killer, share the blame. Certainly, the heroine is shown to be a cold, unfeeling illiterate monster, but equally, the family whom she kills is portrayed not just as literate but as *outlandishly* and *provocatively literate*.

The first line of the novel is this:

> Eunice Parchman killed the Coverdale family because she could not read or write.[24]

Illiteracy defines Eunice. Illiteracy, says Rendell, drove her to murder. The title of the novel is explained at its end. The moment when the family are shot dead by Eunice and her strange (and by this stage, insane) friend Joan at the end of the tale, they are watching a performance of Mozart's *Don Giovanni* on television. In that opera, the unrepentant Don meets his end at the hands of the stone figure of his father, the Commander, whom he had invited to dine with him. It is the statue that condemns him to eternal perdition: a stone judge, indeed. It took me a while to notice this connection. The second connection is more explicit and more shocking: Rendell wants to show us Eunice as a stone figure of another kind: a primitive, 'stone-age woman'. In the scene when she and Joan have just pulled a gun on the family, the metaphor is made explicit. There are screams. Joan turns off the television and the music is over:

> [The silence] held Eunice suspended. It petrified this stone-age woman into stone. Her eyelids dropped and she breathed evenly and steadily so that, had she had an observer, he would have supposed her fallen asleep where she stood. A stone that breathed was Eunice, as she had always been.[25]

This is a picture intended to horrify. However what is the portrait Rendell gives us of this cold murderess? This is given early on in the novel. Eunice Parchman came to work for a well-to-do family who live in a vast house and have a lot of two things she has never had: books and money. The Coverdale family is not just literate but exceptionally so. The parents, Jacqueline and George, share a passion for Victorian novels. The son Giles, who is 16 with acne and no friends, knows more Latin and Greek than his teacher and 'had got so many O levels that there had been a piece about him in the national newspaper'.[26] The vague sexual fantasies he nurses about his half-sister Melinda are fed by his choice of reading: Byron, Evelyn Waugh, Oscar Wilde and Charlotte Bronte. For her part, Melinda (who is studying Middle English at university) is shown as having less talent for academic study but more physical attractions than Giles; her reading life alternates between *Sir Gawain and the Green Knight* and letters from her boyfriend. Giles not only reads at the breakfast table, he is seen sitting at the kitchen table poring over a book while Eunice chops vegetables. To Eunice, the house itself is not just full of books; it seems to have as many books as the Tooting Public Library, where once, and once only, she had been to return an overdue book of Mrs. Samson's:

> One entire wall of the morning room was filled with bookshelves; in the drawing room great glass-fronted bookcases stood on either side of the fireplace and more shelves filled the twin alcoves. There were books on bedside tables, magazines and newspapers in racks. And they read books all the time. It seemed to her that they must read to provoke her, for no one, not even school-teachers, could read that much for pleasure.[27]

Like Dickens, Rendell links illiteracy to sightlessness. Eunice, aged 17, had lived with her invalid mother in 'a narrow twilight world, for *illiteracy is a kind of blindness*';[28] her father is portrayed as 'conspiring' with his daughter in her not learning to read and preventing others from finding out that she could not:

> When a neighbour, dropping in with a newspaper, had handed it to Eunice, 'I'll have that' he had been used to say, looking at the small print, 'don't strain her young eyes.'[29]

As an adult woman, in the Coverdale home, Eunice uses short-sightedness as the excuse for not reading notes or lists left in the kitchen for her. Urged on by the good intentions of George and Jacqueline, she has to pretend she goes to an optician for an eye test and bring home a cheap pair of glasses she buys in a chemist. Through a variety of subterfuges, Eunice manages to keep her secret until very near the climax of the story. It is Melinda, the least academic reader of the family, who (literally) 'sees through' the lenses of her shop-bought glasses in a scene in the kitchen where she is making one more attempt to 'be nice' to the uncommunicative Eunice. Sitting at the table with a magazine, she attempts to engage her in answering the questions in a quiz ('Twenty Questions To Test if You Are Really In Love'). Eunice has no pen. Melinda finds a pen. Then Melinda wants Eunice to ask the questions as she can see the answers at the bottom of the page: 'You ask me the questions'. Eunice says she has not got her spectacles. Melinda points out that they are sticking out of her pocket. When Eunice stumbles over reading-out the questions, Melinda notices that the lenses of her spectacles are made of clear glass and the truth suddenly dawns on her:

> Her eyes went to Eunice's flushed face, her blank stare, and pieces of the puzzle, hitherto inexplicable – the way she never read a book, looked at a paper, left a note, got a letter – fell into place. 'Miss Parchman', she said quietly, 'are you dyslexic?' Vaguely, Eunice thought this might be the name of some eye disease. 'Pardon?' she said in swelling hope. 'I'm sorry. I mean you can't read, can you? You can't read or write.'[30]

Rendell's twist on Eunice's character is then to have her become, not embarrassed, miserable, or ashamed, but angry, hostile and aggressive. At the start of the next chapter, Eunice at first says nothing, and still Melinda has not realised how her discovery might feel to her. As Rendell puts it, 'she was only twenty'. She was also – as the rest of her family – cocooned in a world of privilege. Her next move is to suggest that she could teach Eunice ('It'd be fun. I could begin in the Easter holidays'). Eunice's reaction is to threaten her with blackmail, using what she had overheard from a phone conversation between Melinda and her boyfriend days before. She tells her that if she reveals what she has just found out to anyone else, then she, Eunice, would tell her father that Melinda was pregnant. Melinda is shocked, turns white, leaves the kitchen, and almost immediately goes to confide in her parents. The result is that George and Jacqueline, far from being shocked at their little darling's sexual activities, are appalled at the blackmailing behaviour of their servant and decide to give Eunice the sack. When George tells her she has to go, he also intimates he is aware of her inability to read (for which his only feeling is pity) – and in so doing he and Jacqueline join Melinda to become Eunice's ultimate enemy: they now know what till now only her parents and one neighbour had ever known. This, Rendell tells us, is the motive that drives Eunice to the final act: these are now people who must be punished.

Rendell, as always, has done her research on her chosen topic: the way in which children can slip through a school system and not acquire literacy; the way a particular family structure of feeling might prevent learning; the way someone, as an adult, might seek above all things not to be *found out*; these were features of the experience of illiteracy that were being given particular limelight in the early 1970s. What she did with the character of Eunice Parchman, however, was to add another ingredient, that of pathology. She paints a character who is devious and amoral; who is drawn to televised scenes of violence on summer afternoons with the curtains drawn; who finds a kind of satisfaction in blackmailing others for their secrets; yet lives, not in terror, but in horror of her own central secret being exposed. What Rendell chose to do was to make, not just illiteracy, but the fear of her illiteracy being found out the cause of her essential inhumanity:

> All the springs of warmth and outgoing affection and human enthusiasm had been dried up long ago by it. Isolating herself was natural now, and she was not aware that it had begun by isolating herself from print and books and handwriting. Illiteracy had dried up her sympathy and atrophied her imagination.[31]

Eunice is a monster; and she is a monster because she is illiterate. Yet she is not the only one who is unable to imagine. For all their education, the Coverdales also seem to have this problem. It simply never occurs to them to consider that Eunice's resistance to taking messages or her odd behaviour in dealing with notes left in the kitchen could have any explanation other than some kind of stubbornness. They are, in fact, unable to imagine Eunice as a person at all. She is a servant who delights Jacqueline because she is more efficient at cleaning and cooking than her predecessor. Theirs is a complacent self-referential world with little acquaintance with lives beyond their own, so that *it never occurs to them* what life without a whole public library in their home might feel like. It is outside their imagination.

A Judgement in Stone begins and ends with another literary reference. Early on we are told that, after their murder, the Coverdales' home became:

> … a bleak house, fit nesting place for the birds that Dickens named Hope, Joy, Youth, Peace, Rest, Life, Dust, Ashes, Waste, Want, Ruin, Despair, Madness, Death, Cunning, Folly, Words, Wigs, Rags, Sheepskin, Plunder, Precedent, Jargon, Gammon and Spinach.[32]

In *Bleak House*, it was Miss Flite, victim of the interminable trial winding its way through the Courts of Chancery, who has birds with these names caged in her garret in one of the back streets nearby – the birds to be set free on the day of judgement, when that comes. In referring the knowing reader to this work, Rendell offers an invitation to us to see parallels with another novel that, while pathologising illiteracy, also suggests the ignorance of which literates are capable. On the last page of *A Judgement in Stone*, the bird-names appear again. Eunice has been tried, found guilty, and sentenced to life imprisonment. To the last, she is committed to her illiteracy and therefore doomed:

> They have tried to reform Eunice by encouraging her to remedy her basic defect. Steadfastly, she refuses to have anything to do with it. It is too late. Too late to change her or avert what she did and what she caused. Dust, Ashes, Waste, Want, Ruin, Despair, Madness, Death, Cunning, Folly, Words, Wigs, Rags, Sheepskin, Plunder, Precedent, Jargon, Gammon and Spinach.[33]

Like Hanna Schmidt, Eunice is found guilty. Unlike her, she has a pathological inability to relate warmly to any other human being, and a commitment to remaining illiterate. In those terms, *A Judgement in Stone* has done no favours to reforming any fixed ideas that her readers may have about illiteracy and Rendell herself could be found guilty of having perpetuated a false stereotype, equating illiteracy with stupidity, narrow world views and worse. *A Judgement in Stone* is a clever book, which does, in part, provide a satire on bookish literacy. I suspect that most readers, however, will remember, not the Coverdale family, but Eunice Parchman, the one who could not tolerate the shame of her hidden illiteracy being discovered.

Alternatives

The millionaire

The Verger is the title of a short story by Somerset Maugham that was first published in 1929, later reprinted in anthologies of the author's work[34] and, more recently reproduced in simplified form as a reader for learners of English.[35] The story shows illiteracy as a drawback causing distress, not to the illiterate – who ultimately becomes a millionaire – but to the literates around him. The main character, Albert Foreman, is a respectable middle-aged man working as a verger in a church. For a long time his illiteracy was of no importance; his wife dealt with any paperwork, he felt no need for literacy. The vicar for whom he worked had always known that Albert could not read and write and did not mind. After he retired, however, the new vicar finds out and calls Albert to a meeting with him and the parish council. They have to sack him, he says:

> Understand me, Foreman, I have no complaint to make against you. You do your work quite satisfactorily; I have the highest opinion of your character and your capacity; but we haven't the right to take the risk of some accident that might happen owing to your lamentable ignorance. It's a matter of prudence as well as principle.[36]

The other men at the meeting, although agreed that this is the right decision, are clearly perplexed at Albert's position:

> 'But don't you want to know the news?' said the other church-warden. 'Don't you ever want to write a letter?' 'No, me lord [answers our hero], I seem to manage very well without. And of late years, now they've all these pictures in the papers, I get to know what's goin' on pretty well. Me wife's quite a scholar and if I want to write a letter she writes it for me. It's not as if I was a bettin' man.'[37]

After leaving the meeting, Albert walks home and suddenly fancies a cigarette. There are no tobacconist shops. This strikes him and he goes home to think about what today would be called a 'market opportunity'. For the rest of the tale, Maugham shows him going on to open a shop, start a chain of tobacconists, and (eventually) become a millionaire.

It is in a scene with his bank manager that Albert has to reveal that he cannot read or write; and – in an echo of the earlier scene with the parish council – also has to reassure him:

> 'And do you mean to say that you've built up this important business and amassed a fortune of thirty thousand pounds without being able to read or write? Good God, man, what would you be now if you had been able to?' 'I can tell you that, sir', said Mr. Foreman, a little smile on his still aristocratic features. 'I'd be verger of St Paul's Neville Square.'[38]

Albert's 'aristocratic features' fit with his previous work in service, first as footman, then as butler; Maugham gives him, earlier in the story, 'clean cut and distinguished' features, and describes him as 'tall, spare and dignified', deferring to the vicar as 'me lord' and (even after achieving his wealth) the bank manager as 'sir'. It is a skilful character portrayal, with others in the story cleverly caricatured beside him. Beside him, the parish councillors come across as servile and the vicar himself as a posturing fool, leaving the last laugh with Albert – who is too well-trained actually to laugh. Enough for him to enjoy a 'little smile' at the irony of his career.

Albert's story was not Maugham's own invention. It derives from an oral tradition. According to folklorist Jan Brunvand, after Maugham was accused of stealing the plot of his 1929 short story, he explained that he'd heard the tale from a friend, and that it was a well-known bit of Jewish folklore.[39]

Maugham's tale, and those told by penniless Jewish immigrants in New York, turn out to contain three common ingredients. First, a main character who, *because* as much as *in spite of* their illiteracy, achieves untold wealth. Second, one or more subsidiary characters who, like Maugham's parish councillor and bank manager, are astonished at this. Third, and for our purposes most important, a hero who has to educate others into the world he lives in: a world where it is possible to achieve worldly success while at the same time being unlettered. Here is how Jan Brunvand recalled hearing the tale:

> My grandfather used to tell about a country lad who went to the big city to seek his fortune, but had no luck finding a job. One day, wandering through the red light district, he spotted a Help Wanted sign in a window. They were looking for a bookkeeper, but after

the madam quizzed the boy about his education and discovered that he could neither read nor write, she turned him away. Feeling sorry for him, she gave him two big red apples as he left. A few blocks down the street, he placed the apples on top of a garbage can while tying his shoe, and a stranger came along and offered to buy them. The boy took the money to a produce market and bought a dozen more apples, which he sold quickly. Eventually he parlayed his fruit sales into a grocery store, then a string of supermarkets. Eventually he became the wealthiest man in the state. Finally he was named Man of the Year, and during an interview a journalist discovered that his subject could neither read nor write. 'Good Lord, Sir', he said, 'What do you suppose you would have become if you had ever learned to read and write?' 'Well', he answered, 'I guess I would have been a bookkeeper in a whorehouse.'[40]

Both these stories suggest that native wit may sometimes be rewarded by prosperity, whether basic skills are there or not. It is a suggestion in direct contrast to the idea of literacy as an economic lever: one which dominates other narratives of illiteracy, such as the film *Stanley and Iris* referred to in the Introduction. They also show something else: that the alternatives to persistently negative images of illiterates may best be found, not in literate accounts, but from within oral cultures and storytelling traditions.

The scientist

The other example of an 'alternative' portrait of illiteracy is by no means one of rags to riches. But it is also one about power. It shows someone whose lack of reading and writing is supremely irrelevant to her standing in a community. It appears in a journal article published in the year designated International Literacy Year, and it is an exceptionally fine piece of writing among what might be termed 'the literature of basic skills and literacy'. (By this I mean the publicity and research documents produced to promote basic skills and describe what the 'problems' are for those who lack them.)

In her article the author, Lalita Ramdas, argues for the need for international policies on women's literacy to give proper attention to women's lived realities. Her purpose in writing this portrait was to illustrate this argument. My purpose in sharing it here is to show the power of combining more than one view of the subject to transcend two-dimensional stereotypes. In order to emphasise Ramdas' achievement the extract has been divided into five pieces.

First, she introduces the woman, by setting out her background, her working life and family circumstances: a plain enough form of introduction:

> Chintamma is a para-veterinarian working in a small village in a backward and underdeveloped area in the south Indian state of Andhra Pradesh. Chintamma, like millions of her sisters, never went to school as a child; she still cannot read or write. When a small non-governmental organisation began to persuade women to come out of their homes and involve themselves in programs of animal care and income generation, Chintamma was among the first to join. She has brought up her five children single-handedly since her husband died some years ago, leaving her a widow at the age of 35 years. She owns a tiny patch of land, keeps a few sheep and goats, and has struggled to eke out a living.[41]

This is information set out as a list. By the end of this piece, we know facts and figures about the woman: what she does, where she lives, and so on. She cannot read and write, yet she joins a training course. She is a widow with five children, yet she manages to feed them all. The impression so far is of someone who is stuck but determined, someone to be admired a little and pitied a lot, from a distance. What Ramdas does next is to add another layer: the layer of people's view of her in her own community:

> But Chintamma has a standing in the village which has no bearing on her economic or educational status, and therefore when she volunteered to join the para-veterinarian training, many others were inspired to come forward too. Chintamma exudes a confidence and strength that comes from having survived in the toughest possible circumstances…

This is new information; we have to adjust our admiration and pity. Now we find ourselves feeling slightly in awe of this woman. But Ramdas is skillful; what she does next is to rein us in and remind us of our previous position, formed by long experience of television broadcasts and newspaper reports from distant places where floods and famine happen – but not to us. She says:

But statistically speaking, Chintamma is one among the approximately 280 million illiterate women of India, a statistic viewed by many with horror, dismay and even shame.

All the more powerful, in contrast to this, is the turn that the writing takes next. Back with the woman herself, we now learn something more. It seems this is someone who is not 'uneducated' at all, she is a respected scientist, and a woman with authority:

> Yet Chintamma knows more about the plants, the trees and forests, the clouds and rain patterns, than most of us 'literate' ones. She knows how to heal the sick in her village where no doctor comes; when to sow and when to harvest; and is present at the births and deaths of both humans and animals where her knowledge and experience are seen to be invaluable. It is said that Chintamma can interpret the signs in the environment to predict floods and drought. (The sophisticated meteorological forecasting systems have not yet reached her village).

Lastly, Ramdas tells us of Chintamma's own views on literacy. In these few lines, she puts paid to the campaigner's thoughtless zeal. The reader must pause and consider:

> Today, after four years as a para-veterinarian, [Chintamma] feels she is ready to learn how to read and write so that she can maintain an account book and keep a diary. She is not yet sure, however, as to the value of sending her children to the village school when they could be helping to augment the family's meagre income instead.

Ramdas' message is clear. You have a literacy programme? You think illiterate women will want it? Wait. Listen. And look. It was 4 years before Chintamma decided it suited her. And as for her children, she's still thinking about it.

Chintamma is illiterate. Of all we may want to know about her, or that she knows of herself, this turns out to be the least interesting or important piece of information. In providing us with a sense of her social relationships and some glimpse of the various fields in which she is expert, Lalita Ramdas offers here some inspiration for alternative ways of writing about illiteracy.

The examples of the 'literate mistake' in this chapter are from a journalist's passing remark, from novels set in rural England and urban Germany, posters intending to promote literacy's attractions in developing countries, an introduction to a policy report and a radio programme. The intention has been to expose the limits of the habitual literate's imagination. The next few chapters move out into another way of seeing the world, the relationships of give and take, push and pull, dependency and mutuality that actually go on when writing (and reading) is undertaken collaboratively.

1 Ong, 1982, p156.
2 Millard, 2000.
3 *Making News* was a regular information sheet produced and distributed by a consortium of some 13 London literacy schemes in the late 1970s. The issue I wrote in 1979, inspired by Mel, was called *Jury Service*.
4 DfEE, 2000, para 129: 'In all cases, people who take the Test will be properly supervised to ensure that there are no opportunities for cheating'.
5 Barton and Hamilton, 1998, p230.
6 Brice Heath, 1983; Gee, 1990; Graff, 1979; and Street, 1984 are among a whole crowd of scholars who between them have brought the disciplines of sociolinguistics, history and anthropology to challenge and refute false ideas of 'the great divide' between literacy (rational, economically productive, innovative) and oral societies (primitive, unproductive, stuck in traditions). They have shown (as Barton and Hamilton have done) how the uses of literacy vary everywhere with purpose and context, making it, some argue, preferable to talk of plural literacies, rather than a singular literacy.
7 Mitchenall, 1999.
8 As a bit of an addict myself, I recommend the solution of soaking off the labels of things you buy for bathroom and kitchen; and admit that it is not just to keep the mice away that I decant cereal and sugar into plain containers.
9 Barton, 1994, pp20–21.
10 Giere, 1992, pp80–81.
11 *Ibid*, pp80–83.
12 *Ibid*, p114.
13 Dickens published *Bleak House* in 19 monthly parts between 1852 and 1853. This extract comes from p182 of the 1994 edition: *see* Dickens, 1994.
14 *Ibid*, p167.
15 Schlink, 1998, p60.
16 *Ibid*, pp130–1.
17 *Ibid*, p185.
18 *Ibid*, p186.
19 Moser, 1999, p3.
20 Johnson and Finlay, 2001.
21 *Op cit*, pp22–3, para 3.4.

22 BBC Radio 4, Monday 27 March 2000, *The Great British Secret*, presented by
    Vivian White.
23 Mace, 1979.
24 Rendell, 1978, p1.
25 *Ibid*, p161.
26 *Ibid*, p26.
27 *Ibid*, p55.
28 *Ibid*, p31.
29 *Ibid*, p44.
30 *Ibid*, p136.
31 *Ibid*, p48.
32 *Ibid*, p9.
33 *Ibid*, p190.
34 Maugham, 1951.
35 Milne (ed), 1992.
36 Maugham, 1951, p941.
37 *Ibid*, p941.
38 *Ibid*, p944.
39 www.snopes2.com/business/genius/bookkeep.htm: the 'Urban Legends' pages
    © 1995–2001. Website of Barbara and David P. Mikkelson, updated September
    2000, visited February 2001.
40 Cited in website referred to in Ref 39.
41 Ramdas, 1990.

CHAPTER TWO

Who is a scribe?

(and what do they get out of the work of scribing?)

It can be helpful to think of scribing as a role, rather than a job. At different times, any one of us may take it on. When a doctor listens to our symptoms and writes a version of what we say on the record card, they are, for the time being, taking on the role of scribe. If you help me to find the words I need as I write a letter, you are being my scribe. If I help you by copy-typing out the letter you've drafted, I am being yours. The important thing is that, just because I turn to you, or you turn to me, this does not mean that we are either helpless or illiterate. It is simply that there are writing situations in life when someone else's collaboration is a welcome resource. It is true that for much of human history illiteracy was common, and scribes were just one category of people with a craft, to be hired when needed.[1] Today, you might think scribes are a thing of the past, but scribing is still a useful way of working in all sorts of situations. Now that literacy is more widespread, it seems we are less easy about using someone else to help us craft a text. There is a feeling that it is (that word again) *cheating*.

To get free of this idea, it is helpful to look more closely at the different meanings that we can see for the role of a scribe. It is also important to explore the issue of dependency a little. If you help me write my letter, I feel (or could feel) dependent on you. However, maybe, you get something from this too. This chapter sketches a mix of ideas that see the scribe as *journalist and messenger* – alternately copying and composing texts with and about others. It is then suggested that the feeling of 'mutual exchange' reported by people who exchange scribal help is the kind of thing you hope for from a *Good neighbour*; different again from those who are turned to as *Professional* scribes, doing the job for a living. In the last section three *Roles* are suggested for scribes: as copyist, transcriber and witness, returning us to the scribe as journalist – who, sometimes, gives voice to experiences for which no words have yet been found.

Journalist and messenger

A journalist writes about the death of another journalist. The deceased had been well known and in some circles admired, so this death was a news item. There had been many tributes and obituaries extolling him: 'the greatest journalist of my generation', 'a genius' and other such phrases were used. Nevertheless some disagreed: among them, another journalist, Polly Toynbee, a widely-respected writer on policy issues and matters of social justice. Driven by the excesses of these eulogies to write what she felt to be a more accurate version, her piece filled several column inches:

> The world of Auberon Waugh [she wrote] is a coterie of reactionary fogeys centred on the *Spectator* and the *Telegraph* who affect an imaginary style of 1930s gent...Effete, drunken, snobbish, sneering, racist and sexist, they spit poison at anyone vulgar enough to want to improve anything at all.[2]

'Their language', she goes on, clings 'to the prep school and nursery of the 1940s and 50s'; their standard of writing is 'empty and destructive'; Waugh's own political analyses were no more than the 'knee-jerk abuse of any politician'; and:

> the limited vocabulary of this little tribe of scribes is reduced to those blasé upper-class generalities – ghastly, boring, silly, disgusting, odious, repulsive, bogus, hideous or goody-goody – house style *passim* in most of the *Spectator* and *Telegraph*, lazy in-words of an exclusive clique.[3]

It is an eye-catching phrase – 'this little tribe of scribes'. Toynbee wants us to recognise this group as less important than they think they are ('little'), a defensive and self-perpetuating gang ('tribe') and, above all, as members of the lowest kind of writer, the opposite of the great editors and columnists of good journalism, mere 'scribes'.

The status of a scribe in all kinds of societies seems often to have ranged between two extremes, with that of lowly hack being one of them. At this extreme, a scribe may be the lowest of the low: a mere copyist, labouring away to reproduce a version of someone else's text. The vast industry of scribes in mediaeval Europe was one of hard labour; the act of writing itself being:

an act of endurance, requiring three fingers to hold the pen, two eyes to see the words, one tongue to speak them, and the whole body to labour.[4]

These were scribes bound to the twin tyrants of accuracy and legibility. By contrast, other scribes in other places were elites, occupying the lofty role of tribal elders, high priests, those who interpret the law: the ultimate authorities. So perhaps it is not surprising that the status of journalists should swing from one pole to other; at one moment that of mere 'scribblers', knocking up copy to meet deadlines, making sensational headlines out of nothing, cooking up opinions with no basis in fact, and so on; at another, our guides and mentors in a complex world. As Margaret Meek puts it:

> Journalists break down, for common perusal, the impenetrable speeches of judges, the reports of doctors, the researches of scientists, even the new arcane speech of computer-buffs, and present their findings and opinion to both the expert and the lay reader, with a finely tuned perception of their audiences.[5]

'Scribe' is an old word, not often used in ordinary conversation; Polly Toynbee's choice of this word has an archaic association to it. Yet, in present times, scribes appear in many forms, even if we do not designate them by this term. They are letter writers, paid or unpaid. They are calligraphers, casting a poem or a certificate into careful lettering with exquisite care. They are ghost-writers, turning the dictated or rambling words of a celebrity into coherent autobiographical prose. They are secretaries, producing formal, correctly written documents for others to sign. They are advocates, helping someone to word their answers to questions on an application form in a way that will most convincingly justify a claim. And they are literacy teachers, working with their learners to produce a written text for the learner's use and development. The one thing all these activities have in common is that they involve one person writing down the words of another; all of them, in one guise or another, appear later in this book.

To call journalists 'scribes', as I have discovered, is not always a put-down. Sometimes it is a more neutral term, as in: 'Scribes have their way at PM's meet'[6] and 'New Privacy code shackles on freedom of scribes in Britain'.[7] Both these headlines come from the Indian press. The first headed an account of a change in protocol in allowing journalists to report on the Prime Minister's visit to 'India's nuclear flagship' (the BARC). The second concerned a stricter code for newspapers (including a new offence of 'persistent pursuit') following the death of Princess Diana. For headline purposes, the word 'scribes' is excellent as a short alternative to either 'journalists' or 'reporters'. It is unusual to find this use in the Western media. In another news item (this time in an American newspaper, but still referring to journalists in India), the word 'scribes' carries a further meaning: calligrapher. The report carries the headline 'Urdu Scribes Strike at India Newspapers':[8]

> New Delhi, June 3. Several dozen calligraphers went on strike last week along India's newspaper row, reminding the Asian publishing world that there is still one language that has eluded the typesetter: Urdu. Although experimental computer typesetting is being studied here and in Pakistan, where Urdu is the national language, newspapers in both countries still rely on accomplished scribes called *katibs* to handwrite the news with artists' pens.

Highly trained though these calligrapher-scribes had been (turning out 'their handwritten news columns at the rate of about ten inches an hour'), they were less well paid than the journalist-scribes, those who had composed the text of these columns. Since 1968, the report goes on, the court had classified these calligraphers as journalists; but this change in classification had not been followed by a change in pay. The protest, which was the subject of this report, concerned the failure of the newspaper proprietors to pay the calligraphers the wage of journalists.

This story dramatises the collision of the two primary roles of the scribe, paid separately yet seen as one; both copyist and composer; the one who *letters* and the one who *creates meaning*. The work was being treated as low-paid and menial – that of a mere clerk, copying; the complaint of these scribes was that the employers were denying them the status they were due – that of meaning-makers. Wherever a scribe is at work, there is some tension of this kind. A scribe is often expected to be a mere mechanic, taking down words from speech or copying them from another document. Yet, in practice, they may also be wordsmiths in their own right, and sometimes are expected to be so. In the history of Northern Europe, countless documents have been produced by scribes writing at the instruction of others. By the sixteenth and seventeenth centuries, although literacy was still the province of the urban elite, a great many documents were being produced to manage everyday transactions among the people at large. These were documents that had to be composed, not merely copied, the writing sometimes having been produced, not by elite specialists, but by 'ordinary people':

> Archives throughout Europe bulge with voluminous bodies of paper produced mainly by professional scribes *but also by ordinary men and women*...petitions, bonds and oaths. All across Europe, groups of people banded together to beg, cajole or threaten those in positions of power over them to grant favours, to agree on a particular course of action, or to assert their loyalty to a cause.[9] (My italics.)

Historians, such as Rab Houston (who wrote this), are readers on our behalf. They search and find and scrutinise, seeking to establish the meaning and value of each document, so that they can discern patterns and make statements such as these. 'Throughout Europe' – what a sweep that is; what pictures we can glimpse when we read on: 'groups of people banded together...'. Here in the midst of the group is the scribe as advocate, as well as copyist, writing on their behalf, entrusted with a literacy task that is important and public. When Houston says the writers of these documents were 'ordinary men and women' his readers have reason to believe him, for at every other turn in his argument we have seen his caution. 'We know this...but we have no way of knowing that', he says; and 'bias in these sources show...' and 'other sources permit the historian glimpses...'. This is someone whom we trust to know if manuscripts are written by 'professionals' or by 'ordinary men and women.' This is how he tells of the writing of wills – with his geographical pen sweeping wide, once again:

> *All across Europe*, the sick, the dying or simply the careful, expressed hopes for their souls and wishes about the ways in which their goods and chattels should distributed after their death... These documents were sometimes written by the testator himself though it was more common to have the task carried out by a scribe or notary, amateur or professional.[10] (My italics.)

Our imagination is at work. What we begin to imagine is the key issue at the heart of the scribal relationship: the issue of *trust*. How might I, unlettered myself, be able to trust that the scribe at my side will write what I ask? Whether they are a chosen individual in a group or a paid professional, scribes have to have the trust of those for whom they write. As copyists and clerks, they may occupy a low status; but as secretaries – those who take dictation from others who may not have the literacy to read back what they have written – scribes are in a powerful position. For some, the exercise of power may be its own reward. For others, the idea of providing a service may also be a satisfaction. Whether acting as copyist, as secretary, or as advocate, the scribe is assumed to subordinate any text they may want to write themselves, in the service of this other for whom they are the conduit. At times, certainly, the scribe may be – may even have to be, in the case of a ghost-writer – the person who composes sentences or even entire passages of text. However, the central idea is that the text to which the author gives their name is one that somehow carries *their* message, with the scribe who gets it down acting as the anonymous messenger.

In practice, as we will soon see, scribes are humans and not machines; they get tired, or have their own ideas about the best way to put things. Yet what is it that a scribe gets for the work of producing another's writing? What is their reward?

Good neighbour

At first sight, the relationship looks uneven and, often, it is. 'Illiterate', for this particular task, the author or client in the relationship is dependent on the scribe. This experience is not exclusive to literacy, however. It can also apply to other kinds of situations when one person delegates a task that they do not enjoy or find difficult to someone else. A priest whom I interviewed about her scribing activity reflected on it in these terms:

> When it comes to two people in a partnership, there is a tendency, I think, to let one be the dominant one when it comes to reading and writing. It's like two women I know, both retired. One had been head of a junior school, the other, the head of an infant school. One had never learned to cook. The other one was ill, had to go into hospital, and this one didn't even know how to put a slice of toast in a toaster. As for trying to boil potatoes…! She's an educated woman, but the cook person in her life had fallen ill and she couldn't even work the microwave.[11]

Whether there is a 'cook person' or a 'writing person', you have to wait for them to be in the right mood. Adult literacy classes the world over are populated with people whose primary ambition is to be free of this waiting, free of a dependency on others, in the family or the neighbourhood, to read and write their business. To be free to write and read your own letters is to be free from the moods or attitudes or disagreements of another, on whom you have, perforce, to be dependent. What we have to consider is that sometimes this can be an arrangement that suits both people. As I reflected earlier, what the priest did not mention in our conversation was what it was that the non-cook in the partnership was able to do that the cook could not: what she gave, as well as what she took.

In 1983, Hanna Fingeret of North Carolina State University published the results of a study she had carried out over a one-month period with 43 adults with limited literacy. In contrast to the dark and secretive world suggested by tabloid headlines, her findings told her:

> most of… [them] create and maintain social networks that are characterized by reciprocity.[12]

The location of her study was a place she characterises as 'a medium-sized northeastern urban setting' in America. The group she met consisted of native English speakers (of whom 27 were white, 16 black). When the study began, half the group was attending literacy programmes. Her approach to them was that of an apprentice. She asked them (she says) 'if they would teach me about their lives'[13] and they responded. In addition to spending some 2 hours with each person, she talked with their friends and families.

The story Fingeret goes on to tell is that of a researcher being led, through her research, to change her mind. At the start of the study, as she put it, she had the idea that illiterate poor adults were 'cut off from the social world, perhaps connected to the umbilical of television':[14] exactly the stereotype we saw illustrated in the character of Eunice Parchman. What she found instead, among these poor communities, was that these were people living in 'a web of social relations that provide security and support'. The illiterate adult made choices as to how often and whom they would ask for help, and most of the adults in the sample were treated as equals within their networks.[15]

Fingeret's idea of *reciprocity* or *mutual exchange* in the business of literacy and social life emerged from comments made to her by interviewees such as Kevin, a 40-year-old man working as a barber, speaking about what he did when he needed any help with reading or writing something. 'I never asked my friends for anything I didn't return in some way', he began, going on to explain:

> Some of my friends, they need haircuts. I need firewood, or a bus ticket, or I have some forms that need to be filled in. There's an old saying – one hand washes another.[16]

Another of her interviewees spoke of a neighbour for whom she sometimes acted as scribe. The neighbour, Diane, was seen as someone who can be turned to for support and ideas. As this woman saw it, in comparison to her role as the community's counsellor, Diane's need for occasional literacy help was minor:

> We come here when we need someone to talk to – she listens and helps you figure out your problems. No matter how hard it gets, you know you can come here and have a friend, get some ideas, some help, so you can face it... Sometimes I read the mail for her, or her daughter brings the paper and we sit and read together, talk about what's going on. We don't none of us have much, but we help each other, what we can.[17]

This analysis is very different from that of the concealed illiterate, hiding their shame and embarrassment. True, there is a category she characterises as 'cosmopolitans' who mixed with educated people and went to some pains to 'pass as literate' themselves. In that company a man called Tony felt he had to 'lie' all the time, pretending to have read this or that when he had not. To Fingeret, however, this did not make Tony dependent. He was simply operating in a different social network to her other category, those she refers to as 'locals'. These 'locals' she groups as unskilled or semiskilled labourers having little contact with 'cosmopolitan literate adults'. Often living in poverty, they 'must confront the stress of making ends meet while maintaining some positive self-concept'. Diane, above, was one such 'local'.

The value of Fingeret's study is hard to overstate. The article is not long, and her later published work[18] took a different focus (on the process of life-change provoked by adults gaining new skills in literacy, described through the experience of five participants in adult literacy education). The 1983 article, however, provided many adult literacy educators who read it with a new pair of spectacles, to see what was around us. It made a specific contribution to a newly burgeoning literature[19] on how people actually use reading and writing, on the social contexts within which it occurs, and on the idea of 'practices' as a way of expressing both value systems and behaviours associated with reading and writing. 'Cosmopolitan' contexts, Fingeret said, are those in which people with only partial literacy might have an acute sense of difference and dependency. The same people, with the same limits on their reading and writing, relocated in a 'local' context, with other more urgent priorities to deal with, might barely give this a thought. Fingeret's analysis gave us a fresh outlook on the notion of independence, and a way of seeing literacy as one of several kinds of reciprocal exchange.

This study suggests that the reward of the scribe in poor communities seems to be that of a friend and neighbour, exchanging goods and mutual help. No money changes hands. No extra status is granted. The matter is a simple one: 'you scratch my back, I scratch yours'. In settings where life is hard and literacy merely another craft in which you either have or do not have the skills yourself, a 'writer', even a published one, does not automatically command respect, let alone awe. The black American writer Toni Cade Bambara tells a good tale of such a one being brought down to size when she turned her hand to scribing:

> Some years ago when I returned South, my picture in the paper prompted several neighbors to come visit. 'You a writer? What all you write?' Before I could begin the catalogue, one old gent interrupted with – 'Ya know Miz Mary down the block? She need a writer to help her send off a letter to her grandson overseas.' So I began a career as the neighborhood scribe – letters to relatives, snarling letters to the traffic chief about that confederate flag hanging in front of the school, contracts to transfer a truck from seller to buyer etc. While my efforts have been graciously appreciated in the form of sweet potato dumplings, herb teas, hair braiding, and the like, there is still much room for improvement – 'For a writer, honey, you've got a mighty bad hand. Didn't they teach penmanship at that college?'[20]

No chance of 'the writer' getting above herself here. Her catalogue of publications belonged in another world. Here, what mattered was things getting done, relatives getting news, bureaucrats being stood up to – in handwriting that would be good and clear. This is the scribe as copyist: judged again by those hard rules of accuracy and legibility; her reward, this time, were the skillful products of other crafts – tasty things to eat or drink, a hairdo done the proper way.

Between neighbours, the sense of mutual help (as Fingeret found) means that the scribe's rewards are less tangible, as I discovered myself, when I talked with two women in London who worked together as scribe and author. One Sunday morning in December we sat drinking tea in Liz's sitting room talking with her neighbour Eileen.[21] A tall woman in her 70s, with a deep voice, Eileen had been born and bred not two streets away from where we sat. Liz, the smaller of the two, had (as we agreed when I replayed back part of the tape) a much higher and lighter voice than Eileen. They had been neighbours, they told me, for '10 or 11 years'. The story they told was of the trouble that Eileen had been having problems with her housing. There had been damp. The repairs had been a long time coming. When they had finally been done, they had failed to solve the problem. Unable to get satisfaction from her phone calls to the housing department, Eileen had finally knocked on Liz's door. When asked what had made her choose Liz, she told me this:

> A friend of mine introduced me to Liz, and we just hit it off. I mean, if I need something, Liz will help and if she needs something, I'll help.

It is an ordinary thing to say. It is how two good friends are to each other. The fact that one might be a writer and the other might need writing done was simply the extension of ordinary help that each gave the other. Liz then worked with Eileen to write the first of several letters to the Council's housing department, to press Eileen's case for repairs. The writing process was done like this, Eileen said: 'We talked about it and then Liz wrote it up for me and then I copied it out'. First, the talk, with Liz scribbling a note, then the 'writing up'. For Eileen to copy it out, she would also have had to agree with the finished version, so this was a middle stage I had to assume was there. For Eileen could read all right. It was just that she could not write, at least not to her own satisfaction, and not for official purposes. This did not worry her. It simply meant she would have to find someone else to do that kind of writing. She was quite clear about it:

> I can write and I can read, but I'm no good at spelling. I can't spell to save my life. Don't matter how hard I try, I can't spell.

Liz (she said) had worked for many years in social services, where much of her daily activity was in advocacy and finding out information, so it was easy for her, in her words, to write in 'sort of administrative-ese'. It was for that kind of writing that Eileen knew she needed someone else. There was no problem with sending anything in her own script to someone in her family, or a friend, but not to 'some authority':

> I've got by all my life and I can't spell and it's not done me any harm. I can spell some words. I mean, I can write a letter to, say, Liz. But to send it to some authority, it's no good, I'd have to have help… It doesn't bother me. I mean, everybody who knows me knows I can't spell. I mean, I'm on the committee on the club, our club, and they know I can't spell so they don't ask me. Tenants association…

For Liz, the task of writing to the Council was familiar to her in the job she used to do: writing for someone else, on their behalf, to gain access to services to which they are entitled. However with Eileen, she felt there was a difference, they were working as equals:

> It was important to do it together. It was different from the work I did as a social worker because there you did things on behalf of people who were too anxious, too battered about to sit down and help you to do it, so you had to do the whole thing on their behalf; checking just dates. But this was not like that at all. It was something we got together and we had a few laughs.

Having 'a few laughs' is a reward in itself. Was there any other kind of 'payback' for Liz, I wondered? Eileen had said earlier, 'If she needs something I'll help'. 'What kind of something?' I asked. This was the conversation that followed:

E: Well, sometimes Liz is a bit bad with arithmetic. I'm alright with arithmetic so I usually sort her out.

J: What, bills?

E: No, not bills. But in change and things like that. I mean I've met her down the market and I'll say, that's the money, put that one. She's slow at…she can reckon up, but I don't think she likes it myself! I think she can do it, but I don't think she likes it because it taxes her head and that's not what she wants.

J: (to Liz) Is that right?

L: That's right. The whole area of figures and arithmetic just frightens me. It makes me anxious. So if Eileen's around I don't have any adding up to do, or any situation where money's involved and I think it isn't right...

It was so pleasant to spend a morning with two people who obviously enjoyed each other's company. To Liz, the reward was more than the help that Eileen gave her with managing her change; it was a matter of shared laughter and friendship. They obviously did have some 'laughs' together. Equally obviously, they had a lot of respect for each other. Here is Eileen talking about Liz's handwriting:

E: I've always told people that I can't spell. When I met Liz, she wrote and I said, Liz, don't write me notes if I can't understand them, because I can't spell very well, so you'll have to print them properly so as I can read it.

L: So tactful about my writing!

E: No, Liz writes quick, and I have to figure it out. Now I know Liz's writing now. But when I first came here I did say to you, didn't I, if you're going to write me a note, write it so as I can understand it.

Eileen had had to deal with damp, with poorly-built accommodation, with the effects on her own ill health, and with numerous delays and frustrations in seeking answers to her legitimate claims for repairs, over a period of years. As a Council tenant, she had to deal with people in offices at the end of a phone and, repeatedly, in order to persist with her case, she had to 'put it in writing'. Many times Liz had been her scribe, talking about it with her, writing it up, and then giving it to her to copy in her own writing. This had clearly helped her a lot and (eventually) brought the results she needed. As for Liz, she had gained the 'laughs' they had together and the help with reckoning up that she sometimes needed. She had also received one other 'reward' from her work as a scribe:

I think if you've grown up with books as I did, there's an atmosphere and attitude that when you talk you'd better have something to say...So when you meet somebody who can talk and maybe encourages you to talk, it's a new experience.

Professional

Scribes are first found in the family and then among neighbours, like Liz. Beyond these are the paid professionals. For the professional scribe, the rewards are in cash. A scribe might charge more for a long than a short document; their charges will vary from one scribe to another. Some might make different charges for different kinds of letter.[22] Known in Peru as *escribanos*, in India as *sarkari ahikari*, in hot countries such as these they sit at small tables, outside post offices, railway stations,[23] law courts or government buildings. While the large majority of these street scribes have been men, this may be changing. A colleague who revisits her home in India every year told me she had noticed more women among the scribes in New Delhi:

> When people have to engage in formality – when someone dies or goes into hospital – that's when these scribes are working. Until recently they were always men. Now it's changed, there are some women doing the work, too. In the law courts it's like a bazaar. All these advocates set themselves up under the big shady trees with their old-fashioned school desks with the legs cut off. The women just do the women's writing work. You only see them at the law courts.[24]

As she was at pains to point out, these are the scribes you would see in public. In domestic settings, where women have had some education, as she had done, they might be called on to write for others from a young age.

In the public arena, though, most professional street scribes are men: some writing by hand, others typing. Judy Kalman, who carried out a study of street scribes in Mexico City, found that some did both; first drafting by hand, then, after reading back the text to the client, making corrections and copy-typing the end result. For weeks at a time, Kalman observed the *mecanografos* in the Plaza de Santo Domingo, watching them working with their clients, interviewing them about their work and collecting copies of the writing they produced. She had found there to be a preconceived view of street scribes, that what they did was sit all day and take dictation from ignorant illiterates. She had a feeling that there might be more to it than this – and sure enough there was.

What she found was that there were a range of arrangements that client and scribe would come to, and that, within these, there were moments when the so-called illiterates' contributions to the text showed a sophisticated grasp both of audience and purpose in its composition. As to the scribes, Kalman came to group their style of working in four categories. At one extreme was the scribe who took charge of the text and was its 'composer'; at the other extreme, he would behave, or be expected to behave, as a 'hired hand'. Clients varied in their approach, as well. Some were spectators, choosing to stand back and leave it all to the scribe; others (she calls these 'foremen') would want to make the decisions themselves as to how the text was written.[25] Across these different positions she found there were differences as to who held or withheld control over the text at a given moment. There were also disagreements. Sometimes the client wanted something written that the scribe did not think was correct. At other times she saw the scribe wanting to change something in the client's proposed text, which the client refused to allow him to change.

The people Kalman saw working as street scribes were all men and some of them had been doing the work for many years. All had schooling above the national average; all except one had intended to train for other professions or trades. Pedro (age 72) had been an office worker, Rafael (age 48) had previously been a musician. From this work they made a good, but very modest living. (A fair day's work might bring in about $33 or about $180 per week; this compared with the then minimum wage of $100 per month.)

Although some clients were unable to write their own letters independently, Kalman found that this did not stop them having sufficient 'social literacy' to know the function and power of certain ways of writing. Among her examples was a group of residents from a desperately poor area outside Mexico City who wanted to protest at a corrupt councillor who was selling-off plots of land, evicting families in the process. The three men and one woman could evidently read, but wanted the hand of the scribe in composing the kind of letter that would make their case. In their exchanges with the scribe, and their thinking about the best way to construct the letter, Kalman observed a clear grasp of the different effects that could be achieved in different ways of expressing an argument.[26] Similarly, Marta, a union rep, was well aware of the value of making a claim for improved conditions in writing, rather than orally. The importance of having on record the date of a letter and the date of any response was obvious to her, even if she had to turn to the scribe for the technical business of producing the appropriate wording on the letter.[27]

The clients in Plaza del Santo Domingo varied between businessmen and working-class people with limited education. Although they varied in the way they worked with the scribes to produce their documents, what they seemed to have in common was an attitude of practical respect towards these men. Scribes, as they saw them, were people who were there to do a particular job. As Kalman put it, this set of attitudes fits with an understanding that literacy itself is no simple matter:

> it is a complex language practice, no one characteristic makes a person literate. Rather, it is the orchestration and weaving of multiple factors that make up written language use and literacy.[28]

You might think that professional scribes of this kind only appear today in those developing countries with a low literacy rate or, when it comes to other parts of the world, that they are figures from a distant moment in history. At least in France, if this is the case, it is soon to change – by 2003 there will be scribes who will be able to boast a university degree in the subject. In September 2001, the Sorbonne University in Paris announced that it was launching a new degree course for professional letter-writers:

> 'Scribes were common all over Europe before literacy became widespread and national tongues took over from Latin as the official language,' a spokeswoman said. 'Nowadays people are again not used to writing proper letters.'

For such programmes to be launched, institutions usually have to be convinced there is a market. Reporting on this, a newspaper journalist suggests that the French's interest stems from the government's 'famously incomprehensible state forms' and the 'austere, obscure and unfriendly language civil servants employ in their letters to the public'. The co-director of the 2-year programme, Jean-Pierre Berry (a teacher at the Lycee Maurice Ravel) is quoted as saying:

> It will be good for many ordinary French people, as well as immigrants, to know that professional help is available with the complexities of written French[29]

Roles

Many of the street scribes Judy Kalman watched took pride in their work. They drafted and checked, reworded and corrected, with the aim of producing a good piece of craftsmanship. The clients they wrote for paid them. They might not always agree about the best way to write but, to varying degrees, the scribe engaged in the content of what they wrote. At a remove from this is the scribe who we might think of as a 'mere' technician, someone who 'only' copies what they see in front of them or 'simply' writes down the words someone says, word-for-word. This last section of the chapter considers again the different roles a scribe may actually perform, whether paid or unpaid, so that we can get beyond this mechanistic approach. First, the scribe as *copyist*, then as *transcriber*, finally (returning to journalists) as *witness*.

The copyist

The mediaeval copyist-scribe was not always a menial and lowly labourer. They were also artists, illuminating the words in front of the reader, decorating with pictures and ornament the lettering of holy messages. 'However humble a scrivener he was', writes Michael Clanchy:

> the medieval scribe was an individual artist, who had to discipline himself to achieve anonymity and uniformity.[30]

Founded in 1921 with the aim of 'advancing the crafts of writing and illumination', the Society of Scribes and Illuminators (SSI) thrives today as a professional association for those who are already, or aspire to be, professional scribes. Their craft is that of the copyist, their pride, the aesthetic pleasure to be had from beautiful shapes and lines. These are men and women who work with ink and paint, providing us with lettered surfaces, which include glass, brick walls, canvas, silk and many kinds of paper. Theirs are the subtle distinctions to be found between the stroke of one tool and the line of another, as this example suggests, from an article by one of their members:

> With this script, the brush achieves a calmer transition from one letter to the next due to the greater flexibility and twisting permissible; the pen can guarantee more regular repetitions of shapes, precisely because of the lesser degree of these two attributes.[31]

Until the late nineteenth century, that was what writing was: learning writing at school was learning to copy. Yet copying with this kind of care is a different matter altogether. It is slow, detailed and creative work. No mere joining and looping here. The calligrapher's job is to give attention to a 'calm' transition from one letter to the next, to a 'regular repetition of shapes', and the particular flexibility and twisting made 'permissible' by the specific writing tool being used.

So it does lead you to wonder, do calligraphers care either way as to what it is they are copying? If all their love and care is being devoted to the form, how much does the content matter? One answer that appealed to me, when I found it, is provided by a short contribution to the newsletter of the Society of Scribes and Illuminators, asking 'Can the Scribe THINK?'. The writer makes a plea for a return to seriousness from the triviality and superficiality he perceives to be creeping into his art. Integrity, he argues, derives from three things: artistic maturity, respect for tradition and – last but not least – an appreciation of the writing being copied. At the risk of sounding pompous, writes the author, the best scribal work is done by people who 'care about the words they have chosen to write'; the scribe who produces the best work is the one who:

> *felt deeply* about the words, was 'moved' by the words, perhaps even changed by them.[32]

The transcriber

Transcribing the spoken word is a demanding job. For the reader, the transcript is usually a silent code, the original voice having to be imagined, but not always. In an oral history study of the lives of slaves in the American South, writers and journalists under the aegis of the Works Progress Administration (WPA) interviewed over two thousand former slaves. The interviews told of experiences in plantations, cities and on small farms. From the verbatim transcripts of these, it is possible to see and hear an interview extract at the same time. The effect is extraordinary. On the screen, the text is displayed (Baltimore, Maryland, 11th June 1949). Out of the computer an old man's voice suddenly speaks the words on the screen:

> My name is Fountain Hughes. I was born in Charlottesville, Virginia. My grandfather belong to Thomas Jefferson.

Further down, another highlighted passage in the written text invites the viewer to click for sound; once again, this dusty voice, lower this time, speaks from a June day over 50 years ago:

We had no home, you know. We was just turned out like a lot of cattle. You know how they turn cattle out into pasture? Well, after freedom, you know, colored people didn't have nothing.[33]

The scribe who took down Fountain Hughes' words wrote down what he heard, and we have the evidence of the voice to prove it. The man's age was not precise; it was certain, however, that he was over 100 years old. Having heard his voice giving an account of the routine ways his people were treated, I felt I would always hold an extra sense of the meanings that the word 'belong' could be put to. We use it lightly: 'I belong to this organisation', 'you belong to me'. Yet here, the word weighs heavy. Belonging meant 'being the property of', 'having all rights removed'. The speaker was thinking in a past tense; but the presence of his voice, added to his Creole use of the present tense of the verb, gave me, as I listened, a living meaning to what he said. I cannot know if the scribe in this case was 'moved' or 'changed' by what he wrote, but I was.

Translating the spoken words of this man into writing had given a kind of permanence to his voice; the audio recording of him spoke across the span of half a century to me at my desk. Future developments in technology will allow this to become a more ordinary experience.

The witness

Finally, to return to journalists and their everyday transcribing activity of quoting what other people say. There are reporters who are doing more than repeating what others say to them. Those who report from areas of conflict or war have to find a way of writing beyond this. Some such reports are transcriptions as a kind of *witnessing*: a testimony to the pain that the rest of us can only guess at. The start of this chapter showed how calling a journalist a mere 'scribe' can be disparaging. However sometimes journalists, as witnesses to the sufferings of others, are also scribes in the more honourable sense. Two newspaper clippings from my collection illustrate this.

Uppadathil Divakaran, known as Diva, was loved by family and friends; people liked calling in at the shop in which he worked with his brother. Then, one Sunday evening, he was brutally attacked and died. A bunch of bored kids had nicked something from his shop. Running out after them, Diva fell over. They kicked him unconscious, then kicked him some more. Two days later, he died. The journalist who reported the court case that sentenced his killers decided to write about Diva's life and times, reporting the court case, interviewing his surviving brother. When he spoke to Diva's widow, he found that grief had almost literally robbed her of the power of speech. The journalist, in writing what little she said, acts as her scribe:

> I ask her if she feels she has begun to get her life together. 'No. Not yet. No.' She was asked to write a report for the court about how his death had devastated the family. 'You can't put that into words can you?' The seconds pass slowly. 'No words', she eventually says.[34]

In a war zone, another journalist chose to revisit the desolation and brutality in Chechnya. She listened to harrowing accounts of maltreatment by Russian troops: 'stories so horrific that one's hand refused to jot them down'. While she was there, she herself became a victim of this treatment. She was detained, seized by soldiers and then interrogated for several hours:

> I omit the disgusting details of the interrogations, because they are utterly obscene. But it is these details – and my tormentors couldn't have imagined it – that provided the key proof that everything the Chechens had earlier told me about tortures and man-handling were true.

This is a scribe who does more than report; unwittingly, she becomes part of the story. In writing it, she allows herself only the barest commentary, leaving the original text to speak for itself – and sometimes editing out those things that are unspeakable, because her hand 'refused to jot them down'.[35]

Both these scribes were affected by the people they listened to. Mere machines they were not. For a short instant after the events of 'September the Eleventh' and the criminal attack on the 'twin towers' in New York, media coverage consisted only of pictures on television screens. The next day, some newspapers took over entire front pages with images alone. Almost immediately afterwards, however, there followed a torrent of words building up to and following the bombing in Afghanistan a month later. Journalists covering these events were engaged, as journalists of front-line conflicts may never have been before, in countless scribal moments. Aided by numberless unnamed translators, these writers gathered the news and interviewed scores of victims, relatives of victims, commentators, firefighters, soldiers and politicians. The word 'avalanche' seems the only one that will do: for the rest of us, the viewers of screen and readers of print, there seemed to be only one thing we could do: read, read and read again, hoping somehow that if we kept on doing so, comprehension would eventually arrive.

1 Ong, 1982, p94.
2 Toynbee, 2001.
3 *Ibid.*
4 Clanchy, 1978, p217.
5 Meek, 1991, p228.
6 *Indian Express*, 1997a.
7 *Indian Express*, 1997b.
8 *Humanist Archives* vol. 3 103 (49), Willard McCarty, Tues 6 June 1989, citing an article from the *New York Times* by Barbara Crossette, Sunday 4 June 1989, with this web reference: http://listsvillage.virginia.edu/lists_archive/Humanist/vo3/0102.html
9 Houston, 1988, pp120–1.
10 *Ibid*, p122.
11 Mother Pat Vowles, 8 May 2000, South London.
12 Fingeret, 1983, p145.
13 *Ibid*, p134.
14 *Ibid*, p135.
15 *Ibid*, p136.
16 *Ibid*, p137.
17 *Ibid*, p139.
18 Fingeret & Drennon, 1997.
19 Among others, Heath, 1983; Street, 1984; and Barton, 1994.
20 Bambara, 1992, p68.
21 Eileen and Liz in interview with me, December 2000, East London.
22 Kalman, 1999, found that in Mexico City, street scribes charged more for business letters than love letters.
23 See Chapter 7 for a discussion of the widely acclaimed film portrayal of the station scribe in Brazil.
24 Noyona Chanda, interview with me, 17 April 2000, London.
25 Kalman, 1999, pp86–8.
26 *Ibid*, p121.
27 *Ibid*, p111.
28 *Ibid*, p13.
29 Henley, 2001.
30 Clanchy, 1979, p227.
31 Knight, 1983.
32 *Ibid.*
33 WPA, 1998.
34 Hattenstone, 2001, pp1–3.
35 Politkovskaya, 2001, p3.

CHAPTER THREE

The letter triangle

In this chapter we consider the writing and reading of letters. With phone usage that must be nearly impossible to measure in the early twenty-first century, you could be forgiven for thinking that personal letter-writing is a thing of the past. However, for those who are separated from family and lovers by reason of migration or imprisonment, letters remain sometimes the only option. For some of those people – whether because of language difference or because of lack of writing practice – the help of another, more experienced letter-writer is welcome. This chapter first discusses what the payback might be for the scribe in this, expressed by one as *'Sort of like a favour'*. The two activities of *Composition and transcription*, so often in tension within one person, can, as examples suggest, be separated between letter-scribe and client. Meanwhile, how does the scribe convey *The author's voice* in personal letters? Sometimes the reader, the third figure in these 'letter triangles', is only too aware of the scribe behind the letter. Despite the phone system, letters remain a key means for *Family ties* to be kept up across *Time and distance*.

'Sort of like a favour'

In search of Fingeret's 'reciprocal networks', I sought out letter-scribes in a setting where I thought I could most easily find some persistence of the letter over the phone call. To have little or no access to a phone is one of the deprivations imposed by a prison sentence. Limited to once a day or less for making calls, with others competing for access, and strict limits on phone-card currency, it is in prison that letters take on again the importance they had 30 or 40 years ago. The post arrives each day and the old lessons apply – you only get letters if you write them.

Suddenly, people who may have never bothered to write a letter in their life need to write. From 'inside' they must find a way to write to those 'outside'. One way of achieving this is to turn to someone else, more handy with the pen, more used to putting words on paper: someone willing to be your scribe. In her study of how prisoners use reading and writing, Anita Wilson talked with and observed inmates in several penal institutions in the North of England. She found that, while the payment of scribes in one form or another is very common, the currency varies (and rarely ever – for obvious reasons – involves money). She also found that the scribe may sometimes accept less (in apparent value) than they are offered. This is what one scribe told her:

> Last week I wrote a letter for an illiterate guy to his Mum and I said 'say this and that' but he knew what he wanted to say and would not let me rephrase anything, so I wrote it as he spoke it…he wanted to pay me some roll-up tobacco or Rizla or chocolate but I told him to get me an envelope and a carrier bag as both would not cost him anything – the envelope being prison issue and the bag to put my sewing in.[1]

Both people in the arrangement were agreed that some kind of recompense was expected. Cigarette or chocolate were offered and refused. What the scribe wanted more were two things that 'would not cost…anything' but for which he had more use.

With the help of colleagues in the prison education sector, I talked with seven people about their experience as scribes: five women – Maria, Lorraine, Lucy and Tanya (Lucy's 'author'), and Alison; and two men – Gerry and Harold.[2] Among these people, attitudes towards pay seemed to differ, along a spectrum, from: 'this is a gift, I want nothing in return' to scribing as a commercial operation. At the latter end of this spectrum was Maria. A young black woman in her early twenties, Maria talked to me nearly a year after she had left prison. For most of the 18 months she had spent in jail, she said she had been always writing letters for one or other of the 30 other women on her wing. At first, she had done it with no payment ('it was a gratitude thing'). However, as the demand for her services grew, she decided she had to put some limit on it:

> There were quite a few girls who really could not write. Which is why I had to make a business out of it. Three times a week, some

of them. I was, like, sitting in my cell writing and writing and I had to stop writing to my own pen pals.

Maria's charge for her writing services was usually units on a phone card. Phone cards with 20 units on are worth £2, as she saw it:

Seven units (70p) was not bad for a letter. They'd use up 13 units and then give me the card.

At the other end of the spectrum was Gerry, a tall, Scottish, grey-haired white man, serving a life sentence, and introduced to me as someone who is a regular scribe for others. As far as Gerry was concerned, satisfaction seemed to be (to coin a phrase) its own reward. An exception to the experience Anita Wilson reports, he refused any kind of payment for the writing he did:

People who can't write tend to gravitate to other people who can't write, so the word goes round – get Gerry to give you a hand. I don't want anything in return; I don't do it for the money. They'll say, 'Do you want any tobacco?' I say, 'No, I don't do it for that.'

Payment by money or any other means, as one education officer told me, is strictly discouraged. To exchange a phone card for a written letter may seem fair exchange, but for an inmate to be found with another's phone card may have nothing to do with letter-writing. As the officer pointed out, 'it could equally well be for other services rendered' – or the result of trafficking or bullying. The 'give and take' entailed in gaining someone else as a writer, particularly a writer of personal letters, is often more subtle than that. The payback for the scribe can be other gains. It gives her or him something to do. It may even 'save her hide', as this fictional story from a novel by Sara Paretsky suggests.

Private investigator V.I. Warshawski is working undercover in a women's prison outside Chicago. She is on the case of a young Filipino woman called Nicola who had been found dead one night, having supposedly 'escaped' from this prison. Warshawski's cellmate is a woman called Solina, a woman whose mood swings from high to low, depending on the 'in-house crack supplier'. Paretsky has not presented Solina as illiterate. She can read, but she is uneducated, unsure of writing, of how to write formally. In this scene, Solina has just heard from her caseworker that her children are about to be moved into foster care. Warshawski suggests she could write and tell them how she would have a proper home for them to go to, arguing her willingness to go into rehabilitation. Solina is suspicious, but eventually accepts V.I's offer to draft a letter for her. As V.I. reflects, 'it would give me something to do, besides shooting baskets and occasionally practising my singing'. Without access to typewriters or word processors, she handprints the finished version on lined paper. Solina, as V.I. notes, 'was touchingly awed' by the result:

> She read it over and over and took it down the hall to the cell where she spent most of her day and showed it to the group around the television.[3]

Just as Maria had told me she had been in a real-life British prison, in Paretsky's version of a fictional American one V.I. is inundated with more requests for letters ('to the State's Attorney or the public defender, to different welfare agencies, the children's caseworkers, the employer, the husband or boyfriend'). Any kinds of drugs were offered as payment; when she turns these down, she is offered alcohol, chocolate, perfume – luxuries hard to come by. For V.I. the luxury she craved more was fresh fruit or vegetables. What she gained, as well as these 'fees', was something even more important:

> It was my letter writing that really saved my hide in Coolis. The women I helped began constituting themselves into an informal set of watchdogs, warning me when trouble was lurking.[4]

In this version of 'give and take', Sara Paretsky portrays V.I. the scribe as the centre of a world of illiterate or semi-literate others, revered and protected. The first payback for her is that the letter-writing gave her 'something to do'. Basketball and singing practice had been some kind of occupation in the long hours of enforced idleness behind bars; with Solina acting as her informal agent, she soon had another, acquiring in the process a status for herself of someone to be watched over and warned 'when trouble was lurking'.

Most of the real prison scribes I spoke to wrote for more than one other person; only Maria went so far as to say that she 'made a business out of it'. For the others, the activity was as Paretsky portrayed it: a way of passing time for themselves, and (to some extent) part of an attitude of give and take. Maybe this attitude was a factor of the context of our meetings: namely, within the education section. Each of these people had chosen to use their time in prison to develop their own education, and had a sympathy for others with less than they had. As Lorraine put it:

> I wrote in Holloway for other people... It's sort of like a favour. In Holloway, there's no plug sockets in the cells, so there's no TV or radio and everyone reads. So if you can't read, you feel left out. There was this woman and I could see she couldn't read the letters she got. So I put it like this, so she wouldn't feel bad. I'd say, do you want me to read you one of my letters?' and then I'd read hers for her. Or I'd say, let's write some letters together.

Lorraine knew the signs that suggested the woman could not read her letters. She could also read those that said she might feel 'bad' about it. She had an idea about how to make the reading easy – and that the woman might want to write in response. To Lorraine, someone being unable to read or write and feeling awkward about it was familiar territory. She had grown up knowing that her father, whose childhood in Jamaica had not included schooling, could not read or write:

> The first time I realised he couldn't read all that well was when I was in primary. He had left a note for me. I had a key to the door and I was coming home. He'd written something about leaving me something to eat. I could see the way he had written it, his writing was funny. He'd written, 'Hope it's enough' and spelled 'enough' wrong. But he hadn't left when I got in, and he came in and crumpled it up. I could tell he didn't really like me seeing it.

Later on, Lorraine and her two sisters would take turns to read letters for their father. But it was that child's glimpse of the hastily crumpled paper in the kitchen all those years before that had taught her the delicacy with which to speak to the woman who could not read her letters in Holloway.

In the previous chapter, I introduced Eileen and Liz as a partnership of scribe and author, where Liz, the scribe, gained Eileen's support in situations where she needed help in equal measure to Eileen receiving her help to produce official letters. Among prison scribes, Lucy was in a similar position. She wrote for only one other; they were friends and, in return for her writing, Tanya had been her guide to life in prison and mentor when she had first arrived. Lucy's was a first offence (fraud) for which she was serving a relatively short sentence (months, rather than years). Having had experience as a journalist, writing was not a difficulty for her. Entirely new to prison life, she had been grateful for the help she had got on arrival from Tanya in the cell next door, who 'was very good to me. She would always give or lend me stuff'. Lucy became Tanya's scribe as a way of returning the favour. An older woman with blonde-grey hair, dressed in tracksuit and trainers, Tanya sat next to the younger woman and laughed, agreeing with her account of their relationship:

> Tanya calls me her personal assistant. I'm her PA. My complaint forms were always very wordy. Tanya laughed at first, but she saw that mine got results. So now I write hers, and she just signs them. It's because she's a diabetic. She has to have her medication in order to live, but it's not been on time. She wasn't able to express herself without shouting. I find that if you ask properly, either verbally or written down, you find officers respect you. I'm not being submissive. It's how it works. I wouldn't respond well myself if someone was effing and blinding me.

'We got the answer back', said Tanya: an apology, and after that the insulin was delivered on time. Lucy had help from Tanya; Tanya, in turn, from Lucy – as Tanya put it: 'I do things for Lucy. Lucy does things for me.'.

Composition and transcription

Published accounts of teaching and learning writing and literacy in prison settings are few and far between. Among the most vivid is an account by Andrea Loewenstein of a creative writing residency in a women's prison near Boston, Massachusetts. She first sets the scene. She saw the women she worked with there as falling into three groups: hustlers, 'crazies' and 'model prisoners'. In the first group would be pickpockets, robbers, prostitutes and dealers of drugs or goods. Those labelled 'crazies' might often be repeatedly self-destructive and sometimes bizarre and violent towards others. The women seen to be 'model prisoners', sometimes shocked by the language or behaviour of other inmates, might have been convicted for the first time 'for some violent and usually, even to them, inexplicable act', and would probably be serving the longest sentences. In prison she saw women abandon the protection of pretending things in their lives are okay. In prison they dropped 'the illusion that everything is fine', which they had used to manage life in 'exploitative or destructive marriages, or deadening or programmed lives'.[5]

Of all the different kinds of writing that might be needed in such a time and space, Loewenstein found that letters (for these women) were the most important, the substitute for any other kind of contact when telephone communication is forbidden or limited. Letters received would get shown to others; letters to be written would be done with help. Such arrangements could mean a 'give and take' that was entirely about writing, where one woman's writing strength could complement the other's compositional weakness:

> June, who could not write at all but was known for her wit and ability with words, and Pat, who wrote neatly and correctly, but had trouble expressing herself well. June composed Pat's letters for her and Pat wrote down June's. A group tended to gather during this process, and the letters created were truly communal.[6]

We have here the reconciliation of the two writing activities known as 'composition' and 'transcription'. It was another American writer, Frank Smith, who set out the activity of writing in this way, and argued for a resolution to the impossible struggle of an unpractised writer who attempts to hold the two together.[7] In a book that influenced much adult literacy teacher-training in the 1980s, he developed two key propositions: first, that composition is the process by which we transform thinking into writing, and second, that writing itself is a means to work out what we think. 'By writing, we find out what we know', he argues, 'writing does more than reflect underlying thought, it liberates and develops it'.[8] It is the means by which we can untangle confused ideas and straighten out muddled thought. The difficulty, as he put it, is that many less practised writers struggle to combine the two activities of composing and transcribing in one, expecting themselves to get it right all in one go. The result is that the effort to find out and express what they want to say is utterly overtaken by the effort to present their writing in an acceptable form. The whole thing is dominated by the effort of transcription, in which they struggle, at every step, to produce the correctly spelt and punctuated, grammatically perfect piece of script – in the process either giving up before they have started, or killing off the expressive power of what they are capable of saying. Too much writing, Smith argues, suffers from an excessive anxiety with this business of transcription. The anxiety interferes with the work of expression and composition. His message is unequivocal:

> Composition and transcription must be separated, and transcription must come last.[9]

If you, dear reader, happen to be someone who cares about good spelling and punctuation, and feels depressed at poorly-written work, you may be raising an eyebrow here. 'Would that more people *did* worry about these things!' you may be thinking. Frank Smith's answer (and mine) is that the work of composing has its own rigour, too. Smith helped teachers to recover our confidence and remember the improvements there are when some of our students in adult literacy classes, for a moment, get free of worrying about these other things and focus, instead, on thinking: on what it is inside their head that they have to reveal and connect; on putting meaning into words, irrespective of their uncertainty about whether they can spell those particular words. We remember the pleasure when such students grasp the idea of a draft – which no writer gets perfect first time – and produce the raw material that, when the time is right, can be read, amended and developed.

When a person sits down to write, Smith saw these two roles in tension with each other. In order to dramatise this tension, he suggests we think of one person split into two: an author composing and a secretary (or scribe) transcribing.[10] We can see how this idea illuminates June and Pat's partnership. June helped Pat compose. Pat helped June transcribe. It looks like a very convenient and comfortable kind of give and take.

Anita Wilson's interviewee reported a situation where the author had very definite ideas as to what he wanted to say. He would not allow the scribe any influence on how he said it, 'so I wrote it as he spoke it'. In Judy Kalman's terms, he was behaving as a 'foreman' dictating a work that has no need of being 'perfected', but needs to be transcribed. Very often, however, it seems the scribe has to do more than this; they have to tease out of the author what it is they have to say, to the point when sometimes, they may have to remind the author whose letter it is that is being written. Such 'spectators' seemed to proliferate among Maria's clientele. Some would write something themselves and want her to improve it, but many of them, she told me, wanted her to write the whole thing. They would ask her: 'Can you write to my boyfriend?' or, 'I've just found out my little girl's in hospital and I've got to tell my mum. Can you write it for me?' In the 'please improve it' category were those who had made a start on a letter, faltered, and turned to her for its completion – 'I've written a letter to my mum. Can you make it longer?' or 'I've written the letter, can you go through and check it?'. At one stage Maria had to institute a 'boyfriends' day' to put some limits on the demand. 'Can you write to him today?' 'Not today. Tomorrow, that's boyfriends' day.' Her other solution to this pressure might at first seem cynical:

> Really, I would be writing the same thing to them all, but they wouldn't know. It would be: I miss you, I still think of you every night, I'm counting the days till I get out.

'Writing the same thing to them all' – was Maria cheating her clients? The scribe here has power, of course. If her author is entirely unable to read any text independently, then she is in the hands of the writer. At one extreme, the scribe could, theoretically, read back to her a wording that has no relationship whatsoever with what she had actually written. At the other, the scribe is faithful to every word written, and checks back with the author that this is the wording she herself would choose. Somewhere between these seems to be the strategy that Maria employed. She had limited time to do this writing and limited interest in offering her own creativity to the task. If the author herself got stuck, her solution would be to produce the ready-made phrase of a greetings card – 'I miss you, I still think of you every night, I'm counting the days till I get out'.

The scribe is a tailoring service, made to fit the individual, with her particular relationship. The whole arrangement is based on an idea that this letter or message is unique: personal and exclusive to the author. It seems at odds with the off-the-shelf words of greetings cards. However, as Mary Hamilton and David Barton suggest, the choice of a greetings card (which crosses the line between reading and writing) mixes both mass-produced and personal. They report that:

> the manager of one of the city centre card shops...confirmed that many people spend time choosing cards on the basis of the words printed inside and would sometimes come into the shop and ask for a card expressing particular sentiments.[11]

They go on to argue that this work of choosing the right (pre-written) message is itself a form of writing, similar to the nineteenth century practice of copying out ready-made letters or more recent invitations by computer software, inviting you to 'make your own greeting'.[12] The sense that this message is special to that person is achieved by the handwritten addition by the author.

Handwriting, in both literal and metaphoric senses, provides the personal touch. (The greeting card industry plays on this concern by designating the specific person to whom a card may be addressed: 'Happy Birthday, *Daughter-in-law/Aunt/Brother*'.) It is there to overcome the impersonality conveyed by the printed word. It was Maria's feeling for the personal force of the handwritten word that provided a balance to any danger of formula writing by her. She applied a firm rule. If the letter was supposed to look as if it had been written by its author, then it followed (as she saw it) that the finished version should be copied in their handwriting:

> None of my final letters ever got sent out. I don't care if you can't write very well, and okay I wrote out what you wanted. But you've still got to copy it. It's your letter. I used to make a point of saying that to all of them.

The author's voice

Gerry's account of scribing with a man called Arthur depicts an activity with some shared work going on:

> I suppose he was 35 or so, Irish. A traveller. He didn't even know the letters of the alphabet when he started. He didn't have a *clue*. The only letter he knew was X. He didn't know anything. Mind you, he wasn't a stupid person. But one day, he'd got a legal letter, and he said, Gerry, can you explain this for me? At first I thought he couldn't understand what the letter said. Then, something made me ask, can you read? And he said, no. He had a wife and seven kids. After a couple of times helping him with the VOs [Visiting Order], I said, why don't you write a letter to her?
>
> We just wrote a basic letter, telling her what it was like here. He dictated it but we sort of worked on it together and built it. He started with things like: 'I'm alright. Look after the kids. I'll be

coming home soon'. And I said, 'Oh come on, Arthur, you can do better than that!' I suppose I wrote half a dozen letters for him.

Then I said to him: 'Get your bum into gear. Use your time here. Do the education and go home and impress your wife.' He was in here for two or three months, coming to this class every day. By the time he left he could read little books. Once we'd got him over the initial hurdle, he was away.

Two things about this story seemed to give Gerry a lot of satisfaction. One was the fact that he had been the person to motivate a man who had started by only knowing the letter X to go to a basic education class and learn to read. He was pleased with that, I could see. The other thing was important, too: the way that the two of them had 'sort of worked on' the letter to his wife, found a way to say more to her and *build* a letter that was more than basic. Yet Gerry was someone who said that he did not enjoy writing that kind of thing for himself. He used the prison library to the full ('I read five, six books a week out of the library', he said); but then told me:

I hate writing. I've been away three years now and I've got to dig deep to find something new to say. I'm a telephone man.

When he said more, there were other kinds of writing that he did with a different ease:

I don't mind writing for other people. And I've got no problem writing official letters. I've spent a year writing the story of my trial. There's 220 pages there. People have said to me, you could write a book about it. But it's not like a book. It's more like a transcript.

Another scribe I met who had an interest in motivating his author to their own literacy was Harold. A 'lifer', like Gerry, Harold gazed at me steadily as he talked. He too recalled with pleasure the part he played in helping one of his clients learn to read and write independently:

Many years ago (maybe '86, '87), I was in a cell with a man who could not read and write, in Lewes prison. We were in the same cell for 45 days. I taught this guy to read and write and after I was moved to another prison, I got a note from him. I was touched. I thought, well at least I did that.

He'd been getting letters and just putting them on one side. Then one day he'd been low, and I said, 'What's wrong?' and he said, 'All these letters I get, I can't read them'. So I said 'Here we are, 23 hours a day banged up together, I'll teach you'. I think he was surprised, thought I was going to say he was stupid, couldn't even read and write. But I said, 'Why? Why should I think that?' He had the motivation. It was touching to get that note.

At the same time, Harold also had a firm 'get your bum into gear' approach to others:

I say to them: 'Don't rely on me to be your personal secretary. Show me that you have an interest to learn'. If they say, 'Harold, this is the letter, please can you reply?' I say: 'Is he writing to you or to me? I came here to do time, not to do secretarial work'.

As Harold saw it, trust is central to the relationship. To be unable to write is to risk losing pride; to ask someone else to write is to risk their mockery. In an important sense, as he pointed out, it is also to risk their cheating you:

The thing is, there has to be trust. If I say to you I want you to write a letter to my solicitor and say 'I was there, but I didn't commit the crime', and you write, 'I was there, and I committed the crime', there are two words missing and everything's changed.'

For some scribes, trust itself is the reward for this work. Alison was the last of the women scribes I interviewed in prison and she told me that the trust invested in her was worth more than any other kind of recompense. In giving her trust, the woman for whom she wrote gave her something that, for her, had a particular value:

This woman, Jan, I used to write for her. Maybe it was 11 months that we were together. She would write to her sister, sister-in-law, children. I don't usually trust anyone. So her trust meant a lot to me. It gave me a faith in human nature.

At this point it is time to introduce the third party in the scribal relationship: the reader. Jan's relatives knew that Jan could not write independently and were well aware of Alison's role as her secretary. In their letters back to Jan, they would sometimes address her, too:

Sometimes letters would come back that would begin: 'Hello Alison, I hope Jan's not giving you writer's cramp'… That sort of thing.

When Alison moved prison, she and Jan were separated. Alison then had the experience of receiving a letter from Jan scribed by someone else:

It was really weird. I've got no idea who wrote it for her. That's going to be the first question I ask when I write back. She can't read and write at all.

Two other stories where readers detect the scribe in a letter lead us into the role that family members play in all sorts of communities to keep alive connections across distance. The first, still from within a prison context, shows Lorraine, once a scribe herself for her father, now on the receiving end of letters from him that her sisters had written. Unlike Jan, she knew the other scribes well enough to be able to know which of them were doing the work:

When I get letters from my dad they're always written by someone else. I can tell which sister has written for him when I get one. Serena is more grammar perfect. My dad might say, 'I hope you are fine', but she'll write 'I hope you are feeling well'. Cheryl writes what he says, in his way. Like, 'I'm glad to get your letter', not, 'Thank you for writing'. And I think, 'Yeah, that's it'. I can picture the whole situation. I can picture him at the kitchen table dictating to her and her getting impatient with him. His favourite word is 'um'. He'll be saying, 'Tell her I'm glad she's ok. Um. Um.' I think he gets shy. He gets writer's block without even picking up a pen.

Having been one of her father's scribes herself, Lorraine knew the process at first hand. In the letter written by one sister she could practically hear his voice. In the letter written by the other, she received a formula, but no picture. Serena was the kind of scribe who wants to improve on the text, turn it into something 'properly written', formalise it. Cheryl, on the other hand, wrote in her father's voice, waiting (not always patiently) for him to produce the words before writing. While Serena imposed an alien style on her father's words, when Cheryl wrote for him, she kept his style. As Lorraine read it, she could picture him in the kitchen, dictating and pausing; getting stuck as all writers do; lost for words one minute, surging forward the next: 'Tell her I'm glad she's ok'. Reading the letter, Lorraine was reading his voice; well aware, at the same time, that she was reading it through the handwriting of a sister, invisibly there, penning the letter from him to her. This is not merely two styles of writing, it is two styles of *scribing* – two different ways of handling both script and author.

The second story concerns the reader of a letter written by two people. The first time Tara began to receive letters from her parents was when she left the family home in Trinidad to live in Britain. This was in the late 1950s. Like many other parents, Tara's father and mother wrote a joint letter. The letters were written as if from both of them. Tara, however, was well aware who actually put the words on paper; for she knew that her mother could not read or write:

> In a situation like that, when I got letters, I had to read between the lines what it was my mother said, and what was my father. Because he never said, 'Well, your mother said this' or, 'I'm saying that'. It was just one letter, as though it was written by one person. But I could tell when it was her voice saying something and I could tell when it was his voice saying something. He used to deal with the business side of it. You know. 'Have you got enough to eat? Have you got enough clothes? Is it warm for you?' And my mother would give me news about – well, about my other brothers and sisters, and how she's feeling. Different. One letter, but different.[13]

Tara's mother's writing was only a partial contributor to the letter; but the picture Tara suggests is of both her parents composing together, attempting between them to imagine her, the reader.

Family ties

Like Lorraine's father, an author may write with the help of more than one scribe. In research about women's literacy in the early twentieth century, I was told this story by a woman in Swansea, Wales. It is a recollection of how her own mother, Peggy, would write letters to her father (Peggy's husband) when he was away at sea in the 1940s. Peggy would be in the kitchen, trying to write a letter. Her scribes, upstairs in their bedroom, were her small children:

It was a time they both dreaded. They would both be banished to bed and she would settle herself at the kitchen table ready for this mammoth task. After a few minutes, Peggy would call out: 'Glen, Glen!' 'Yes, Mam?' 'How do you spell *please*?' Glen would diligently call out the letters one by one. Next minute you'd get, 'Glen, Glen!' 'Yes, Mam?' 'Which way does the P go – up or down?' This would go on until the letter was finished.[14]

This is a humorous story, told with affection. The roles are reversed: the children called on to resolve their mother's spelling and hand-writing troubles; the mother (having 'banished' them to bed) disturbs them with her calls to help her. However, the trouble with having other people in your family be scribes for your personal letters is that you may not want them to know your business. For Peggy, the situation may have felt less amusing at the time than her daughters found it, recalling it later. Writing to a husband far away, working out what to say and what to leave out, she had to stop and start and ask before she could get at least some version of what she would really have liked to write on the page.

Someone with interesting, different scribes in her own family is Sandra. She grew up in Edinburgh; we met in her front room one Tuesday morning in November, in South East London. A woman in her fifties, she had attended classes in literacy and basic education for some time. Until recently, she had turned to others to be her scribes: first Dave, her husband, and later Mandy, her daughter. Soon after they married, Dave had persuaded Sandra to try to overcome a barrier she had about writing anything, convinced as she was that she was no good at it. Based on his promise that he 'would not laugh at her' Sandra eventually agreed to write a few words. At first she would not let him read what she had written. Only when he had promised that 'he would not laugh' did she show her writing. He replied, also in a note, also left on the table. This became a habit. She would leave a note for Dave and Dave would leave one, in return, for her:

I thought it was worthless. I just wrote two lines. And I couldn't write any more. I wouldn't show it to him either. The person I'm married to and I know well, but I wouldn't do it. Then he came up with the idea. He said, 'Sandra. I want you to write something down. Don't matter. Six words. Write it down. And when I come back – and I promise I won't laugh, or anything like that. No matter how wrong it is. You try and do it.' And it got to the stage when we were doing it all the time.

It became, it seems, an almost everyday thing. Two or three decades on, although they no longer lived together, Sandra would call on Dave when she had any difficult writing to do. How did they work together? I asked. Her answer suggested a partnership. Sometimes she would dictate to him; sometimes she would write some words down very rough, to start things off.

> I'd say, 'I want to say that'. Or else he'll say, 'What are you trying to say?' And I'll say, 'I'm trying to say...etc. etc., but I'm not sure' and I've got my words all jumbled up. So he says, 'Don't worry. Let me suggest this'. So he suggests it to me. 'Yeah, that's just what I'm trying to say'. So I feel good when that happens.

In more recent years, Sandra had turned more often to her daughter, now a mother herself. In this account, Sandra again would 'rough out' what she wanted to say – but this time out loud rather than in writing. Her daughter then had a go at improving on it, sometimes, but not always, with Sandra's agreement. Writing a letter to Sandra's friend Janet, in Birmingham, they were writing to someone they both knew:

> To begin with, she writes, you know, the address, the name. And the general bit what everybody says, you know, 'How are you? How's the family?' So she'll start the letter off herself, without me: and I quite accept that. And then the middle part is where my information comes in. I say to her, Mandy I says, how does this sound? and she says, 'Well yeah, mum, that's good'. And then maybe if I say it the wrong way, Mandy will say, 'Well mum', she says, 'it's up to you, you know, if you want to say it that way, it's your letter. But it would sound better like this, you know. What do you think of it?' So I says, 'Well, Mandy, that makes sense. But you know what like Janet is'. And maybe I'll *want* my word in. And then other times: 'No Amanda. Yours sounds good. Put that one down!'

This is an account of give and take, first between wife and husband, then between mother and daughter. Each scribe gave her a different kind of encouragement. With Dave, she would rough something out and then feel she had got her words 'all jumbled up'. He would suggest a way through. Mandy, on the other hand, would take the pen and make a start on the letter herself. Then Sandra would try something out aloud for her to write down and Mandy would either agree or suggest an alternative. With Dave, Sandra was half-drafting the words herself to start with, and then turning to him to offer alternatives. With Mandy, she was more in the position of author and secretary, with the secretary taking down what she said but suggesting occasional improvements.

As I said earlier, there are disadvantages in having to rely on family members as scribes. An author may have private feelings to share with her friend or relative that are, perhaps, even about the person they use as their scribe. In some situations, too, authors know that the person they are writing to has to rely on another to read it out for them. Such a case was described by Adama, who attends a literacy class at the same centre as Sandra. Adama came to Britain from Sierra Leone in July 1992, since when she had written regularly to her mother, sending her much-needed money. The war in that country meant her writing a letter that she knew would take over two weeks to arrive; because of her own uncertain spelling, it also meant using a scribe. 'The spelling is hard for me', she said, so she depended on her husband to help her, each time she wrote ('I tell him and he writes it').

Adama also knew that her mother could not read and that, once her letter arrived, her mother would have to rely on her son (Adama's brother) to read it to her. Now, there are things that a daughter (a mother herself) might want to tell her mother, but, as Adama put it, this meant that her writing was constrained by having to remember the presence of not just one other reader (her husband), but also a second (her brother) – two other people to think of when she chose her words. 'Sometimes if I want to say something I can't', she said, 'because I don't want [my brother] to see it'.[15]

Time and distance

At the beginning of this chapter I mentioned the telephone. As far as personal communication is concerned, it seems the single most important invention to have happened in the last few hundred years. However, actually the history of this invention is still short[16] and we would do well to imagine the scale of the half a century earlier when, for the first time, ordinary people could afford to post a letter. The revolution that a cheap postal system brought about in the mid-nineteenth century is now beyond living memory. Telephones and email so dominate our lives in the early twenty-first century so that it can be hard to imagine what it meant: writing and posting letters with an envelope and a stamp, not dialling a number and holding a piece of plastic to your ear, was how a family sent and received messages from its members. The labour of composition, even so, might be costly. Ursula Howard cites a memory recorded in one man's autobiography of his mother and brother working all evening on a letter to a 'far-away sister', 'the mother painfully composing the sentences, the lad painfully writing them down', the whole evening's work only to be tragically destroyed a moment later as they held up the letter against the candle flame to dry the ink. The letter caught fire and 'the work of three laborious hours [was] destroyed in three seconds'.[17]

Until the middle of the nineteenth century, most people in Europe could not afford to post letters. The cost was born by the sender; it was tied to the distance it travelled. Added to that, until a system of railways was established, letters took days, or even weeks to arrive, travelling at the speed of a horse on a road. Nevertheless once letters and postcards became commonplace and relatively cheap to send in the early years of the twentieth century, the work of mail systems grew and grew. In the same period, ownership and use of the telephone was still only for the minority. Right up to the 1950s, more people were writing letters than making phone calls; then, in the 1970s, things changed. This is how the historian David Vincent put it:

> By 1928, for every hundred mail items, there were 25 telephone calls and just one telegram. As late as 1950, there was two and a half times as much work for the postman as for the telephone operator. Not until 1972, almost a century after its invention, did the telephone finally gain pre-eminence over a still expanding postal service.[18]

Maybe letter writing is once again a minority occupation. But long-distance phone calls have not yet become so cheap that letters between family members are a thing of the past. For Adama, writing to her mother was a lot cheaper than paying the cost of a call – even if her mother had access to a telephone: so she wrote, despite the disadvantages. For Teresa (from the same literacy class as Adama in South London), the cost of calls to her family was less, since they lived in Portugal, where she had grown up herself. In answer to my question about her letter writing habits, she was very definite (at first):

I do not write letters. Always I use the phone. I prefer to ring, because I hear the voice and I know the answer straight away as well. With letters, I need to wait. I am waiting on the answer and sometimes you don't receive.

What came out next, however, was a different use of letter writing than anyone else had so far mentioned to me. Teresa wrote letters to herself. She never posted them and, when she had written them, she would throw them away, for they had served their purpose:

You know what I do? I do this all the time. I have some problems. I don't go to the doctor or something to ask for help. I just stay home and write the letter, like I'm writing to someone. Like a diary. And after I have written everything, when I feel more comfortable, zum! I rip it up and put it in the rubbish. I write it in Portuguese. Like, if you upset me, or I have some problems with my husband or with my family or something. I write down everything.

J: So it's like writing a letter to yourself?

Yes. Just to myself.

J: Do you say, 'Dear Teresa'?

No, I just put London, 13th or 12th of the... I do the letter, that is okay. Everything is okay. And after, what has happened. And what is the news. And after, one is to ask questions, example. When I finish to ask the questions and everything, I start 'about myself' and then I start my diary. I don't start today. I start everything in the past, the present, I do everything like that. And after that I do – like that [*gesture tearing up paper*]. But after, I feel okay.[19]

It seems to me encouraging to think of a woman who exploits the medium for her own purposes – with no other reader than herself. For Teresa, it is enough to have written, not a diary, but a letter, recounting family news and other stories and then letting down her hair about herself. And when she has finished, she tears it up and throws it away. The letter has arrived at its destination.

The writer writes into the future; the reader reads into the past; they meet at two separate present times of their own, in separate rooms and, even, separate countries. When it comes to the reading and writing of letters, this reality has its own poignancy. The letter writer stays still: it is the letter that travels. From a foreign country to a distant home, from village to city, across seas and skies, it is apparently a one-to-one contact. What we have seen, however, is that behind any number of letters and their signatories, there maybe the unwritten name of husband, neighbour, daughter, wife or friend – a third figure in the relationship, creating in effect a triangle of participants. What Teresa shows us is a resolution of the tension between composing and transcribing together with a fusion between all three actors in the letter-writing drama: author, scribe and reader.

1 Quoted in Wilson, 2000, p61.
2 In Chapter 6, I quote from Kelly, another female prison scribe; Harold appears again in Chapter 9.
3 Paretsky, 1999, p375.
4 *Ibid*, p376.
5 Loewenstein, 1983, p35.
6 *Ibid*, p37.
7 Smith, 1982.
8 *Ibid*, p33.
9 *Ibid*, p24
10 More on this in Chapter 9.
11 Barton and Hamilton, 1998, p123.
12 *Ibid*, p150.
13 The contributions from Tara (a literacy teacher) and Teresa (one of her students) both derive from a tape discussion in Bede House Education Centre, South London, 14 February 2001.
14 Cited in Mace, 1998, p143.
15 From a scribed conversation between Adama and her literacy teacher, Jacqui, March 2001, Bede House, South London.
16 Alexander Graham Bell took out a patent for his telephone in 1876. He had, it seems, a particular interest in the voice. His father was the inventor of 'visible speech', a system for guiding the deaf to learn to speak. His mother, a gifted musician, began losing her hearing when Graham (the name the family used for him) was 12. www.cybercomm.net/~chuck/bell.htm (the Telephone History website: visited 22/04/01).
17 From *The Life Story of Will Crooks* by G. Haw (1907), cited in Howard, 1991, p102.
18 Vincent, 2000, p3.
19 From the tape discussion at Bede House, 14 February 2001.

PART TWO

Scribes and situations

CHAPTER FOUR

The office scribe

T hese words come from a scene set in Palestine in the 1940s:

> I'm the typewriter. I write letters for people. I have four keyboards, Roman, Hebrew, Cyrillic and Arabic.[1]

This short speech is striking. It says: 'This is who I am. This is what I do.' The speaker is a man, in a street. On the table in front of him are four machines, also called typewriters, each of them with a different script (Roman, Hebrew, Cyrillic and Arabic). His choice of job title ('typewriter') catches the ear. The tool defines the worker. It is as if a dressmaker were to say, 'I am the needle'; or a carpenter, 'I am the hammer'. Like those whom Judy Kalman observed in Mexico City, this man is a street scribe; unlike them, he has the tools to type in any one of four scripts. His texts are:

> love letters and letters to creditors and letters to doctors and letters to mothers and letters to sons. And sometimes to fathers.[2]

Street scribes in the present day, as we have already noticed, are mostly men. Office scribes, however, are usually women. It is with *A matter of gender* that this chapter begins. From some office scribing experience of my own, I follow this with *A short autobiography*, in which I discuss some of the changes brought about for office scribes by various *Machines in the office*. There have been careful distinctions made between different expectations of office scribes. The section *Secretary or typist?* offers three people's views about how these are expressed. The idea of a secretary's loyalty to her/his boss is given a humorous twist in an anecdote from 1950s New York. The chapter ends with the task of being the scribe for a group, the person who has to write the *Minutes of a meeting*; a role which very many people experience as having a lot of responsibility and very little power.

A matter of gender

When the first machine for producing writing appeared on the mass market in America, its manufacturers took the decision to train women (or 'girls' as they were then known) to demonstrate them. Firms who bought the machines wanted to hire the operators with them. Keyboard and keyboard technician then, as in Palestine half a century later, were one and the same; at this time, the technicians were to be overwhelmingly female:

> The typewriter was introduced to the public in 1873, and Reming-
> ton had the revolutionary idea of training girls to demonstrate it.
> Called 'typewriters' themselves, the girls created a sensation, and
> the firms that bought the machines wanted the operators too.[3]

In the civil service in Britain, specialist hand-copying had been done before then by temporary workers known as 'writers' or 'copyists': 'men and boys who...were in practice used as a sort of mobile reserve for overspills of low-grade clerical work.'[4] With industrialisation came increased paperwork. The typewriter offered an efficient way of dealing with this. Clerical work, till then a largely male occupation, was suddenly opened up to women – cheaper to employ and 'less troublesome' than male workers.[5] Clerical work, inevitably, became deskilled.

Well, that is one version of the story. Meta Zimmeck, the author of a study of secretarial work in the British civil service, disagrees, calling it a 'trite scenario',[6] which 'begins with male clerks copying manuscripts by hand and ends with operators keying in computers'; these women, and the jobs they do, becoming 'deskilled' in the process. In her view, this scenario oversimplifies a complicated story. Her study looked at the way in which the civil service in Britain made decisions about how to organise its clerical staff. Her findings, she tells us, show that:

- it took a long time for typewriting to take over from hand-copying (the change began in 1878, in the 1930s hand-copying still survived);

- typewriting was actually first taken on by men and boys; transferring to boys only, and then to women and girls, with these stages overlapping; and
- the advent of the typewriter did not mean deskilling, since typewriting was actually 'hand-copying by other means' (the Treasury and other departments already saw hand-copying as low value, and simply carried on with the same attitude when it came to typing and shorthand writing).[7]

There were, and still are, strong feelings about the difference between being a secretary and being a typist, not to mention marked pay differentials between them. As far as the different status of 'writers' and 'copyists' is concerned, Meta Zimmeck leaves us a little tantalised; what she does say is that they were men or boys 'hired on a daily basis directly through departments or subcontracted through law stationers'[8] and that both categories of employee were expected to have skills in 'handwriting, spelling, and the power to copy'.[9] I still wonder whether 'writers' were better paid than 'copyists'. I wonder too, if writers were expected to go away and actually compose a document – I don't know. By the 1930s, a clear line seems to have been drawn. The female clerk or 'stenographer':

> needed only the intelligence to understand what was being dictated to her and what she was supposed to do with it...within the relatively unimportant range of routine dictation... The secretary, by contrast, was all that the stenographer was not, and performed a much more demanding job.[10]

And by the 1950s, one person who saw herself as a 'secretary' was even clearer. In a letter to the Times newspaper, she wrote:

> Sir,
>
> By all means let salaries for secretarial staff be stabilized at an economic level; but in this process let us not lose sight of economic justice. A financial distinction should surely be made between the *unskilled and semi-skilled typewriter or punchers, of little or no education*, and the women of genuine education and background who bring a professional skill, sense of responsibility and capacity for initiative to bear on their work.[11] (My italics.)

No question about who is who, here. The 'financial' distinction is being measured by a distinction of class. The use of the word 'typewriter' to denote the person at the machine (first used when 'girls' came into office life) here has a clear suggestion of a menial factory worker (a 'puncher'), lower in the ranks than 'women of genuine education and background'. Later in the same letter the writer goes further. Revealing herself as one of 'the secretary…class', she deplores the (evidently younger) 'flibbertigibbets' she is forced to work with.

By the 1990s, with the impact of new technology in offices large and small, there was an assumption that far more men were now becoming, if not scribes for others, at least more in the habit of doing some of their own scribing. There was even talk of male secretaries. However, the vast majority of people *typing for others* today, evidently, are still female. As one reporter put it:

> There is no physical reason why the vast majority of secretaries are women, but the fact remains that they are. It is such a glaring discrepancy that some try to deny it. Agencies will claim that things are changing, and that 15 to 20% of clerical jobs are done by men these days. Closer examination reveals, however, that this includes such positions as accounts clerk. When secretarial work only is taken into account, the percentage of men involved becomes so small that it barely registers.[12]

If we stick to our definition of a scribe as someone who *writes* and who *writes for others*, the days of the male 'writers' and 'copyists' seem further and further away. One point of view has it that the whole idea of 'touch typing' is abhorrent to most men. In a piece that argues for more children to learn touch typing at an early age, this (male) writer claims that:

> one of the initial problems of selling the computer was getting men to put their hands on keyboards. No manager would be seen dead with a keyboard on his desk or even in his (*sic*) office. Five-finger touch-typing was for sissies…
>
> When real men, such as Fleet Street journalists, absolutely had to do it, they would adopt a flamboyant 'hunt and peck' two-finger style. I suspect the hacks still do – although the rakish fedora, the 'office bottle' and the cigarette drooping from the mouth have gone. Tough guys don't touch type.[13]

We will pass over his omission of all the *female* managers that you and I can think of who get on with touch-typing: some of us (arguably) colluding with the resulting layoffs of secretarial or 'support' staff when organisations feel driven to make 'cuts' or false economies in their budgets. However, I digress. The argument here is that no kind of rhetoric about 'the computer revolution' is of any use until and unless students can 'find 'v' on the keyboard without 5 seconds' hesitation'; and it is a good one.

A short autobiography

The occupation of typist intrigues me, maybe because I have been one myself. I love the way writing that looked a mess can be made to look so fine, simply by copy-typing it. I like typing my own writing; I have taken pride in typing other peoples'. My career as a typist, if I can call it that, has been much like that of many other women I know. It has moved from paid to unpaid and then back to paid again. As a young graduate in the 1960s, I joined a 6-month 'graduate secretarial course' and got a job soon after as secretarial assistant in an art gallery. Later, I earned my living as a 'temp', typing for an art historian, doing odd typing jobs for friends, and a short spell in a travel agent. For a couple of years when my children were small, I was the (unpaid) editor for the newsletter of a campaign organisation.[14] As an adult literacy tutor (unpaid and then paid) in the early 1970s, I typed worksheets, newsletter articles, reports. Later, I seem to remember switching back to the role of unpaid typist, tapping out my husband's MA dissertation and later still, CVs for him and our children as they grew up.

Some of this was a chore, but most of it I enjoyed. I like the mix of manual and mental, the translation between rough copy and finished text; I could not count the number of reports, letters, articles and minutes of meetings that I have typed in the years since that secretarial course. A dear friend and colleague of the time, now head of a study skills unit in a large higher education institution in New Zealand, had (like me) moved from earning her living in temporary work as a secretary to becoming (via voluntary work) the Director of a voluntary-sector Adult Literacy Scheme in South London. We would compare notes about the offices we had worked in. Now as office-heads ourselves, we would get on with being our own secretaries, typing our own letters, reports, newsletters and articles, and typing out, too, the painful writing of our literacy students, so that they (like us) could experience their own text in formal dress. (I sometimes think that the 'language experience movement' discussed in Chapter 9, might never have happened if there had not been a critical mass of women working first as volunteers, later as paid tutors and organisers, who had this conjunction of experience: education and office work, teaching and typing.)

Back in the 1960s, as a student on the secretarial course, I also learned shorthand. Painstakingly, I copied the outlines with my well-sharpened HB pencil. Laboriously, from my seat on the top deck of the bus that took me home each evening to my Finsbury Park bedsit, I would mentally translate into straight and loopy lines all the slogans on the advertising hoardings I could see outside the window. Conscientiously, on my candlewick bedspread in the evenings, I sat copying the same outline into my shorthand pad, pushing the pencil up and down a little faster each time. I do not even remember now what speed I arrived at. By March, it was all over. Just before the course was due to end, with the awful climax of exams and tests, I got a job. I bunked off – and never used shorthand again. Somehow none of the typing jobs I went on to get asked it of me. Before long, I had moved from being an office scribe, to become a classroom one, instead.

I am less sorry about this than I might have been. Shorthand and I were not meant for each other. To do it properly, I had been taught, you always needed a sharp pencil. A biro would not do, as there would be too little distinction between thick and thin lines. For the writing I went on to do myself, I have been too much on the move, too little committed to the art of consistent, accurate outlines, too fickle with my writing tools. It was not until years later, speaking to a professional shorthand writer in research-ing this book, that I learned an alternative to this dogma of the pencil:

> Anybody with any sense would not use a pencil in court. You use a fountain pen. When you're fully proficient, thick and thin doesn't really matter all that much. It won't be like it is in the book. One or two people can do that absolutely copperplate stuff. The majority of people cannot. Some people can write beautifully, others don't; but they can still do the same thing.[15]

Machines in the office

What became the serious craft of a courtroom shorthand writer apparently originated in the nineteenth century as an enjoyable and absorbing pastime, like crossword puzzles or jigsaws. It was only after it had taken on practical use for 'the taking down of sermons for publication', later extending to newspaper reporting, that shorthand became common in offices in general.[16] The office scribe, today, may use shorthand a lot more than I ever did: but the technology of pencil or pen is small fry compared with the array of machines she has to contend with. A little more history here, to provide some perspective on how the clerk or secretary's work as scribe has altered over time.

After typewriters, the photocopier and the dictaphone are regarded as the two pieces of equipment that made the main changes to the way that office writing progressed in the first half of the twentieth century. In an interesting account of power relations in the office, Rosemary Pringle suggests that the photocopier was 'perhaps the most underestimated piece of technology to slink in in the 1960s'.[17] Documents that had to be copied for legal purposes no longer had to be retyped. There was no longer the need to make a lot of carbon copies.

Let me stake a claim, however, for that other, less stream-lined means of copying: the ink duplicating machine. One of the few poems of mine to have been published was written after a long evening of typing articles for a newsletter for some friends (somehow it got into the hands of the editor, so they printed it in the newsletter with an affectionate tribute to the author). It begins with the lines:

Hello, writers of collective prose.
It's me, the typist.
Homeworker of the vanguard,
my labour, invisible,
gives your paragraphs of worried scrawl
the dignity and symmetry of type.

It is the second verse that tells of the technology I was using at the time:

Playing out the thunder of your manifesto
late into the evening's quiet,
I sit here
(checked by the ringing bell)
and punch out your abstract syllables
into the spongy skin of the stencil's promise.[18]

The date of the poem was 1980. The 'ringing bell' and the 'thunder' were the sounds of a particularly heavy secondhand electric typewriter I had only recently acquired at the time. I can remember the feel of the Gestetner stencil between finger and thumb, and the smell of the pink correcting fluid that was needed to patch up errors. It was the punch of the typewriter key through the stencil on the typewriter carriage that would pierce letters through the stencil 'skin'; these, when the stencil was fitted onto the duplicating machine, would allow the ink through to print the text on the paper being fed through. Reading this, you may also be of a generation to be able to share a certain nostalgia for the smell of that ink and the piercing of those stencils. You may also remember the pleasure in abandoning the whole business in favour of laying a sheet of paper on the glass top of the photocopying machine and watching the copies pour out at the touch of a button.

It took 20 years before the photocopiers that 'slunk in in the 1960s' became cheap enough for smaller organisations to be able to throw away these ink duplicating machines. The community education centre where I worked in the 1980s[19] was part of a higher education college, 2 miles up the road. I remember feeling shocked the first time I saw how staff in the 'main building' of the college would make photocopies with such ease and extravagance. I would return later in the day to finish work on a community newsletter, to be printed on our inky machine, the wrinkled stencil resisting all efforts to smooth it round the drum. It wasn't long before we got our own photocopier, of course, and since that time I have become as profligate as anyone else in pressing the copy machine button.

At the same time, the profligacy that shocked me then, with the introduction of electronic mail still to come, was soon widespread. Memos, minutes and papers were suddenly copied on a huge scale. Pigeonholes fill up with a copy for everyone. Plans for reorganisation, efforts at consultation, all this meant the ideas had to be 'circulated' – a confetti of paper was everywhere. In an attempt to make sense of our part in creating some of this paperwork for others, Ruth Lesirge and I wrote an argument for its purpose in the organisations where we then worked. We said:

> Much of this writing frequently seems like sheer bureaucracy; but in reality it should, and often does, have a purpose. We want to argue that managing and developing adult education is a creative process; and that this means that in an important sense this everyday, internal paper-pushing has a vital significance. The 'outcome' – in the form of published prospectus, policy statement,

budget, research report, conference paper, book – has the status of a public product. But for any of these documents to have value, the process of their production is crucial.[20]

We needed to convince ourselves, as well as our readers. Technology (the photocopying machine) could not be called the 'cause' of the problem. Technology was what we, and others, were using (and continue to use) as a means towards some effort at democracy. The price we continue to pay is the added pressure we give ourselves and others to have read and formed a view on all the documents that photocopying enables us to circulate.

Typewriters meant the shift from handwriting to keyboard tapping: legibility guaranteed. Photocopiers and duplicating machines meant no more carbon paper. Word processors, when they came in, introduced the wonder of the delete button. (Only if you have had to hand-correct not just a top copy, but three or four carbon copies, each time a mistake was made, can you fully appreciate the relief that meant.) However what the dictaphone machine did was to change how speaker and scribe had to work together. In that sense, they may have had an even bigger impact than any other machine on the scribal work of offices. It was the dictaphone that made possible the idea of typing pools, where typists processed text from disembodied voices on tape, rather than from the man (usually) pacing up and down in the office in front of them. Scribe and author are now separate from each other; the 'author' now free to dictate in another time and place from their scribe. From a commercial point of view, the advantage of dictaphones over handwritten shorthand in the 1960s and '70s was increased productivity:

> The manufacturers…argued, for example, that an executive can put his ideas down in longhand at a maximum speed of 15 wpm, dictate to a secretary at twice that rate, and to a machine at 60 wpm after a few days' practice.[21]

The advantages of speed and increased output are a recurring theme in the story of changes in office technology. With this calculation, manufacturers made their pitch at employers' interests in increased productivity. The thing that the busy executive can do with a dictaphone is *save time* – or rather, save *his* time. As we shall shortly see, audio typists sometimes have to spend more time than they might have as copy typists, simply having to replay badly recorded texts.

In the early 1930s, when The Dictaphone Company was first marketing its wares, they used an advertisement with time-saving as its main message. A bespectacled man in suit and tie, with a hair-parting of military precision, sits at his leather-topped desk holding a microphone, attached by a snake-like tube to a machine on his desk. In his right hand he is holding a sheet of paper, which he is evidently reading. The microphone is large and held close to his mouth. Beside his right elbow stands an upright office telephone (the kind where the receiver must be removed from the stand with one hand while the other hand firmly grips the upright). The words beneath the picture are clearly addressed to someone identical to the person in the picture: another man, with important work to do:

> You cannot afford to overload your memory with the clogging details of your work.

Man-to-man, picture and text seem to say: 'You and I know how the world is. We are busy men with a lot on our minds, some of it too trivial for us. We need someone else to deal with these "clogging details"'. The caption continues:

> The best of private secretaries – silent, tireless, supremely efficient – is ALWAYS with you if you dictate to THE DICTAPHONE.

> Doctors, lawyers, authors and business-men deal with all details of their work – letters, instructions, memoranda, press articles – the instant the need arises.

Foreshadowing later sales talk of increased productivity, this promise follows:

> OVER 200,000 DO THINGS THE DICTAPHONE WAY saving 50% of the cost of handling everything they dictate and winning for themselves two extra hours every day.[22]

So much for the promises. The next section returns to the present day.

Secretary or typist?

Dictaphones and photocopiers are still in use, email and all sorts of computer software have elbowed their way in. Office scribes may be producing text already composed, or having to do much composition themselves. One example of how a secretary may have to learn to alternate these roles comes from Jess, a woman in her thirties who had worked as a secretary in a publishing company for 3 years. This his how she described to me the ways in which she would be asked to produce a typed and finished text:

> One would be the letter written out in longhand, and my job would be to copy-type it. The second would be, the woman would dictate some and vaguely tell me what she wanted to write for the rest ('Say something like that'). And the third would be: 'Can you just write to them and say…?'

These three approaches seem to ring a bell. They are remarkably similar to the requests that Maria, in the previous chapter, said her clients in prison made to her. (Women asked her, 'Could you go through this and check it?' or, 'I've written this – could you make it longer?' or: 'Can you write it for me?'.) In office settings everywhere, the practice of handing handwritten texts to secretaries for typing is common. As a strategy for producing texts fast and efficiently, it has weaknesses: not least, the difficulty many secretaries have in reading their boss's handwriting. Of the three approaches mentioned here, taking dictation from the person in the same room is the most labour intensive. Two people are caught up in the process at the same time. As Jess describes it, the woman who chose this option with her found a way out of this – by leaving the composition of a good part of the letter to the secretary. With the third approach, the responsibility for composition is entirely with her.

The claim that audio typing might save time and be a more efficient way of working than any of these three holds water as long as the 'dictator' themselves provides a coherent and intelligible dictation. Jess's experience of audio typing from such a tape was a mixed one:

> One company I worked for, I had to work as audio typist for the chairman and the director. One of them (the chairman) wanted all of it edited, the other didn't want any of it changed. The chairman tended to dictate in a way that was clipped, but friendly. The

director's letters were much more formal and at the same time more chaotic, and needed quite a lot of correction – but he didn't think he needed it. So it was strange: one doesn't want it but needs it, the other needs it but doesn't want it.

If we compare this with the distinction between 'secretary' and 'stenographer', Jess is clearly behaving like the former: the one who had the 'genuine education' to correct the employer's mistakes, even though, as Jess suggests, not all employers are aware that they might benefit from such correction. The secretary at the keyboard has to make judgements and choices all along the line. She has to remember that the chairman wants her to edit and improve his text, while (in her view) it works well as it is. She then has to consider that the director wanted her to take his dictation down without changing it at all, even though, as she listens to it, she found she was being asked to transcribe a 'chaotic' text that (if she made no corrections to it) would make a poor impression on its reader.

For Sharon, the difficulty with the audiotape she was given to work from was the intelligibility of the speaking voice itself. She had worked for 14 years in a major London teaching hospital. The department for which she works employs some 180 staff. Her job (which is part-time) is to type for any one of some 15 managers in the department. The work mainly consists of writing up clinical trials, with procedure and protocol and background information. Occasionally, she has audio typing to do, but it was not her favourite kind of work. As she put it, some of the managers have got 'the most horrendous voices':

J: In what way?

S: I don't know: the pitch, the tone of the voice and stuff. The more you rewind to see what they said, the worse it gets and you really can't understand a word they're saying.

Re-winding and re-playing a tape to catch the exact turn of phrase is tiresome, frustrating and time consuming. The idea of audio-typing is fine as long as both people involved in it – both 'dictator' and typist – have the skills it needs.

The 'take a letter, Miss Smith' image of a typist taking dictation in her shorthand pad may not exist any more, if it ever did. People in a hurry are more likely to depend on a secretary to do the composition themselves:

they start a text maybe (as Jess's female boss did), and then leave her to do the rest. In Sharon's experience, she would be asked, not so much to 'take' a letter but to 'do' it – then and there:

> I might have someone standing over my shoulder and they say: 'Can you just quickly do this letter?' I hate it. If they're talking and I'm typing, I hate it. It just puts me off. Quite a lot of people have said that… They say, 'I've got this in my mind. Can you just quickly bash it out?' I hate it. The manager's standing in the door with this look on his face. 'Er – have you got five minutes?' And you think: 'Oh no, he wants a letter'.

When I asked Sharon: 'Have you ever typed something and thought: "I think this needs improving"?'. She began by questioning whether she was qualified to correct things, 'my grammar's not good', she said; then added, 'but I can normally pick up mistakes'. So it would be that, despite her claim to be 'not good' at correct English, she might have a very good sense of what would read properly:

> I might say, 'This doesn't sound right' or 'You've used that word too many times already'.

For routine situations that keep recurring, Sharon's department keeps what she calls 'master letters' (for example, for when an employee is looking for somewhere to rent privately and the letting agency writes to her department for a reference to confirm the salary and reliability of that individual). For other kinds of composition her boss has a personal assistant. That suited Sharon fine. She is a copy typist, with no interest in making secretarial work her career. Her ambitions lie elsewhere (she is taking a qualification in massage therapy). Meanwhile, she is a fast and efficient typist; so fast and efficient that her spelling on a keyboard sometimes outstrips that which she produces by hand:

> The funny thing is, I can spell 'sincerely' when I'm typing but I can't spell it for the life of me when I'm writing.

One of Jess's bosses preferred to give her handwritten text to copy-type. Many boss/authors prefer this to dictation, and busy people may be only too glad to have corrections or improvements offered by their office scribes, particularly if the letter is to someone on a routine matter – in which case they might go along with secretarial amendments with which, in their heart of hearts, they do not agree. When there is more at stake, the boss/author may prefer to keep a close eye on how the letter is worded. This is how John, a retired junior-school headteacher, recalled working with his secretary:

> I couldn't dictate. I would write it in longhand. She'd say: 'You can't say that!' I'd say, 'Yes I can'. But she would sometimes improve it.
>
> There was a mutual respect between us. She thought I was a good headteacher, and I thought she was a good secretary. So I was prepared to leave it to her sometimes. But if it was someone I knew or wanted to influence, I'd draft the letter myself. For example, a parent of a child who was being bullied. I'd want to write to invite them to come in and I'd want to convey concern about their child. So I'd prefer to write 'Please could you come in and see me tomorrow', rather than, maybe, 'Kindly come and see me tomorrow'. I didn't want to give them an abrupt note; I had to convince them I was on their side. Mothers can be savage in defence of their own children. They wanted to know that I knew the child. The fact that I knew the child's name and remembered they'd had a tummy bug last week would mean more to them than if I were to say, 'I see Deirdre's in the top quartile of reading ages'. It was a middle-class thrusting area and some parents – especially fathers – wanted to know that, certainly. But mainly, in the letter, what I had to do was convey that it was their child I was writing about.
>
> The secretary did tend to be a bit terse. She was more succinct than I was. Which was fine if it was to a supplier, maybe, asking them to send us a copy of their invoice; more a letter from secretary to clerk.
>
> Sometimes she'd say – 'Well you haven't got time'. It was me that felt I wanted to control everything, be a control freak, and write it all myself. She was trying to rescue me from not delegating enough.

The 'mutual respect' between these two people meant that, sometimes, the author left the scribe to write it her way. When John wanted to win the trust of his reader, influence them or 'convince them that he was on their side' however, it felt important to him that he should compose his own letter. The choice of words would influence the result. Once again, the issue of trust is mixed up in this. He wanted his reader to trust him. So everything depended on who it was he and his secretary were writing to.

The balance between author and scribe changes according to context and personality. John's account comes from the other side of the counter to Jess and Sharon's. All three suggest some moments when the secretary is expected, by mutual consent, to produce a first draft, others when the boss prefers to compose the text him/herself, and others again when there is give and take between the two. So it seems that, even if not evident to the reader, the resulting text must always be a mix of two people's work – a different picture from that of the stereotyped secretary in the advertisement of The Dictaphone Company: 'silent, tireless, and supremely efficient' – a mechanic who churns out words verbatim.

The signature may be the boss's; the secretary may be the letter's true author. From the autobiography of Broadway star and writer Mae West comes this story of the slightly misguided loyalty of her secretary (a man) in dealing with her correspondence:

> There was a business letter from a manufacturer, who had visited the Royale Theatre in New York. He was a crude type, a vulgar, loudmouthed individual nobody liked very much, who was charmed with himself and blind to his own faults. The letter offered me some kind of a business proposition. It was phrased in common terms and contained many expressions of over-familiarity.

Imperiously, the star turned to her secretary and gave him direction as to how she wanted to reply:

> I said, 'Take a letter to this obnoxious lout and tell him not to bother me again. Period.' I made certain off-the-record remarks that were unflattering to the man's character, brains, and I even questioned his legitimacy. Lee scribbled away on his pad. He knew no shorthand. 'Send that out right away'.
> 'Yes, Miss West.'

The purpose of her letter to the manufacturer was clear: she wanted to send him packing. But a few days later she got a reply that surprised her:

> Dear Mae Baby:
> I have received your letter and it is the funniest and cleverest letter I have ever gotten. One of my associates read the letter, that nearly tore his insides out laughing, and put it up on the bulletin board. I am getting a lot of ribbing from the other associates in the firm, but you sure can (and a great deal more).

Wanting to recall what she had said that could have been so amusing, she asked her secretary for a copy of what she had written in the first place.

> He said, 'I didn't make a copy of it, Miss West – no carbon paper – but I put in everything you said.'
> 'You don't mean you put in all the low-down things I said about him?'
> 'Sure. I read his lousy letter after you threw it in the waste-basket.'
> 'I better burn my mail after this.'
> 'Only a bum could write a letter like that to a lady. You said – remember? – if he ever opened a book on etiquette the pages would fall out, and that you wished you could think of him as just a poor, good-natured bum, but he wasn't poor and he wasn't good-natured. And you signed it, "Cordially yours".'[23]

He wrote it; she signed it; the recipient found it clever and Mae West's reputation for being outrageous was kept intact. What more could a secretary do for a boss? She let him off with an admonition to 'let me read over what I say in my letters from now on'.

Minutes of a meeting

While the business of writing letters must still be the most common task of a secretary, other writing is also required of secretaries – not least, as writers of minutes from meetings. Not forgetting, of course, you do not have to be a paid-up professional typist to get drawn into being the secretary of your trade union branch, parents' meeting or local community group. The dread of being called on to 'take the minutes' is often the single thing that puts off people going to some meetings in the first place. As suggested elsewhere, a good chair of a meeting should not be 'a police officer of talk', but a facilitator who, among other things, keeps in close touch with the minutes secretary during the course of the meeting, checking that she or he is clear as to what the meeting expects to be recorded:

> It comes as an extraordinary piece of news to many people to know that the word 'minutes' early on in a meeting agenda is there to indicate a moment 'when the whole meeting takes responsibility for checking the accuracy of the minutes of the previous one'. If there are omissions or mistakes, it is the job of the group to check and amend them. This activity is there, not in order to pass judgement on the minutes secretary's failures to do a perfect job, but precisely in order to recognise that the record of a collective group is a collective responsibility.[24]

Office scribing is not confined to people paid to work in an office. David Barton and Mary Hamilton, in their study of the different kinds of literacy that get used in everyday life, came up with a category they called 'meetings literacy'.[25] By this they meant all the kinds of reading and writing work – bills, accounts, reports and correspondence – that form part of the activity of an association of people doing their business. Much of this paperwork is essential to an organisation, however small, if it wants to be accountable to its members. I mentioned earlier, an article that Ruth Lesirge and I wrote about this. We were trying to consider how some at least, of all the seemingly unending paperwork in some organisations, is supposed to be useful, to enable people within them to be informed, to influence decisions and even to participate in the shaping of ideas and policy.

Of all the paperwork that might achieve such democratic intent, the minutes of a meeting must be the most essential. Yet the taking of minutes, in itself, cannot guarantee democracy. Barton and Hamilton illustrate this in their account of a meeting they observed of a local allotment association. There was a chair, a minutes secretary and the group of members. There was a cardboard box of papers on the floor by the chairperson. While there was reference to minutes of the previous meeting, copies were neither distributed nor read out. Nor did the minutes secretary appear to be taking any minutes of the meeting that was happening. What appeared to be his practice was to write up the minutes after the meeting, keep one copy, and neither copy this nor read it out at the next meeting. As Barton and Hamilton put it, the way things were organised here meant that there was no more than a 'veneer' of democracy.[26]

The business of writing minutes is a three-part process. First, the minutes secretaries, sitting in meetings, take notes. These are and must be a selective version of what is actually said. They are likely to be entirely illegible to anyone else. Every now and then they ask the chair a question, such as: 'Do you want me to minute that?' or, 'Could you give me a moment while I get that down?' This is the first part of writing minutes and goes on during the meeting itself. The second part, later that day or the next day (the sooner the better; the more time passes, the less you can read your own scribble), is when the minutes secretaries read back their notes and copy out a neat version, editing as they go. The third stage can take two directions. Either this draft set of minutes goes to the chairperson for checking, or it doesn't, but is copied and gets circulated to everyone. The important thing at the next meeting is that anyone who wants to make an amendment does so in the spirit of a shared responsibility for this record.

In practice, too many meetings in too many organisations ruthlessly sideline the minutes secretary. They are ignored and forgotten in the heat of discussion: a discussion that does not allow them to join in due to the worry about getting the writing done right. Minutes secretaries are expected to turn everything they see and hear into the third person; know enough about the story being discussed to select what to leave out in the minutes; and pick out what counts as a decision – not forgetting to note who it is who has agreed to act on it. All that, and then face the risk that at the next meeting, when they get to see the minutes, people will say they got it wrong. It's no wonder people are nervous of being landed with the job. It is for the chair, if they are doing *their* job right, to remind the meeting of the support that they owe to the minutes secretary, by saying things like, 'We need to agree how much of this discussion we want Sesheta to put in the minutes'. Or 'Sesheta, have you got a minute of that alright?'. It is for the meeting as a whole to provide the proper 'give and take' to the scribing work of their discussion and give thought to the person doing it. Adult literacy education offers an ideal opportunity to rehearse this way of behaving. More of us could ensure that this kind of scribing role is open to anyone. We need to write scenarios and role cards and persuade our students to act out the parts of a group of people struggling with an agenda, who show that they also take a shared responsibility for the production of a written record of that struggle. To be a good minutes secretary is not about being good at spelling; it is about the individual having the practice of doing it and the group having an awareness of the support they owe the individual.

Government policy-writing about adult literacy education seems not to say a lot about this kind of literacy. The focus seems to be on an individual showing an ability to achieve individual learning targets unaided. In a comparison of public policy-writing about adult basic education in English-speaking countries, Sue Gardener pointed out that the idea of literacy competence that stresses mutual support is only evident in Australia. Here, the process of setting up a framework to describe and define what makes someone competent in their basic skills did not start, as in Britain, by developing a set of standards or programmes. Instead, they began the exercise by carrying out 'an analysis of communication skills and practices in the workplaces of the new economy'. It was this analysis that, in turn, led to the concept of something they called 'collaborative competence', which laid emphasis on the 'teamwork principle'.

In Britain, by contrast, the stress has been on expert performance as 'unassisted and solitary, on the model of the final exam'.[27] Yet this is a democracy that bemoans electoral apathy and yearns for more participation. One way to make such participation in local activities more attractive would be to make the literacy of meetings much more attractive – with the role of community scribe promoted as a supported one, in which the task of producing writing with or for a group is a collaborative activity. Inspiration for this sense of mutual responsibility, as shown in the next chapter, is there to be found in the Quaker approach to writing minutes.

1 Grant, 2000, p219.
2 *Ibid.*
3 Benet, 1972, p39.
4 Zimmeck, 1995, p5.
5 Crompton and Jones, 1984, p.21; and Zimmeck, 1995, p16.
6 Zimmeck, 1995, p3.
7 *Ibid*, p21.
8 *Ibid*, p5.
9 *Ibid*, p7.
10 Davies, 1982, p129.
11 Letter from 'Marie Trevett', published in *The Times* of 21 January 1956 and reprinted in a collection edited by K. Gregory, 1976.
12 Saunders, 2000.
13 Sutherland, 1999.
14 Campaign for the Advancement of State Education (CASE): the newsletter was (and still is) called *Parents and Schools*.

15 From an interview with Walter Hemingway, shorthand writer and transcriber with the Courts of Justice from 1950–2000, February 2001, Chancery Lane, London. Further from WH in Chapter 6.
16 Benet, 1972, p42.
17 Pringle, 1989, p183.
18 Mace, 1980.
19 The Lee Community Education Centre, Goldsmiths' College, London. For an account of the Centre's work, see Mace, 1992, p46 and p68.
20 Lesirge and Mace, 1991, pp236–7.
21 Pringle, 1989, p182.
22 This advertisement featured in *Punch*, or the London Charivari, 4 May 1932.
23 West, 1996, pp142–3.
24 Mace, 1992, pp138–9.
25 Barton and Hamilton, 1998, pp214–7.
26 *Ibid*, p229.
27 Gardener, 2001, p21.

CHAPTER FIVE

Religion and scribing

eligious life is very much about voices. Worship of the divine finds expression in praise and lamentation, in prayer and prophesy, in solos and choruses. Divine revelation is performed through words – spoken or written. In Islam, Qur'anic revelation came in the form of a written text shown to the Prophet (who did not read and write) when he was asleep. Ordered to read it, he replied that he could not; but Gabriel, who brought the message, 'throttled' him until he could, telling him that the Lord 'teaches by means of the pen and teaches humans what they do not know':

> And Mohammed said, 'I read it and when I awoke from my sleep,
> it was written on my heart, like a book'.[1]

To make revelations of the divine will available to others not present means reciting, repeating and writing. This chapter discusses religious scribes in four ways. It starts by considering scribes as *Officials*, lawyers and lawmakers in Jewish society, and moves on to the mediaeval scribes working as manual *Labourers* in monasteries all over Europe – with a brief excursion into a drama set in one such monastery. Between reader and copyist sits the more educated *Transcriber*, the one who takes down (apparently from dictation) the words of mystic revelation. Back in the present day, we meet the clerk of the Quaker business meeting who acts as a group's *Servant*, whose scribal task is to 'capture the spirit of the meeting'.

It would be wrong to begin, however, without a brief word about gods who are themselves scribes. According to the legends of many civilisations the origin of writing itself is attributed to 'the intervention of divine or semi-historical beings'; but in ancient Egypt, two of their key deities were also given the formal position of scribes: the ibis-headed Toth and his consort Seshat. Toth, also known as Thoth or Tahuti, was:

...not only the scribe of the gods and the 'master of papyrus' but also the inventor of writing.[2]

Mighty in knowledge and divine speech and the inventor of hieroglyphs (*medju-netjer* in Egyptian: 'words of the gods'), Toth was god of the underworld, recorder of the judgements on the souls of the dead: author, even, of the *Book of the Dead*. Sometimes depicted in human form with the head of an ibis, at other times depicted wholly as an ibis or baboon, Toth is often shown holding a writing reed and palette.[3] His principal spouse or consort, Seshat, was also a divine scribe; the goddess of history, portrayed with a star on her head, surmounted by two long straight plumes, an ideogram of her name – whose meaning is 'secretary'. Seshat (or Sesheta), like Toth, was seen as the inventor of letters. She was called the 'mistress of the house of books'. She was goddess of history and record-keeper for the gods. Sometimes portrayed 'writing the names of the sovereigns on the leaves of the sacred tree at Heliopolis'; at other times she is shown 'drafting the minutes of Jubilee celebrations'.[4]

These are scribes for the holy writing tasks of many gods. In the monotheistic religion in which I grew up, the scribal task appears much simpler.

In the beginning was the Word, and the Word was with God, and the Word was God.[5]

Once upon a time someone wrote those words on papyrus, and between that time and my copying them here on this keyboard, the sentence has been translated many times, copied many more, and been contemplated by uncountable numbers of readers. While Toth was one of several gods, and scribe, stationer and calligrapher for all of them, the Christian God is singular, and the ultimate author of all words.

Officials

All over the Mediterranean world and the near East, scribes were a common feature of religious and cultural life over several millennia.[6] In the ancient world, they were alternately seen as Scribes (with a capital S) looked up to as officials, keepers of the holy laws and scholars (and seen by some as corrupted by their power), or as lowly village scribes, mere copyists and keepers of local documents. In his account of scribes in Palestinian society, Anthony Saldarini suggests a useful analogy between the varied status of scribes and that of secretaries:

> The word 'scribe' in Hebrew, Greek and other languages, had a wide range of meanings which changed over time and could denote several roles. The closest idiomatic English equivalent is the term 'secretary' which can refer to roles from a typist to a high level administrative assistant and on to a highly responsible organizational or corporate official and finally a cabinet officer at the highest level of government.[7]

In Jewish society in the first century AD, the village scribe was 'little more than a copyist who knew how to draw up letters and legal documents'.[8] At the other end of the scale was the wise and respected community leader, looked up to as the source of legal and scriptural knowledge, and turned to for the resolution of both local and national conflicts. Years of training would have been needed to acquire the necessary literacy to perform their job. From this period there are descriptions of such learned men, committed to acquiring wisdom through much study, scholarly in matters of holy law and scriptures. The 'Word' of God enters the thinking of such a scribe and gives him special insight:

> The scribe prays and if God fills him with the spirit of under-standing, he will be wise.[9]

Later Talmudic literature refers to scribes in multiple ways:

> from a copyist who produced Torah scrolls, to a literate person who writes letters and documents, and to a teacher and interpreter of literature.[10]

Examples of the two extremes both occur in a later period. The low-status scribe features in the story of Salome's[11] family, threatened with servitude. The form this servitude was to take was that the mothers in her family would have to weave at the loom at the side of slave girls, and the brothers would become village scribes – a punishment seen to be a sarcastic reference to the low standard of their education. By contrast, the high-status scribe appears in a story of Salome's stepfather, Herod.

For Diophantus, Herod's scribe, to have been found guilty of forging a letter, it has been argued that he would have had to have been a 'highly placed official close to Herod'.[12]

Like others brought up on the Bible, I met the scribes along with the Pharisees in the New Testament, and they were not a pleasant lot. Chapter 23 of St Matthew's gospel is given over to Jesus' famous diatribe against them. It is an invective against duplicity and greed, against those that 'say, and do not' (verse 3) and those who 'love the uppermost rooms at feasts, and the chief feasts in the synagogues' (verse 6). The cry:

> Woe unto you, scribes and Pharisees, hypocrites!

recurs eight times in the chapter, rising to a crescendo of rage with the memorable:

> Woe unto you, scribes and Pharisees, hypocrites! For ye are like unto whited sepulchres, which indeed appear beautiful outward, but are within full of dead men's bones, and of all uncleanness. Even so ye also outwardly appear righteous unto men, but within ye are full of hypocrisy and iniquity. (Verses 27–28.)

Throughout the New Testament, scribes, like Pharisees with whom they are lumped together, are portrayed as officious bureaucrats with a fussy adherence to rules and regulations. Just after Jesus had performed one of his more dazzling miracles (the 'feeding of the five thousand': turning five loaves and two fishes into 12 baskets of food) along they come, complaining that his followers ought to be more scrupulous about the formalities:

> Then came together unto him the Pharisees, and certain of the scribes, which came from Jerusalem. And when they saw some of his disciples eat bread with defiled, that is to say, with unwashen hands, they found fault. For the Pharisees, and all the Jews, except they wash their hands oft, eat not, holding the tradition of the elders... Then the Pharisees and scribes asked him, Why walk not thy disciples according to the tradition of the elders, but eat bread with unwashen hands?[13]

In the Gospel of St Luke, lawyers are lined up alongside the scribes and Pharisees as enemies of Jesus' teaching, all of them:

laying wait for him, and seeking to catch something out of his mouth, that they might accuse him.[14]

In the parable of the woman taken in adultery, scribes and Pharisees challenge Jesus to ensure she is punished by stoning, according to the law of Moses. In this story, there is an interesting glimpse of Jesus choosing to be his own scribe, maybe composing other kinds of legislation:

> And the scribes and Pharisees brought unto him a woman taken in adultery; and when they had set her in the midst, they say unto him, Master, this woman was taken in adultery, in the very act. Now Moses in the law commanded us, that such should be stoned: but what sayest thou? This they said, tempting him, that they might have to accuse him. *But Jesus stooped down, and with his finger wrote on the ground, as though he heard them not.* So when they continued asking him, he lifted up himself, and said unto them, He that is without sin among you, let him first cast a stone at her. *And again he stooped down, and wrote on the ground.*[15] (My italics.)

The scribes portrayed in the Gospels of the New Testament, seemed to be fussy upholders of rules and self-serving keepers of the status quo.[16] Saldarini's comment on this is that, while the gospel writers saw the scribes as a unified group, this is probably not borne out by history. While none of these four writers had any quarrel with 'the role of scribes as learned guides of the community and guardians of the tradition', what they objected to was the Jewish scribes' opposition to Jesus; the parables in which they appear are those that show this and Jesus' repudiation of the bigotry which this opposition embodied.[17]

Labourers

In practice, these officials were only one category of Hebrew scribe. Somewhere between them and the mere copyist were varied kinds of village scribe, acting as clerks and archivists for a community, keeping records and writing out marriage contracts and other documents. 'Mere copyist' does no justice to the training necessary to produce a proper copy of the scrolls. To do this properly, it was necessary to learn the *Masorah*, the system of marginal notes that would allow the reader to vocalise the written script. It was also essential to have what today we would call an obsessional attention to detail. As a Hebrew scholar told me:

> The Masoretic scribe would believe he must copy with no mistake. The text is holy. He would even copy little splashes of ink. If mistakes were made he would write a marginal note to indicate a 'scribe's correction', directing the attention of the reader to this. These were times before Tippex and the labour of writing a column of script was long.[18]

Is this what copying sacred texts is all about? Making a replica, with no variation? Across continents and religions it seems to be so, and the practice seems closely allied to that of learning texts 'by heart'. Until very recently, traditional Qur'anic schooling in Morocco required children to concentrate entirely on memorising the text of the Qur'an. This, in turn, demanded a cycle of reciting, copying, learning by heart, and testing. The goal was the 'faultless reproduction of a sacred text'.[19] In the Judao-Christian traditions, such copying is less a feature of modern school systems; but historically it was certainly central to the publishing of holy texts.

Pity the poor copyist, sitting for hour after hour lettering these texts. It was weary work:

> Hebrew scribes would often add at the ends of books the words *Amen*, *Sela* or *Salom*, meaning, respectively, 'So be it!' 'Pause!' and 'Peace!' Latin monks, in addition to using the now Christianized word *Amen*, added functional terms such as *Explicuit*, 'The End', or *Explicuit feliciter*, 'Thank goodness it's finished!' or other expressions of relief.[20]

Never mind if the light was failing or his stomach was calling, the job was to look and copy, look and copy, with no mistakes, or errors: accuracy was all. Not for him the luxury of Tippex; far away indeed, the touch of the delete button. Scraping the parchment clean of mistakes must have been an arduous business for him as well, spending:

> long winter hours at his desk, his fingers numb around the stylus (when even in a normal temperature, after six hours of writing, the fingers are seized by the terrible monk's cramp and the thumb aches as if it has been trodden on).[21]

For nearly two thousand years, the work of copying depended on this slow and scrupulous check between the reading eye and the writing hand. Not till the Gütenberg Bible (the first complete printed book) was published in 1456, did the print revolution make redundant the manual copyist.[22] And, as the individual scribe laboured away, the temptation to insert his own comments, asides or exclamations must sometimes have been great. For later readers, *explicuit feliciter* in the margin would be the only trace of the hand that had copied the text in front of them: the only moment, in fact, when the scribe is himself a visible author in that text.

A monastery that housed a 'scriptorium' (effectively a factory of scribes and illustrators) would also contain libraries of some size. Texts that it had taken such labour-intensive work to produce would have been closely guarded. In Umberto Eco's clever novel *The Name of the Rose*, set in a fourteenth century Italian monastery, the library is a labyrinth. The person who holds the key to its entrance and to its secrets is Jorge, the blind librarian. Jorge knows the whereabouts of sources and texts like no-one else does. Monks in the scriptorium, working out the best kind of decoration to give their texts, would consult him, 'asking counsel on how to depict an animal or a saint':

> And he would look into the void with his spent eyes, as if staring at pages vivid in his memory, and he would answer that false prophets are dressed like bishops and frogs come from their mouths, or would say what stones were to adorn the walls of the heavenly Jerusalem, or that the Arimaspi should be depicted on maps near the land of Prester John.[23]

Jorge it is who, at the end of the narrative, is revealed as the murderer of no less than seven members of the monastic community. He kills his first victim, the monkish scholar Venantius, by literally poisoning the pages of the 'lost book of Aristotle',[24] which Venantius found and so greedily read, turning the pages with a licked finger and in so doing causing his own death. He it was who also lured the Abbot to the library's most secret chamber one evening and suffocated him to death in a secret passage. For the 40 years since he had become blind, his single purpose had been to control the library and keep hidden its most precious manuscripts: among others, a 'Syriac translation' of 'a little Egyptian book on alchemy',[25] followed by a Greek text on the subject of laughter. The genius of Eco's novel is the creation of Jorge as the enemy of joy: blinded and possessive of all the interest (and the fun) to be found in the library's treasures, he is the engine of death to all those who want to discover what he has taken so long to hide: that is, laughter. For laughter, as he sees it:

> is weakness, corruption, the foolishness of our flesh. It is the peasant's entertainment, the drunkard's license… Laughter frees the villein from fear of the Devil, because in the feast of fools the Devil also appears poor and foolish, and therefore controllable.

This is why Jorge wanted, above everything, to prevent anyone reading the second book of Aristotle; for it 'could teach that freeing oneself from the fear of the Devil is wisdom'.[26] To Jorge, it is the will of God that caused him to be the one to find the only copy of this text, buried for years and abandoned in an old library, in order that he could hide it from others. All this account of Jorge's grim self is set out in a late chapter in the book, in which the detective-cum-monk, William of Baskerville (a visiting English friar), confronts him with the murders in the monastery and disputes with him his views on God, the Devil and these manu-scripts. In response, Jorge commits what is, for both these men, scholars and lovers of manuscripts, the ultimate horror. Slowly and carefully he tears up the pages of this manuscript and begins stuffing them into his mouth. As he does so, he suddenly begins to laugh. Adso (William's young companion in this drama) and William fall on him and try desperately to wrench the precious manuscript from his hands (and mouth). Candles fall to the ground and, in no time at all, the entire library is on fire; and not only the library, but the whole abbey. The rest of the buildings suffer less damage than the library, 'doomed by its own impenetrability, by the mystery that protected it, by its few entrances'.[27]

Adso is an old man when he recalls the story, a monk who is no longer a mere copyist, but the composer of his own script. The book ends with him recalling how, years later, he revisited the site of the monastery in Italy to find a desolate scene of ruin and emptiness; yet, with one tower of the library still intact. He finds along one stretch of wall a shelf of books and, after hours of searching, gathers together the fragments of pages and books. In his last declining years he searches patiently for meanings among these fragments, and (as he writes the last page of his own book) feels the despair of not knowing whether there is any value at all, either in what he reads or what he writes:

It is cold in the scriptorium, my thumb aches. I leave this manuscript, I do not know for whom; I no longer know what it is about: *stat rosa pristina nomine, nomina nuda tenemus* [The rose stays fresh in its name; names themselves we hold to be bare].[28]

The kernel of this drama is an issue over God's tolerance of laughter. Eco's introduction to the whole sets up an idea with the reader that this work is not a novel at all, but the manuscript of a real monk that he had found (in the shelves of an antiquarian bookseller in Buenos Aires). In his introduction, he speculates on the origins and merits of the text, and debates the usefulness or otherwise of publishing it. In his chosen persona as scholar/writer, he goes on to say how he decided to do so. Eco wrote his original in Italian. English readers need to appreciate the fact that this explanation is provided for us through the writing of his translator, William Weaver (a name only provided in small print in the title pages):

On sober reflection, I find few reasons for publishing my Italian version of an obscure, neo-Gothic French version of a seventeenth-century Latin edition of a work written in Latin by a German monk towards the end of the fourteenth century.[29]

What persuaded him to go ahead anyway, he tell us, is his perception of a change in literary fashions, from a time in the 1960s (when he 'found' the manuscript), when 'there was a widespread conviction that one should write only out of a commitment to…change the world' to the time of writing when 'the man of letters…can happily write out of the pure love of writing'. Tongue in cheek, he tells the reader that what is in store is a book which is 'gloriously lacking in any relevance for our day, atemporally alien to our hopes and certainties.'[30] Revisiting the book more than once to search out these thoughts for my own book, I kept finding layers of meaning to entrance me. Most of all, I was struck by the idea of a text, any text, being the product of many hands, with authorship a multiple matter and the 'original' author concealed behind subsequent writers and readers.

Transcriber

As you will have noticed, the whole affair so far is very male. As far as I have discovered, that is the way things were for rather a long time. In the Christian tradition at least, both authorities and their scribes were male. The exceptions were a small number of women with claims to hear the divine voice. Here, that other scribal role emerges, that of *transcriber*, whose task is to transform into writing the spoken word.

To copy a holy text is to be its servant; every word must be faithfully copied; errors, if not removed, must be marked as such. To transcribe words from speech, a scribe in the service of religion may have to edit, or select; for the pen does not exist that can move as swiftly as the mouth can utter words. In mediaeval monasteries, the word *dictation* could sometimes mean a monk reciting aloud a text he knew by heart (a kind of 'self-dictation' and at other times, the same monk dictating to the whole *scriptorium* (monastic scribe-factory).[31] Writing in Latin, an eleventh century bishop used the word *dictaveram* with the meaning 'I had composed', using the word *scriptitare* to refer to work of 'copying', making a fair copy on parchment. The verb *dictitare*, it seems, was used to describe what we would now call the process of 'drafting' on wax tablets.[32]

This is the story of a woman who dictated the story of her mystic experiences to not one, but two scribes. Here the word 'dictate' is used in a more modern sense: that is, of one person speaking aloud to another, who writes down what they say. First, a summary of what is known about the woman herself. Her name was Margery Kempe, and she was born of a merchant family in Norfolk. Her father was elected mayor of Lynn five times. Her husband was well-to-do and they had 14 children. The book she wrote (which strictly speaking is two books, written at different stages) was intended to tell others of her visions and meditation, and inspire others to turn to a better life. She had been encouraged to write it by 'worthy clerics'. Having held back for some time from doing so, she only consented in the end when she felt that God was encouraging her, too.

> And so it was twenty years and more from the time that this creature first had feelings and revelations before she had any written. Afterwards, when it pleased our Lord, he commanded and charged her that she should have written down her feelings and revelations, and her form of living, so that his goodness might be known to the world.[33]

Her book was scribed – that is (apparently) taken down from her dictation – for Margery could not read and write herself. Later on, scribe/copyists copied the finished text. The manuscript, it seemed, then disappeared. However publication in the modern sense took longer. It was not until some five centuries later, in 1934, that the manuscript came to light in a private library, was read again, recognised as a valuable text, translated out of the spelling and vocabulary of Middle English for the benefit of a twentieth-century readership, and published in printed form.

The dates are these. Margery was born in 1373. She married John Kempe in 1393 or 1394 at 20 years old. At the age of 40 she set out on pilgrimages, first to the Holy Land, later to Italy; after that to Santiago. In 1431 a scribe, who might have been her own son, began work writing down her journey towards God. Soon after that, the son and her husband died within months of each other and the work was put aside. Over the next few years she travelled again, this time to Germany. In 1436 a second scribe began work revising and amending the first scribe's work and soon after that began 2 years of work with Margery to write her second book. Margery would then have been in her 60s; the date of her death is thought to have been 1441.

Reading Margery's text in a printed paperback book, I thought about her scribes. The first, as I said, may have been her own son. The 'Proem' from which I have just quoted goes on to tell of this man who 'having good knowledge of this creature and of her desire' agreed first to undertake the task, moving his wife and family in with Margery's household and writing 'as much as she would tell him in the time that they were together'. After his death came the second, a priest. In this passage, the scribe has written about his own doubts (to Margery's dictation, we must presume) about her authenticity as a mystic:

> Among these people was the same priest who afterwards wrote down this book, and he was resolved never again to believe her feelings. And yet our Lord drew him back in a short time – blessed may he be – so that he loved her more, and trusted more in her weeping and crying than he ever did before.[34]

So much was this scribe (apparently) convinced by Margery's sincerity that at times when he was in the midst of writing what she said he would be overcome by emotion:

> he that was writing for her could sometimes not keep himself from weeping.[35]

Scribes who took down the words of another as they were spoken had a different task altogether from the scribe as copyist. We can only guess how it worked in this case. Did Margery first speak a few words and then wait, while her scribe wrote? Or did he ask her to stop and pause so that he could catch up? Did she pace up and down, or did she sit in a trance and gaze out of the window as she dictated? Did the scribe add anything to what she said? Did he read back to her what he had got down? After all, if the 'dictator' happened to be, as Margery was, entirely illiterate, the scribe might have often have been tempted to improve on the text he was hearing.

As you may already have noticed, the narrative puts Margery in the third person. This was how the Middle English manuscript worded it. No-one except Margery and her scribe could say whether this was how Margery herself dictated to him. It could be a form of words which the scribe, with what Barry Windeatt calls his 'bookish concerns', felt was more fitting; for as he puts it,

> it would be misleading to take the *Book* as if it were the transcript of conversations in which a medieval Englishwoman remembers her life. The writing has clearly been much more edited and shaped than this – edited by the bookish concerns of the scribe, and shaped and focused by that spiritualizing lens through which Margery looks back at her experience.[36]

Whether it was Margery's original voice, or the bookishness of the scribe, almost all of her many translators seem to have kept the third person formulation. As it happened, the first version I came across myself was the work of one of the rare exceptions, John Skinner. The same passage you have just read, cast by Windeatt in the third person, appears in Skinner's version as follows:

> Among this group [who spoke against me] was the same priest who later on agreed to write this book for me; but at that time, he made up his mind never again to trust and believe in my inner feelings. And yet our Lord drew him back on my side in no time at all – blessed may he be! From then on, he loved me all the more and trusted in the sincerity of my weeping and shouting more than ever before.[37]

When I first read this, I took it to be an authentic version of the manuscript. To my inner reading ear, 'I', 'me' and 'my' felt comfortable. I have grown up with first-person autobiography; it is around me on a daily basis, in television interviews, print journalism, celebrity memoirs, and so on. In my own academic discipline – education – the first person is encouraged. Reflective practice has soaked through into many of the human sciences: we expect 'I'. Presumably John Skinner felt all this would be sufficient justification to make this choice in translating Margery: for he gives no other.

So it came as a complete surprise to me some time later to learn from further reading that the original text had been written entirely in the third person, making frequent use of the strange phrase 'this creature' which Margery chose to refer to herself, as in:

> Thus...*this creature*, who for many years had gone astray and always been unstable, was perfectly drawn and stirred to enter the way of high perfection, of which perfect way Christ our Saviour in his own person was the example.[38] (My italics.)

Fully to appreciate the difference in effect between first and third persons, I compare now the same text we have just looked at in Skinner's translation with the translation by Windeatt. In both accounts, the person writing on the page (and his translator) places himself in the third person:

> Among this group was the same priest who later on agreed to write this book *for me*; but at that time, he made up his mind never again to trust and believe in *my inner feelings*. And yet our Lord drew him back *on my side* in no time at all – blessed may he be! From then on, *he loved me* all the more and trusted in *the sincerity of my weeping* and shouting more than ever before.[39]

> Among these people was the same priest who afterwards wrote down this book, and he was resolved never again to believe *her feelings*. And yet our Lord drew him back in a short time – blessed may he be – so that *he loved her* more, and trusted more *in her weeping* and crying than he ever did before.[40]

Looking at the phrases used by John Skinner, we can note that he has five in which the person of the narrator occurs, compared with Windeatt's three:

Skinner	**Windeatt**
For me	
My inner feelings	Her feelings
On my side	
He loved me	He loved her
Of my weeping	In her weeping

There seems to me to be two effects of this stress on the first person: first, an additional emphasis is on the narrator's presence in her story and, second, a greater intimacy between writer and reader. We are being addressed eye-to-eye. At every turn, her priest/scribe reminds us that the feelings and the weeping were hers; that it was for her that he had agreed to write the book; and that he was *on her side.*

In a scribe-written text, any negotiation between scribe and author is usually kept under wraps. The whole idea is to give the illusion of a single authorship. In the case of *The Book of Margery Kempe*, something different is happening. While there is no word or phrase to convey a partnership at work – no *we*, no *us*, no *our* (except in the conventional reference to 'our Lord') – we are clearly told at several points that there are two people at work, one of whom retains a withdrawn position behind his own third person. The effect of Skinner's choice of first person for Margery makes this hidden figure even more remote, as in a passage that follows soon after:

> Yet at times while I was busy dictating this book, I would often be overcome by holy tears and much weeping. And often I would feel a flame just like a fire in my breast, yet even as it enfolded me, it was utterly pleasurable. My scribe, too, would sometimes be overcome by tears.[41]

What Skinner gains by this is the effect of Margery addressing her audience directly; what he loses is the presence in the text of her writing partner in the text. Windeatt's way of translating allows us to see both characters on stage at once:

> Also, while the said creature was occupied with the writing of this treatise, she had many holy tears and much weeping, and often

there came a flame of fire about her breast, very hot and delectable; and also, he that was writing for her could sometimes not keep himself from weeping.[42]

My own discovery of Margery Kempe was the result of a search I was making through the internet, one spring afternoon in 2000, a year that seems remote indeed from 1431. Using the keyword 'scribe' had led me down all sorts of pathways, some of which I have already referred to. When I came upon an entire paper on the subject of Margery Kempe and her scribes I had one of those moments of excitement where, if I had been holding a book I would have had to put it on the table for fear of scorching my hands. As I was reading a computer screen at the time, I could only leave my chair and dance a small jig. The paper is by Andrea Triton. The place it appears is on a website created by an American women's college called Wellesley College, in Massachusetts. To this day I have not tracked down the date of its publication.[43]

The special excitement of Triton's paper was her account of the references, found in the text itself, to Kempe's relationship with her scribes. At that time, Margery Kempe's name was unknown to me. In the field of literacy studies, she had been out of reach. Here, though, was an illiterate woman who had gained authority through a particular use of literacy. Her status as someone who had (eventually) published a book about her spiritual life put her illiteracy into second place. Following the discovery of her work in the 1930s by a scholar in mediaeval studies among the papers in a private library, Kempe has become the subject of a research industry. As John Skinner reported:

> a medievalist friend of mine in Oxford has lost count of the number of approaches he has had to decline from American students wishing to present their doctorate on some new aspect of Margery Kempe.[44]

So there are, again, layers within layers. Margery's priest was enabled to appreciate Margery's behaviour through his reading about another saintly woman. I was able to situate my reading of Margery through my discovery of a community of scholars writing about her. Margery herself, in deciding to write about her life, was likely to have been inspired by several other female mystics before and during her lifetime. Of these, Barry Windeatt mentions four, all of them mothers of large families, all of them turning to a life of poverty and penitence, being prone to falling into fevers, ecstasies or uncontrollable tears at the thought of Christ's death on the cross. Like Margery, at least three of these women – Blessed Angela of Foligno (1249–1309), St Bridget of Sweden (1303–73) and Blessed Dorothea of Montau (1347–94) – were known to have written their experiences through the medium of another, dictating their revelations, in Angela's case, to her confessor, in Bridget's and Dorothea's to their spiritual director.[45]

Also, like Margery, these were all women who saw themselves, in part, as *messengers to others*, needing an intermediary to pass on the message they had been given. Other women, such as the 'Maid of Orleans', were to come to a bitter end for such claims. Joan of Arc was burned at the stake in 1431 on a charge of heresy: the punishment of thousands of other illiterate women across Europe who for more than 2 centuries were found guilty of being 'instruments of the devil'.

Servant

The scribe who receives dictation from a single person has an easier job than the scribe who has to do justice to several voices in the minutes of a meeting. The minutes secretary, as we saw in Chapter 4, has to interpret and select what she or he hears. They have to transform the first person of direct speech into the third person. They have to discover the particular style and voice of the group or organisation for which they are writing. In short, this is very much the scribe in the role of interpreter. This connects with scribes as servants of a holy text in the setting of a meeting of Quakers.

Quakers, or the Society of Friends, need no priests as mediators with their God. The furniture for their 'meetings for worship' is so arranged (in circles or semi-circles) that no one person is seen as the leader. 'We seek a gathered stillness in our meetings for worship' wrote their founder, George Fox in 1656.[46] To sit in a meeting for worship, as I did one Sunday morning,[47] is unlike a silent sitting in any other place. There is a sense of waiting, not as you do in a doctor's surgery, waiting in a queue, isolated from each other, but in a company, seeking, as Quakers put it, to receive the ministry of God. The ministry may be received either in silence or vocally – that is, from listening to another. When a Friend stands up to speak, they do not give sermons or lessons as in a church service. They may refer to an excerpt from the *Quaker Faith and Practice* and say what it means for them. They may tell of a deeply felt experience that they want to share. The intervals of silence between one speaker and another allows a message to sink in. There is, in all of it, an important idea that it is not the speaker who speaks, but the Spirit.

At the end of the meeting for worship that I attended, the elders shook hands, and all present then did, too. There was an informal gathering for coffee and tea, after which some of the gathering returned upstairs for the 'Preparative Meeting'. This is what I came to see: the Quaker way of taking minutes. I had been invited by a good friend, Caroline Nursey, who had interested me in this. A Quaker since 1981, Caroline had served as the clerk of Quaker Peace and Service (QPS) for 4 years and, at the same time, as clerk of the Walthamstow Meeting House in East London for 5 and a half. This is how she explained the clerk's role at 'business' meetings:

> In a Quaker meeting, the clerk of the meeting scribes the minutes made by the meeting in which God has been involved. God's in the process to complicate things. As clerk, I'm not writing down my own thoughts; I'm writing down in a sense the spirit of the meeting. I then read it back. That is, at the end of each item I'll read out the minute. And I'll get comments that range from 'I think you need another comma in the fourth sentence' to 'I think that isn't quite what we meant'. I ask, 'Is the minute acceptable?' and only if it is, do we pass on. It doesn't always satisfy everybody. I've had to write minutes when I don't agree with what is being said. As clerk, you're muzzled.

My own notes of the meeting I witnessed that morning went like this:

> The clerk had given out copies of the minutes of the last meeting. These included a note that the meeting had agreed to invite me to come to this one. Caroline pointed out gently that this should read 'Jane', not 'Jean'. Irene apologised and said: 'minute 0176 should show Jane, not Jean.

That was the only conventional meeting formality I was to see at this meeting. The 'correction' of a mistakenly written minute, in a Quaker business meeting, rarely happens at a subsequent one, the way that minutes get corrected in any other meetings I have ever attended. The Quaker 'business method' has the same person chairing and scribing a meeting: the clerk's job, with the help of the assistant clerk, is to do both. At a business meeting of Friends, as Caroline had told me, the minutes are agreed or corrected as they are written. Sure enough, that day, I saw both these things happen. The minute-writer (clerk) read aloud the minute she had written and the assembled company offered their amendments or their assent *there and then*. The principle of getting written minutes written and agreed during the meeting is a fundamental one to Quakers. The value of this practice is seen to be:

> that the views of all may be taken into account, and a decision may emerge which is beyond what was suggested by any individual.[48]

Such a system may only be possible because of the even more central principle of the use of silence in Quaker worship. The habit of silence is one also used in business meetings, precisely in order to sustain the idea that these take place in a worshipful spirit.

The Society of Friends publishes a number of guides to explain how to carry out these combined responsibilities of chairing and scribing.[49] On the active use of silence, the following advice is given:

> If you are confused during the meeting, or if the meeting is becoming lost or aimless, ask for silence and insist on it. Having asked for silence, lead Friends into it, reminding them of the decision to be made or the specific topic being considered, so that, when the silence begins, they have the item in hand clearly in their minds.[50]

The Quaker habit of silence helps us understand a little of the puzzle that the business practice represents to the rest of us. How does the rest of the meeting tolerate the time spent waiting for the clerk to draft the minute we wonder? Having to sit and wait while someone else writes down what has been said would madden a more impatient group. As for the clerk, there might surely be a sense of pressure, of keeping everyone waiting? Caroline told me more about this:

> It *is* stressful, writing away while the meeting is happening. But you do feel held by the group. It's best if I succeed in separating being me from being the clerk. If I can be the scribe, rather than being me, I feel supported by the meeting.

They ought to be sitting there silent, prayerfully supporting me in the writing of our minute. If they are being restless, I can say: please can you support the clerk.

A practical solution suggested for some items is for the clerk to prepare before the meeting some minutes for some items in draft form, leaving gaps to fill in the names which the meeting actually decides (as in: 'We appoint...and...as our representatives at the next Monthly Meeting at...on 24th November next.').

As it turned out, when I sat in the meeting that morning, I was surprised at the calm I felt, waiting while Irene wrote. She had a pencil in hand and a pad of lined paper in front of her. After she had chaired the brief discussion on the first item she sat and wrote; nobody spoke. We waited for her. After a few minutes, she looked up and said: 'I suggest then that the minute should read: "Carol will arrange speakers on this.".' Again, nobody spoke, so she went on to the next item.

As Caroline had explained to me, the effort of the clerk is to arrive at the 'sense' or 'the truth' of the meeting, rather than some artificial consensus: a principle that applies whether the meeting lasts 2 days (as the QPS does) or an hour (as in the monthly meetings). The task of the clerk is both to bring the discussion to that point (as chair) and to record the decision (as secretary). This is how she described her own experience of doing this:

> I have a feeling of where the sense is coming from. It's not really in the head. The head is saying 'We're not keeping to time' but at the same time something begins to emerge – which isn't consensus. In fact, it is not consensus that we're seeking, it's Truth. Sometimes it's hopeless and we don't get there; but sometimes it's a deep spiritual experience. 'Meeting for worship for business' we call it.
>
> The clerk/scribe is not the author. The author is the whole group, including God. She or He isn't dictating it to me, but God is part of the meeting. What I'm trying to do is to scribe the sense of the meeting.
>
> It's good if you get changes – it gets them to own the minutes of the meeting, so it's not just the work of the minute writer. I take them home to type up but I sign the rough copy in the meeting, during the silence at the end.

From my observation that day in Walthamstow, I was intrigued to learn that there is an important difference in the grammar of Quaker minute-writing and that of the more conventional kind. Whether written formally or more informally, all the minutes I have ever read from any other organisation, have been written in the past tense. Certainly, the agent of the verb may be masked by the use of the use of the passive, as in: 'It was agreed that' or, 'the proposal was seconded'. Certainly, the agent is more evident when minutes are written more informally and use people's names, as in: 'Joe Bloggs suggested that…' or 'Meera Clarke agreed to…' But these minutes, by contrast, were written in the present tense: a custom, I learned, that is not just encouraged, but required. If you think about it, as I did that day, this has a logic to it – the minute-writer is writing there and then, the decision or activity is taking place as the writer writes. Here are two examples from the meeting that preceded the one I attended in June 2001:

01/74 Library

Further to 01/50 of April *we are presently reviewing* our use of the library. *Friends have various ideas* to encourage particularly newer Friends to use our books. *We ask Nominations Committee* to find the names of 2 or 3 Friends by July to work together with the librarian to discuss these ideas and for that group to report to the PM (Preparative Meeting) in September.

and:

01/76 Study of Scribing

We have been told of Jean Mace, a friend of Caroline Nursey, who is interested in how Quakers make written records of their business decisions, and the role of the clerk as scribe of the Meeting. *We are happy to invite her* to attend in July. (My italics.)

At first the present tense passed me by. I re-read and realised the difference. It gave me an odd feeling. The people who made the decision, who wrote this minute together, had made it in a present time. Some of them were in the meeting I was with that morning, in another present time. Those who had agreed to invite me were a collective presence among us. In all of this, the clerk had played a double role: both leader and servant – but only a leader in the sense of being the group's facilitator:

There indeed is the paradox. As one of the gathering the clerk seeks that course most likely to lead to a constructive and creative outcome. As its scribe and messenger he or she is its servant. Yet knowledge and acquired skills lend authority. All a clerk's gifts are to be exercised, yet never rightly for personal prestige, for getting one's own way, or for the pleasure hiding in the successful practice of the techniques of clerking. There is much enjoyment. It comes from the 'prospering of Truth' through the work of the whole meeting.[51]

1 From a translation based on the account in Ibn Hisham's Sirat an-Nabi, Cairo, 1346 A.H., cited in Baynham, 1988, p54.
2 Gaur, 2000, p105.
3 Viau, 1959.
4 *Ibid*, p27.
5 New Testament: St John's Gospel, Chapter 1, verse 1.
6 Saldarini, 1988, p241.
7 *Ibid*, p242.
8 *Ibid*, p274.
9 *Ibid*, p255.
10 *Ibid*, p272.
11 Through the accident of my own middle name, Salome has a personal interest for me.
12 *Ibid*, p263.
13 New Testament: St Mark's Gospel, Chapter 7, verses 1–2 and 5.
14 New Testament: St Luke's Gospel, Chapter 11, verse 54.
15 New Testament: St John's Gospel, Chapter 8, verses 3–8.
16 The extracts are from the 'King James' version of the Bible: the only version I possess, given to me 2 months after I was born by my godfather, a lawyer and lover of literature.
17 Saldarini, 1988, p267.
18 Harry Rosenwasser, April 2001, North London.
19 Baynham, 1988, pp54–5.
20 From *A brief history of scriptoria and the evolution of the book*, New Mexico, Monastery of Christ in the Desert, 1996. www.christdesert.org/noframes/script/history.html (visited January 2001).
21 Eco, 1983, p128.
22 *Ibid*.
23 *Ibid*, p129.
24 *Ibid*, p469.
25 *Ibid*, p467.
26 *Ibid*, p474.
27 *Ibid*, p489.
28 *Ibid*, p502 (I am grateful to my brother Nigel Sommerville for this translation).

29 *Ibid*, p4.
30 *Ibid*, p5.
31 Gaur, 2000, p178.
32 Clanchy, 1978, p218.
33 Windeatt, 1985, p35.
34 *Ibid*, p191.
35 *Ibid*, p260.
36 *Ibid*, p24.
37 Skinner, 1998, p217.
38 Windeatt, 1985, p33.
39 Skinner, 1998, p217.
40 Windeatt, 1985, p191.
41 Skinner, 1998, p296.
42 Windeatt, 1985, p260.
43 www.geocities.com/Wellesley/Garden/4594/margery.html (visited 20 April 2000).
    A 26-page bibliography on Margery Kempe has been published by the University
    of Colorado on www.uscolo.edu/history/seminar/kempebib.htm (visited 17
    December 2000).
44 Skinner, 1998, p10.
45 Windeatt, 1985, pp18–22.
46 Religious Society of Friends, 1995, 1.02 para 8.
47 In June 2001.
48 Committee on Truth and Integrity in Public Affairs, Religious Society of Friends
    (Quakers), 1988, p6.
49 See: Redfern, 1994 and Sharman, 1983; the key source cited in previous footnote;
    and www.quaker.org for a general introduction to the Society of Friends.
50 Redfern, 1994, p24.
51 See above, note 21, p7.

CHAPTER SIX

Scribes and the law

In office and religious settings, secretaries and clerks work to reproduce, alternately, what they see and what they hear, copying or transcribing the words of others. We have seen that there are variations in the way that author and scribe take control of the text. A boss may dictate a letter to a secretary; the secretary may see fit to improve on it. A Quaker clerk listens to what is said; she then offers her own version of it for the meeting to accept. The scribe who copies, also ornaments; and the scribe who transcribes is doing more than matching a spoken utterance with visual marks on the page. At times, she or he exercises a fair degree of power over the text that is produced. Nowhere is this more crucial than in the field of law.

Up until now, with few exceptions, I have not made much of scribes as being powerful. I have shown examples of them – particularly when they work as copyists – as low-status, or at least as anonymous people. In this chapter are three sections. *Statements* looks at the issue of power in the making of statements by witnesses and/or suspects in trials. The scribal work of police officers or lawyers is both highly regulated and oddly free from regulation, and analysis suggests they exert some power over the way the statements are produced. The section on *Courts* suggests that there is less power and more anonymity in the work of the law-writers and court transcribers. The *Rights* section discusses the work of scribes as advocates, writing with or on behalf of clients who very often see themselves as without any power, seeking help from organisations committed to ideas of 'empowerment'.

Statements

When I met Kelly[1], she was 24 years old and had already served nearly 5 years of a 14-year sentence. She had met her first boyfriend when she was 15. The relationship, which was violent, had lasted 3 years. 'I thought it was normal', she said, 'the beatings'. Eventually, she left him. The night of the murder was some time later, by which time she was living with a new boyfriend. Her ex was then living with another woman, who had a child by him. One evening, the woman rang Kelly and asked her and her boyfriend to go round. She sounded frightened, and Kelly and her friend felt they should go. The ex was there. There was a row, in which he threatened Kelly, and Kelly's boyfriend pulled out a knife. 'If he had pleaded manslaughter instead of self-defence', she told me, 'I might not have got this sentence'.

Prison was a shock to Kelly. The fact of being there, of the long sentence in front of her, robbed her of words.

> When I was in Holloway I didn't know how to put down on paper how I was feeling. I didn't know how to *start*. I used to write the same letter to my mum every week. 'Hi mum. I love you. I will see you soon. Bye.'

Talking to her in an empty prison classroom, sitting at the table with my pen and notebook, I was struck by the associations our meeting might have had for her with the experience of having to give a statement to the police, 6 years before. 'How do you remember that process?' I asked her. Her reply told me, not about the stress of being questioned, but about a procedure used to resolve what she called her (then) 'problem with reading and writing':

> I must have spent 7 days at the police station, being questioned. My solicitor told them that I had a problem with reading and writing. So really, they took a lot of trouble. They taped what I said. Then later, they typed it out and the person who typed it spoke it into a tape recorder as she typed. So when I came to read it back, I had her voice on the tape to guide me.

At the time of the interview, I was puzzled why they had not used the tape of Kelly's own voice as a guide to her reading back the transcript. It was only later that I came upon the guidebook on 'those areas of law and legal procedures with which all police officers are concerned'[2] – *Butterworth's Police Law*. From this source I also learned of the other rule concerning the interviewing of suspects, as Kelly had been: that the tape which is made of an interview like hers has to be kept, and shown to the interviewee that

it is kept, in its entirety. It would have been the second copy of the tape –
that 'must be made in the presence of the suspect and without the master
copy leaving his sight' – which the typist had used to make the transcript.[3]
To overcome the difficulty for Kelly in reading back the transcript, the
strategy used was to have the typist read aloud the transcript as she typed –
making a new tape, of her voice reading Kelly's words – so that Kelly could
listen to this as she read her own words back from the written transcript.

If you have witnessed an accident or crime, or been the victim of one,
sooner or later you have to 'make a statement' (even though what actually
reaches court may only be a summary of this). However making a
statement (in the UK at least) means that another person usually does the
writing; you answer questions, read the written result and, once you have
given your agreement to it as 'yours', you sign it. If you have ever had to
do this, you will know that the other person does more than silently write
to your dictation. They interview you, writing as they go along. They ask
questions, prompt, suggest, infer, recapitulate what you just said, and
make any number of other interventions, noting down a version of what
you say in response. For their task is to produce a narrative that gives
facts. It is not to produce a text that is distinctively yours.

If, however, you are a suspect, the text of the statement must be a
verbatim transcript of what you say (though again, only a summary may
reach court). With few exceptions, the Police and Criminal Evidence Act
(1984) made it compulsory to tape-record interviews with suspects. Any
such interview record must include a note of the place, time, date of
interview and names of everyone present; the tape recording must be
carried out 'openly but unobtrusively'; and the interviewee must be
confident that there is no chance of the tape being later interfered with
or altered.[4] There are two particular features of the 'code of practice' on
tape-recording interviews to consider here. One is that, unlike witness
statements, there are certain circumstances in which the interviewer's
questions must be transcribed verbatim as well; and that is 'where an
admission is made'. (Imagine how important this would be in evidence:
the way in which the 'suspect' had been asked a question must certainly
influence the way in which she or he would answer it, let alone 'admit'
to having done something.) The second is the solution proposed for the
witness who cannot read their statement:

> Unless it is impracticable the person interviewed must be given
> the opportunity to read the interview record and to sign it as
> correct or to indicate the respects in which he considers it

> inaccurate ... *If the person concerned cannot read or refuses to read the record or to sign it, the senior police officer present shall read it over to him and ask him whether he would sign it as correct or to indicate the respects in which he considers it inaccurate. The police officer must then certify on the interview record itself what has occurred.*[5] (My italics.)

What Kelly got was something extra: something she could read and listen to at the same time, in her own time.

In legal terms, Kelly had been a *suspect*; for my purposes, she was a *research subject*. Later I thought some more about the differences or similarity between the two interviews she had undergone. Mine was similar, in that while I knew I held to a code of practice about oral-history interviews, I was responsible (as a police officer is) for making sure she also knew this, and had some rights over the transcript too. On the other hand, it was different in several ways. First, there was the fact that I was not there to gather evidence, at least, not in the legal sense. Secondly, between the first and second interview, Kelly had learned to read. I did not have to work out an arrangement where someone else could read back to her what I had written from the tape of our conversation after we had parted company. Instead, I was able to send her, on paper, my transcription of what she had told me and on the second visit I made to the prison she was able to let me have her comments on it.

The third thing that made my position as interviewer different from that of the police officer who had questioned her years before was that I came to Kelly with no prior knowledge of her life, let alone of anything she may or may not have done which had brought her to be behind bars. 'Prior knowledge' is important to police interviews. Whether interviewing witnesses, victims or suspects, the legal questioner routinely brings in such 'prior knowledge' via certain kinds of questions. These may take the form of statements themselves, with a rising intonation, as in 'So you were on duty at...place at ten o'clock on the night in question?' or 'And the defendant became abusive and threatening?'. From her study of police interviews, Frances Rock found this a common approach. Others held back the 'prior knowledge' they had, choosing instead to put the witness in the position of authority, leaving them to tell their tale in their own way.

From email correspondence with Frances, I learned of her research work in three main areas of the law. One has to do with the language used in cautioning and explaining rights to suspects detained at police stations; another, with the language that judges use in their summing-up speeches to juries in crown court trials; the third with what she calls 'witness statement-taking'. As well as the 'prior knowledge' prompts that interviewers use with their interviewees, Rock also noted something she called 'collaborative talk', which was necessary for witnesses to be prompted into providing answers. Interviewers, for example, would remind witnesses of the time at which an incident had happened or prompt them with possible answers (as in: 'So this road that you were on – was it a dual carriage way or single carriageway or what?'). The purpose of the whole exercise, as she observed it, was for interviewer and witness to 'co-construct' an account with as many accurate details as possible. At the same time, she found that interviewers had an interest in ensuring that the resulting text would conform to the discourse or code of police or courtroom language. So, for example, one interviewer she observed who heard his witness say: 'Never met him before in my life' then proposed that this could be reworded as: 'He was a man who I now know to be...' The witness evidently agreed to this; and transcript from the next bit of their interview shows the police interviewer giving him the name of the man they are talking about. So that, indeed, by the time other people were handling the case and reading the interview transcript, it would be perfectly true that the witness would 'now' know the name of the man. Rock saw changes of wording like this as due to a need to get the statement written in 'police-register', not to any devious plot to twist a witness's wording for some other purpose.[6]

Witnesses commonly feel that the finished statements are not their own. This is at the heart of Frances Rock's thesis; for witness statements, as she shows, are artefacts produced out of a complex web of negotiation, compromise and collaborative writing between interviewer and interviewee. As a 12-year-old child, she herself had experience of this. Having witnessed an armed robbery in her local city centre, she found herself being interviewed in her house by a detective inspector who had come to take her 'statement'. She was, she recalled:

> intrigued by the way that the piece of writing which resulted from our conversation captured what I'd said, whilst somehow simultaneously failing to capture what I'd said.

This feeling appeared to be shared with others, as she was to discover when she did her research. A key finding from the study was a feeling of not owning the statement they were asked to sign:

Some are not quite able to pin down what was 'wrong' with the statement that resulted and some, who are used to writing and dictating during their professional or personal lives, describe frustration at not being given a pen themselves or not being allowed to simply dictate to the police officer the words they wished to be recorded.[7]

The written statement of a witness, as Rock showed, is produced to appear as a narrative of what happened, but it is actually the creation of a series of questions, answers, and decisions as to what is or is not 'relevant'. No wonder that a witness may end up with the feeling of it not being their own way of saying it; a feeling echoed by Sue Gardener, in a note to me on her own experience. Sue had been interviewed as the victim of a robbery. Like some of Frances Rock's own 'witnesses', Sue had to sign something she would not have written herself:

A few years ago I was robbed by someone who pushed his way through my front door and held a knife up to my face. He had caught my attention with what sounded like a pitch for a handout. He didn't seem sure what he wanted, and he talked too much while he was there. So when he went and I called the police – who came very quickly – I had quite a lot to tell them.

There was a team of two, and it was a young woman who took my statement. She did it in a way I have experienced before: led me through retelling (and inevitably reorganising) my account of what had happened, and stopped me at intervals to write it down on the statement form. I have always wondered why I couldn't write it myself. As we worked through it, I was aware that it was not exactly my words that were being written down... Checking was for fact, not for forms of words, and when I was given the draft statement to read that was the purpose again. So you sign it, but it isn't your utterance.[8]

As Frances Rock sees it, this method of writing production is not necessarily undesirable. Witness statements have a particular function, which does not include a full account of feelings or thoughts by the person concerned. Yet there is, she found, an idea around that statements such as these are unadulterated words from the witness, written down to dictation. In practice, as she shows in her own evidence, they are more often the result of two people's words mixed together. For Sue, the 'inevitable reorganising' of her account by the police officer was part of the mix. There were, as she also wrote, 'pervasive changes' throughout the text, in terms of vocabulary and idiom and sentence structure, which would not have been her choice. The checks were for 'fact', not for 'form of words'. The purpose was for accurate detail, not for expressive language; the expertise very different from her own, as an experienced literacy teacher and scribe for others. As she put it, 'it was being turned into a professionally acceptable discourse rather than rooted in my perceptions and my way of telling things'.

Legal history is littered with stories of false statements, statements or 'confessions' extracted under duress and so on. The potential for abuse is not confined to witnesses who cannot read and write themselves. Anyone under pressure is vulnerable to the pressure to sign, even while knowing it is not exactly right. In a report on the public inquiry held in Northern Ireland as to what had happened in 1972 (29 years earlier) on 'Bloody Sunday', the journalist Maggie O'Kane gives us a glimpse of the editing that may go on in the making of a statement. Her report pieced together the experiences of that day from diaries and interviews with two young men. She quotes from the diary entry of the day of one of them, 'Private 027' of the British army's Parachute Regiment, in which he recalls the 'exuberance' of other soldiers firing into the crowd, and his sense of bewilderment at the lack of fire coming in return from behind the barricade. Later, Private 027 was flown to Coleraine to meet army lawyers in order to give his evidence. This is what he remembered from that meeting:

> The lawyer and I sat either side of the desk and he wrote the statement as I spoke. I described shooting from the small wall by Kells Walk towards the centre of the crowd behind the rubble barricade. The lawyer stood up and expressed surprise and said something like: 'We can't have that, can we Private? That makes it sound like shots were being fired into the crowd'. I was very surprised.[9]

Courts

Sit in a court at the Old Bailey and you sit watching paper being moved about. Piles of paper stack in front of the wigged and suited barristers. Huge ledgers weigh down the desk in front of his lordship. Clerical fingers tap and tap and tap all morning. Notebooks are written in. Someone, somewhere, will be making a full account of the whole thing. Many people, later, will produce more legal papers for others to read, sign and respond to. The legal scribes who do all this paper-writing are anonymous. It is not their job to be named in reports. I have two accounts of such scribes to offer here. The first, from the nineteenth century, is fictional. The second is an autobiographical account of a court shorthand-writer in the late twentieth century.

The handsome captain

> The one great principle of English law is, to make business for itself. There is no other principle distinctly, certainly, and consist-ently maintained through all its narrow turnings.[10]

This was Dickens' bitter judgement on the legal system that imprisoned his father for debt, a system that made money for lawyers and misery for others. In the first chapter of this book, I introduced Jo, the crossing-sweeper, and Krook, the shopkeeper, from *Bleak House*. 'Nemo', the law-writer and copyist is a third character from the same novel. This is how he advertises himself in Krook's shop window:

> ...There were a great many ink bottles. There was a little tottering bench of shabby old volumes, outside the door, labelled 'Law Books, all at *9d.*' Some of the inscriptions I have enumerated were written in law-hand... Among them was one, in the same writing, having nothing to do with the business of the shop, but announcing that a respectable man aged forty-five wanted engrossing or copying to execute with neatness and despatch: Address to Nemo, care of Mr. Krook within.[11]

The person who gives Nemo work to do is Snagsby, the law stationer, who is employed, in turn, by Tulkinghorn, the lawyer. Snagsby evidently found Nemo did his work well; he had, he says:

> a quick hand, and a hand not sparing of night-work; ...if you gave him out, say five-and-forty folio on the Wednesday night, you would have it brought in on the Thursday morning.[12]

Who *was* Nemo? And how did he come by his curious name? The story is the drama of a handsome captain who, because of an illicit affair with a beautiful woman, is forced to go into hiding and earn a miserable living as a lowly scrivener. He is doomed to a tragic death for a hopeless love; an educated man, doing work beneath his station. The captain and his woman had fallen in love. She becomes pregnant and gives birth to a daughter in secret. The secret must not be known. Somehow (this bit is not clear) her sister convinces her that the baby dies at a few hours old. Hiding her grief beneath a ravishing but stony exterior, she embarks on an endless round of balls and parties until eventually she is courted by and marries a wealthy aristocrat old enough to be her father. All this takes place 20 years before the book opens.

The woman, Lady Dedlock, comes from a rich family herself, but a family about which there were estates and inheritances that are the subject of the interminable court case made famous by Dickens' novel: the case of *Jarndyce v. Jarndyce*. Years after her early tragic romance, sitting in the vast drawing room of their immense mansion, she and her husband listen to their lawyer (Tulkinghorn) telling them of the progress of the lawsuit. The lawyer brings out some papers as he talks and puts some on the table. The husband is staring into the fire, having little interest in the story. The woman, at first also bored and disdainful, is suddenly struck by the handwriting on one of the papers. She recognises it. 'Who copied that?' she asks the lawyer, suddenly. Surprised, he stops what he was doing, which was reading aloud from another document. 'Is that what you call law-hand?' she asks. The lawyer is precise, answering: 'Not quite. Probably... The legal character which it has, was acquired after the original hand was formed.' Soon after this exchange, my Lady is taken ill; a servant is summoned and she is taken to her room, saying that she feels 'faint...only that', leaving her husband to remark on the 'extremely trying' weather.[13]

The handwriting is that of the woman's former lover. Some time later, another letter catches her attention. Sitting in their carriage on the road home to their Lincolnshire mansion after weeks at opera, balls and concerts in Paris, her husband is reading his correspondence. His Lady, merely as a means to lessen the permanent state of boredom, asks him what he is reading, which reminds him that in the letter from their lawyer is a message for her. Her husband reads it aloud to her:

> I beg my respectful compliments to my Lady, who, I hope, has benefited by the change. Will you do me the favour to mention (as it may interest her), that I have something to tell her on her

return, in reference to the person who copied the affidavit in the Chancery suit, which so powerfully stimulated her curiosity. I have seen him.

Once again, 'my Lady' has to disguise inner turmoil, this time with the request that the carriage be stopped so that she can take a walk.[14]

Back in their home, the Lord and Lady receive Tulkinghorn one evening. The scene is a masterpiece of suggestion. The lawyer has something to tell them. He had inquired about the man, he says, and had found him in a miserable lodging, dead from an overdose of opium. His lordship interrupts the story in the interests of protecting the ears of a delicate lady; she, in contrast, uses a languid indifference to mask a raging desperation to hear more. The lawyer, deferential, pauses and resumes, watching its impact on my Lady, already half-sure he knows the reason for it. Throughout the short dialogue she and the lawyer 'looked very steadily at one another'; after it, she gathers up her 'mantles and furs' and leaves the room.[15]

The Captain had not died entirely without possessions. A collection of letters was inside the portmanteau left in his room. His landlord, Krook, stole this. The shopkeeper, though prevented by his illiteracy from comprehending its contents, is canny enough to sniff the possibility of blackmail it represents. The only other person that 'Nemo' spoke to during the time he lodged there was also illiterate: the boy Jo, with whom I opened this book. Jo is tracked down to give evidence for the inquest into Nemo's death and the report of the inquest reaches the papers. Lady Dedlock reads the report. Cloaked, veiled and disguised as a maidservant, she sets off to find Jo, asks him about the man who died and gets Jo to show her the pauper's grave where her lover is buried. She pays him a sovereign and vanishes into the night.[16]

It is the sinister Mr Tulkinghorn who first remarks on the oddness of the law-writer's pseudonym, in the course of his conversation with Mr Snagsby during his search for the identity of the affidavit-writer. Tulkinghorn speaks first.

'You copied some affidavits for me recently.'
   'Yes, sir, we did.'
   'There was one of them,' (says Mr Tulkinghorn, carelessly feeling – tight, unopenable oyster of the old school! – in the wrong coat-pocket), 'the handwriting of which is peculiar, and I rather

like. As I happened to be passing, and thought I had it about me, I looked in to ask you – but I haven't got it. No matter, any other time will do – Ah! here it is! – I looked in to ask you who copied this?'

'Who copied this, sir?' says Snagsby, taking it, laying it flat on the desk, and separating all the sheets at once with a twirl and a twist of the left hand peculiar to law-stationers. 'We gave this out, sir. We were giving out rather a large quantity of work at that time. I can tell you in a moment who copied it, sir, by referring to my Book.'

…he finds the page, and the line in his 'Book':

'Jarndyce! Here we are, sir,' says Mr Snagsby. To be sure! I might have remembered it. This was given out, sir, to a Writer who lodges just over on the opposite side of the lane.'

Mr Tulkinghorn has seen the entry, found it before the Law-stationer, read it while the forefinger was coming down the hill.

'*What* do you call him? Nemo?' says Mr Tulkinghorn.

'Nemo, sir. Here it is. Forty-two folio. Given out on the Wednesday night, at eight o'clock; brought in on the Thursday morning, at half past nine.'

'Nemo!' repeats Mr Tulkinghorn. 'Nemo is Latin for no one.'

'It must be English for someone, sir, I think,' Mr Snagsby submits with his deferential cough. 'It is a person's name.'[17]

The choice of this name is a wonderful device by Dickens to convey the captain's need utterly to erase himself. To save the honour of his woman, he has sacrificed all identity; in order to be as anonymous as possible, he opted to be a scribe for the 'business' of English law. His own views on the world are left to be guessed at. Central to the drama, however, is the fact that his handwriting is unmistakable. The whole engine of the many plots and sub-plots of *Bleak House* turns on this. Anonymous though Nemo is, it is his very personal style of writing that defines him. On this, the motives and destinies of the main protagonists depend. The author of amorous letters, with a very real name and identity for the person he wrote them to, he earns his living by writing 'law-hand', a script that he writes efficiently and fast, but which still cannot quite conceal his own style from the eyes of his mistress, 20 years after she had last seen it. To her, he may be everyone; but (as Dickens would have it) in the world of the law, he is a scribe – he is 'no-one'.

Mr Shorthand Writer

So it was with a pleasant sense of historical irony that I found myself interviewing a living law-writer of another kind, just off the same Chancery Lane where Dickens had placed his drama. This man's own career began a hundred years after Nemo had laboured at the folios for Snagsby the law stationers. We met in the upstairs offices of a firm of transcribers where my interviewee, Walter Hemingway, worked as a senior member of staff. Between 1953 and the mid-1980s, he told me, he had worked as a professional shorthand-writer in the law courts. His first job had been as an office boy in Hull, graduating to work as a typist with a timber merchant, and then with the Army Legal Services:

> There were some shorthand writers there who took the official notes in court martials. They would dictate to me and I became what is known as a 'dictatee'. It would be a transcript of the proceedings…which I typed, on dictation from the shorthand writer… He could take shorthand down. But I could type it faster.

It was after he left the army that Walter embarked on what was to become his professional career, beginning as a trainee in the Royal Courts of Justice. It was a scribe's apprenticeship, which was evidently still very alive to him:

> I went into court with a proper shorthand-writer. He was taking notes. I was taking notes of the same thing. He was more experienced than me. He would show me how to write it in certain outlines in shorthand. He would say, 'Pitmans say write it like that, but write it like this; because you will get a definition and be more sure of that outline'. He would let you in on all the nuances.

'And to ensure your accuracy was greater?' I asked.

> Yes. Because accuracy, of course, is paramount, you see. After a while I became proficient enough to go into my own courts. I sat with the judge and barristers and I took verbatim notes of the whole proceedings. Day after day I would go into various courts, not necessarily the same one, from half past ten to say quarter past four. You'd get a counsel furiously cross-examining a witness (you know, 'I put it to you, you're a liar', whatever is the version) and having an absolute tirade with each other and then the judge would say, 'Well,

I didn't get a word of that, it was far too fast. Shorthand Writer, read that back'. So you got up and read it back...

That would happen quite a few times during the day. The first time I had to read back, I was very nervous... Everyone is looking at you. ' Shorthand Writer, stand up and read that passage. Read it out so everybody can hear it. 'Do you agree, Mr So-and-So, with what Shorthand Writer has read?'... It's a terrifying experience actually, to get up and read, to a judge. A lot of judges, if you were new to them as a shorthand writer, they would say, 'Mr Shorthand Writer, read such a passage back'. You'd read it back. He'd got a note himself, and if you corresponded with his recollection in his note, he never asked you again, because he knew that you were capable of doing the job.

The voices of the court room are the raw material of the Shorthand Writer. Head down, pen moving, his ears are straining to catch every word. As Walter told me, this habit of acute listening results in a surprisingly sharp aural memory:

Years later, when you've taken a note at the time, you've never transcribed it and someone says 'Can we have a transcript of that?' and you think, 'God, what was all that about?' And it comes back. You can hear the voice of the barrister. It's really strange.

I asked him if he was ever tempted to waver in the discipline of accuracy; did he have the scribe's temptation to improve on anything that was said? His answer was interesting. There was an unwritten rule, he told me, that the judge's words – however idiomatically spoken in the original – should always be rendered in standard English. There would be, he said, a 'tidying up' of what judges – and barristers – actually said:

If a judge says, 'Well, er, um, Mr Mrs – oh I'm so sorry, I should have said "Miss"', you would not put all that in. You would clean it up. You don't want him stuttering. And if the judge said, 'I didn't hear that', you wouldn't say – 'I didn't hear it' or 'I couldn't do this' or 'I wouldn't' or 'I shan't', you would put in proper English 'I could not', 'I shall not', 'I will not' 'I do not'. If the defendant says it, you would put precisely what the defendant – or the witness – says. The same with Counsel. You have to brush them up a little bit.

125

> With Counsel, they can use bad English. Just because they are a barrister with a wig and a judge, they're prone to make some grammatical gaffes, the same as anybody. We do try and tidy up Counsel. Counsel and the judge. But with the witness, we must put precisely what he said, because something could turn on that.

I asked him: 'Could not something turn on how the question was asked, though?'.

> We couldn't change the sense of the question. If the Counsel said, 'Um, Mr So-and-so I put to you – well, what I mean to say is, what your version is -' you know, you would think about 'Mr So-and-so what I put to you is'. It's not important. You could leave that out. You have to really use your loaf. You can get a counsel who does slightly stutter and he can say two or three words, or is feeling for words. And the same with the judge when he's giving a judgement. He'll probably feel for words. He may get – he'll say 'In this case the claimant said – I mean, defendant' – and you wouldn't put that in.
>
> If a judge gives an extemporary judgement…at the end of the case, without having had more time to think, we'll type it out in draft form, and it goes to [him], and he is at liberty to alter what is said in print, because he thinks on mature reflection 'Well I didn't really mean to say that' or 'I don't like the way I put it'. Some judges now seem to use the red pen a lot more than they used to, on the judgements. Not on the transcript, they can't alter that; but on their judgement of their findings of their view of the case, at the end. They can tidy up the grammar and probably completely change the sentence. Or in some places completely cut things out, or ask for a rider to be put in, that they meant to mention. When it comes back to us, we correct it, and then it goes out to the client.

'So that is an editing of the transcript?' I asked.

> Yes, there is a little bit of editing. Not that it would affect the substance. This is only in civil cases. Now, in criminal cases, if the judge said 'The sky was green' instead of blue, well it would go in that he said that, because that's for the jury. You've got to put down precisely what the jury heard. So you can't change the language. But in civil matters it has to be good English. Especially if it is

going abroad. On the internet: now, most judgements go on the internet. And a judge doesn't want to see a gaffe on the internet for the rest of his life and everybody else's, where he made some awfully badly grammatical thing on the transcripts. But, as I say, when the jury – you type exactly what the jury heard.

'Good English', apparently, is necessary to a judge's authority. Imperfect or idiomatic English would not do. For him, the court scribe tidies up 'gaffes' in how he speaks; for everyone else, absolute verbatim transcription, whether grammatically correct or not, remain the rule. Most courts now in England – except for appeal courts, where Shorthand Writers are still used – are tape-recorded. You might think that this technology would make impossible any of the careful editing Walter Hemingway described. The tape, like the camera, surely cannot lie. But paradoxically, as he told me, this is not the case. Technical problems caused by court acoustics can make it hard for transcribers to hear every word recorded on the tapes. The rustle of papers too near the microphones or the scrape of a chair and whole utterances are inaudible.

In this interview, I also learned of a machine, introduced in the 1950s and today much in evidence in courtrooms called the Palantype. On this machine, the operator's fingers press several keys at once, rather than one at a time – almost as if they were playing chords on the piano. Every chord represents a syllable, or a complete word or phrase. Nowadays, the Palantype machine is linked to a computer-aided transcription (CAT) system. This means that the computer can transcribe the shorthand notes *simultaneously* and – an asset for hearing impaired people – display the resulting English transcript on screen.[18]

Walter can write accurate verbatim shorthand at phenomenal speed (200 words a minute, he said; the usual expectation for secretaries is 120 or 150 wpm maximum), and had done so for several hours a day, year after year. His account of the 'unwritten rules' about transcribing is of interest – one rule for the lawyers, the other for the defendants. Also interesting is the detail of how a judge might apply his (or her) red pencil to the transcript of a trial. The scene he conjured up of the Shorthand Writer having to stand up to read back to the court the dialogue that had just taken place is now, presumably, no longer practised. However, the sight of one speaker reading out the verbatim words of another is still the ordinary currency of courtroom discourse.

Lawyers certainly seem to speak in a language unlike ordinary conversation; a variety of Standard English that is strange indeed. One morning I sat in the public gallery of one of the courts in the Old Bailey in London. These were the phrases that floated up to me from the man in a wig below:

> The augurs are not particularly auspicious, it seems to me... I don't say this disparagingly... I am bound to say...the Crown have not made orders lightly...There are reasons which I have not put before your Lordship...Precisely the reverse considerations would apply...I needn't therefore go into the interstices of the case.

I then watched the same barrister read aloud from the statement made by one of the defendants. On a certain date in a certain place, this man had threatened a customs officer. The barrister wanted the court to be clear as to what he had said. The words were these:

> We know more than you think, mate. We know who you are and I can fucking find you.

It was funny to hear this ugly menace read out by a man in fancy dress speaking with plums in his mouth. But we were in a courtroom – and no-one laughed.[19]

Rights

We have looked at witness statements, document copying and court transcriptions. There is one other important space in which scribing occurs within a system of law, which I want (as a lawyer might say) to put before you. This is when a client with a problem (often more than one) meets with a legal advisor and together they work out what needs to be said and written in order for it to be solved. The organisation that knows most about this kind of scribing is the National Association of Citizens' Advice Bureaux (CAB).

This is an example of how the CAB might be asked to help. A man comes in and says 'I've been thrown out of my flat'. The advisor's job is to help him retell the story. She asks him to clarify who it was that threw him out (his partner? his parents? his landlord?) so it becomes possible to see the *legal meaning* of the story (has he been *evicted, served a notice to quit, issued with a summons*? has his landlord *obtained a possession order*?). A key task for the advisor is to enable the client to translate his personal experiences into legal categories that bring with them both rights they may claim and/or responsibilities they have to live up to.

The CAB's present twin aims are to provide an advice service and to collect evidence to influence social policy. As its own website puts it:

> From its origins in 1939 as an emergency service during World War II it has evolved into a professional development agency.[20]

With the advent of a newly established Welfare State, 10 years later came additional need for such a service – both to help people through the rules and forms they needed to understand in order to claim benefits and pensions, and to inform the State how the system was actually working. The CAB:

> helped the public interpret new government welfare schemes and...provided feedback for the government on how these schemes were received and administered.[21]

By the early 1970s, the annual number of inquiries was just over 1 million. Thirty years later, this had risen to 5 million.[22] Three principles underpin today's CAB work: it is free, independent and confidential. At the heart of the work is the advisor's skill in enabling a client to fully explore the problem. CAB training stresses this; the advisor is not there to provide solutions or fixes. The Citizens' Advisor is there to help their client to fill out a full picture of their situation, so that it goes beyond the immediate issue she or he blurts out in the first 5 minutes. Arriving at a full picture means the advisor offering back to a client some summary of the story so far, at which point a client may then remember something extra – often offering as an afterthought something that might make all the difference to working out what might be the best thing to do next. Searching through the information system for the appropriate bit of the law that might apply, the advisor's job is then to help the client be clear as to what options are open to her or him, and then help them work out what might be a good way forward.

It is at this point that something may have to be written to someone else about the case. Sometimes the client, now clearer in their mind about what they could say, simply goes away and writes it. Alternatively, it can mean the advisor helping the client there and then to work out what to say, and giving them some notes to take away as the basis for what they can write. Much less often, the advisor undertakes to write something on the client's behalf, ensuring they see a draft first, or agree the wording beforehand. The key to all of this is the idea of *empowerment*, with the advisor's job being, above all, to help clients express themselves to best effect.

From a couple of weeks during my time as a trainee advisor, I picked out four examples of different stances I took as scribe with client. The first two were drafted together with the client; the second two were completed and sent for the client to check after they had left the interview.[23]

Application form to the Home Office for a travel document
A young woman's social worker had referred her to the CAB for help with this form. The client, who had no passport, had come to the UK seeking asylum 3 years before, and just recently obtained 'exceptional leave to remain' a few months. *We drafted replies to questions on the form; I wrote these down in a notebook; she read and checked what I had written, then copied them in her own writing onto the form.*

Draft letter to an employer about the payment of wages
A man in his early 30s, working as a security officer with no written contract, had worked for the firm for 2 months and was still waiting to be paid. His second month's pay was due the next day. He had come into the Bureau to discover what his rights were, should his pay not be forthcoming. *We drafted together the wording of a letter he could write, should that happen; I suggested phrases, he added to them, I wrote them in a notebook and he took the note away with him.*

Letter to a client with extra information on a possible compensation claim
The client who had been off work for some months as a result of a disability, had been in the bureau a few days before to check on his employment situation. In consultation with the supervisor, *I drafted and posted to him a follow-up letter, to ensure he was clear about the time limits on him making a claim, should he wish to, as the disability was work-related.*

Letter to the County Court making the case for the client's repayment of rent arrears to be reduced (backed up by a budget sheet)
The client, a single parent, was due to be evicted in 4 days' time. Her arrears were considerable. During the interview, we drafted notes for a

letter she could write to the County Court setting out a case for leniency. I summarised to her what she had told me, asked if she agreed that would be something to put in the letter and wrote a shorthand version of that. *Later, I word-processed this as a more formal draft and sent this to her for her to check before sending her a final version that she could sign and send to the Court.*

The scribe who is helping their client make use of legal procedures or make a claim for State benefits has to tread a path between pleading and persuading. In the first case, I had to help the client think of the best way to answer questions on the form that asked her to explain why she did not already have a passport and why she could not get one from her own national authorities. There were good reasons for both. They had to look like good reasons to the reader at the desk in the Home Office. The second (a draft that may not have been needed) had to be assertive and yet also avoid risking the antagonism of a manager perceived by the client to be volatile in his reactions. The third (which, because of my inexperience, had to go through two drafts) had to be absolutely clear as to the time limits and as to what might be the client's entitlement to 'care and mobility support'. The last letter took the most time to prepare. I had to make the case for the client's entitlement to sympathetic treatment without, at the same time, seeming to imply that she was weak and feckless.

The CAB's reputation for being impartial was on the line in all of these situations. At the same time, all were the work of a scribe-as-advocate: that is, writing alongside a client, with the purpose of ensuring that they get the results that are in their best interests. People working as other kinds of advisors deal with this compositional effort every working day. One example of this comes from Jessica (who had worked for 9 years in organisations providing services for people in housing need). She helped one man to complete an application for a place in a housing co-op. One question to be answered in such an application asks: 'Why are you interested in co-operative housing?'. Jessica's client did not know what to say. As far as he was concerned, his priority was to find somewhere to live. Till then, he had not given any thought to the difference between co-ops and other kinds of housing. Jessica explained and suggested that maybe he might have an interest in helping to organise the place a bit? Going to a meeting or two about it, perhaps? 'Oh yeah', he said 'I could do that'. So she wrote on the form: 'I understand that members are involved in the management of their housing and am interested in participating in the organisation of co-ops'. As advisor, Jessica was here working as scribe-advocate. This is how she put it:

> What you are having to do is translate a client's life into what the people you send it to want to read. You have to phrase people's experience under the bits of legislation which apply. For instance, in order to increase the chance of a person who is homeless being accommodated by a local authority, you may need to encourage them to accept the legal term 'vulnerable' and be identified as *less able to fend for themselves* in housing terms. You're not there to just tick boxes for the client, though. There has to be a balance between how they see themselves. The label is a powerful one and the person may not like it or have thought of herself in that way before. Once you have collated all the 'relevant' bits of their life together and written about it in a particular way, you draft a supporting letter and say to them, 'Go along to the HPU (Homeless Persons' Unit), take this evidence and say that you're presenting as homeless and vulnerable'. I remember one woman who I did this with and she went, *'What?'*.[24]

The picture Jessica gives here is of the kind of scribing that I had thought CAB advisors did before I became one myself. It is a picture of one person writing on behalf of another to the bureaucracy of the Welfare State, in a language that is foreign to everyday ways of saying things, but has to be used if they are to achieve their rights. At times, that is indeed what the CAB does, but its emphasis is on empowering clients to learn this language and carry out more of their own casework themselves. The difficulty for many CAB clients is very often about literacy; but not all clients would be described as being short of basic skills in the usual sense. In times of stress, any one of us who is trying to disentangle fact from feeling, does not write as fluently or as effectively as we might at other times.

As far as the CAB's approach to providing scribal help for those with limited literacy, two kinds of work have attention recently. One has been the need to provide help, particularly to those on low incomes, on how to manage money better. 'Financial literacy', while not yet fully defined, is the concept being promoted. Following a government report that urged more education in the area, a pilot project was set up with five Citizens' Advice Bureaux in the Midlands, funded by the Basic Skills Agency.[25]

The other kind of work is to set up a basic skills class in CAB premises, to which people might be encouraged to come after they have already been a client in the usual sense. One such project was set up in February 1999. Called 'Never Too Late to Learn', it provides basic skills classes in a room above the advice centre in Castle Point Citizens' Advice Bureau in Essex. It seems obvious that there should be more projects like this. In both cases, people who come in the first place for advice, discover the possibilities that an empowering advice service offers them and can find a way to go further. Clearly, their success hinges on the reputation of the National Association of CAB for being a service to be trusted – and this, in turn, depends on the local bureau's reputation for an attitude of acceptance of a full diversity of people,[26] and an explicit commitment to utter confidentiality.

So the practice of 'citizens' advice' is a lot more than a scribal service in which someone simply calls in to a place to get a bit of writing done and then goes out again. The CAB advisor does not sit with pen or typewriter at a desk outside a station or post office, and the CAB certainly does not charge a fee for writing letters for people. Yet scribes such as those in Mexico City may have something to teach us. What might it be like to have a shopfront scribe service in your local high street? I recently learned that such a service had indeed existed for a couple of years in a small town in western Canada. Funded as a research project, the main work of its volunteers was to help clients deal with filling in forms and preparing resumes (or CVs). It had another agenda as well. Among the purposes for the project was that it should 'reach those individuals who are in need of literacy training and refer them to appropriate literacy programs'.[27] In the 2 years of its operation, a smaller number of people than they had expected seemed to want to follow up their visit by going to join an adult basic education class. Their report regrets this and wonders why it happened. Were they already attending classes? Or did 'the usual barriers' prevent them taking up the suggestion? There is a third alternative, of course. Maybe the scribe service was all they needed. Some people do not want to be their own scribe – at least, not for the time being. The good, possible opportunities for literacy development must be a right, along with any other legal entitlement – but it must always be the person's own choice to exercise it.

When it comes to our most basic right – the right to vote – there is a point of view that says, strictly speaking, people do not need to be literate. It is the bureaucracy of the modern state which requires that there be 'a literate apparatus to record the vote, to count the vote and to control the voting'.[28] This view came back to me when I came across The National Association of CAB's social policy report on Census 2001 – another piece of the modern state's 'literate apparatus'. In Britain, the census is undertaken every 10 years. On 29 April 2001 every adult in the country was expected to have provided information about themselves. Forms were delivered to every home. It was compulsory to complete and return it. There was a fine of up to £1,000 for anyone who failed to do so, or for anyone who gave false information. Thousands of information leaflets were printed in 24 languages; helplines were also set up, in 12 languages. In England and Wales, leaflets were available in Braille and large-print formats. Five days before Census day, the Office of National Statistics issued a press release, appealing to the media and community groups to give help to people in completing census forms. People were having difficulties getting through to either the recorded message or the operator on the helpline. Many people all over the country had trouble filling in the forms and went to their local CAB to get help with them. The National Association of CAB central office's comment on this was to point out something that the Office of National Statistics had forgotten:

> What they do not refer to in any of their press releases is help for those with disabilities or with limited English...

The most shocking piece of evidence that the National Association of CAB had collected about this was the story of one man who said that he had told his census enumerator that he could not read and write. The response he got must have depressed him. It certainly depresses me:

> However the enumerator not only refused to help him or advise him of the helpline number but informed him that he would be prosecuted if he didn't complete it.[29]

1   Kelly was one of the letter-writing scribes I introduced in Chapter 3.
2   English and Card, 1996, pv.
3   *Ibid*, pp74–5.
4   *Ibid*, pp72–81.
5   *Ibid*, p75.
6   Rock, 2000, p27.
7   Ibid, pp1–2.
8   Personal communication, 8 July 2001.

9 O'Kane, 2000.
10 Dickens, 1994, p451.
11 *Ibid*, p43.
12 *Ibid*, p119.
13 *Ibid*, p13.
14 *Ibid*, p129.
15 *Ibid*, pp137–8.
16 *Ibid*, pp186–7.
17 *Ibid*, pp111–2.
18 The manufacturers are called Possum Products; information about the Palantype system can be found on their website: www.possum.co.uk/possum/paltype1.htm.
19 Old Bailey Courtroom no.9, 21 December 2000.
20 www.nacab.org.uk, visited 20 December 2001.
21 Citron, 1989, p2.
22 *Ibid*.
23 In accordance with NACAB training policy, all these drafts were checked with the staff member who was Advice Session Supervisor at the time before giving them to the client or posting them.
24 Jessica, better known as Jess, is my daughter. This is from an interview/conversation we had walking along a London street in August 2001.
25 For information on this I am grateful to Kate Taylor of Nottingham CAB.
26 Training of volunteer advisors requires close self-scrutiny of attitudes and prejudices and a conscious understanding of what 'equal opportunities' means.
27 Skage, 1994.
28 Barton and Hamilton, 1998, pp228–9.
29 NACAB, 2001: with thanks to Chris Dugmore of Castle Point CAB for this reference.

PART THREE

It takes two to collaborate

CHAPTER SEVEN

The scribe has feelings too

So far I have suggested that scribes, whether men or women, alternate between the extremes of copyists and composers. For the most part, their work seems to fall in the middle: they act as invisible semi-authors, improving on the dictation or spoken words of others but, at the same time, committed to ensuring that the public authorship is apparently someone else's. Their job is to create the illusion that they have had nothing to do with composing this text. Their role is to act as the conduit for the voices and feelings of others. Sometimes, as discussed more in the next two chapters, this work entails translation, as well as transcription. In considering the business of bilingual scribes, it is still more clear how much is entailed in the work of producing writing under other people's names. This chapter gets inside the scribe themselves a little. (For convenience, the female pronoun is mainly used: as we have seen, scribes come in both genders and male scribes should feel included as well.)

For hour after hour the scribe writes away, transforming speech into text. Questions, recollections, wishes, accusations, appeals: all must go through her pen or keyboard and, at times, the sheer burden of other people's language wearies her. For the scribe has a life too; she too has feelings. As her hand moves the pen, or her fingers tap the keys, she may feel sad at the author's sadness, glad at their joy, but she may also feel contemptuous of their ignorance, or exasperated with their use of words. She may, in short, fall out of role – and need to take a break. This chapter had two previous titles before I settled on this one: 'The scribe gets tired' was the first. I rejected it because it seemed too narrow a version of what scribes might feel. Then came 'Good and bad scribes'. That was at a time when I saw Dora, whom you will soon meet too, as a 'bad' scribe, cruel and cynical to her authors. However I have thought about Dora some more since then; and the title seemed too judgmental. What does make a 'good' scribe? Remembering I have said that being a scribe is not a full-time job, but a role that any one of us might get into at a given moment, it is a question worth pausing on. My view, now, is that, for the whole system to work at all, for a scribe to be calm and generous and skilled, she needs to recognise herself as an author, and be recognised as such by others. The more she is clear about her own worth as a writer, the more she has the necessary energy to co-author other people's writing.

The kind of feelings that might put some pressure on the calm and generosity of the scribe are reflected in the three headings: *Pain*, *Scorn* and *Fatigue*. A couple of real-life examples show scribes feeling hurt at the pain of other people that they have to transcribe. Those who, in contrast, illustrate a feeling of contempt, which may be a scribe's view of their author, are both fictional characters. The first is from work by the playwright George Bernard Shaw; the second was portrayed in a film set in Brazil. Fatigue is a feeling that any scribe may have, working with a script that is difficult, or with an author who is demanding. First is a woman speaking of the cumulative weariness she felt from having had to be her husband's scribe. Second is a literacy teacher, offering us a glimpse of the occasional weariness that may afflict the scribe in the classroom.

Pain

The journalist who reported from Chechnya found the accounts she listened to by the victims of maltreatment 'so horrific that one's hand refused to jot them down' (Chapter 2). Margery Kempe's scribe (Chapter 5) was so moved by what he found himself writing for her that 'he could not keep himself from weeping'. The spoken words that must be transcribed may sometimes break the heart of the transcriber.

Truth and reconciliation
In 1998, South Africa's Truth and Reconciliation Commission (TRC) delivered its written report, after 3 years of hearings. During that period some 22,000 people had given statements; of these, just 1 per cent had the opportunity to testify publicly. What I know about the TRC I have learned through a mix of listening, reading and discussion. In August 1998, I listened to two South African women in my home talk about its work. In November 1999, along with a packed hall of others at the Institute of Education in London, I watched Archbishop Desmond Tutu speak of his experience as Chair of the TRC to Helena Kennedy, QC, in a

public interview. Two months later, I read his book.[1] Nearly a year after that, I listened to two researchers discuss some aspects of the TRC's work at a conference: notably their findings on how both victims and perpetrators of crimes under apartheid perceived the idea of 'forgiveness'.[2] That evening in London, Tutu made a striking reference to those who had to interpret for the witnesses who came to the TRC.

Interpreters, of course, deal in spoken language; I am not recruiting them here to the category of scribes, who are dealing in writing. The power of the courtroom testimonies in the TRC's work lay in the drama of speech, and Tutu's first point was about that. Interpreters, he said, had to 'switch identities'; becoming, in their own first person, the person for whom they spoke. As he put it in his written version:

> It was particularly rough for our interpreters, because they had to speak in the first person, at one time being the victim and at another being the perpetrator. 'They undressed me; they opened a drawer and then they stuffed my breast in the drawer which they slammed repeatedly on my nipple until a white stuff oozed.' 'We abducted him and gave him drugged coffee and then I shot him in the head. We then burned his body and whilst this was happening, we were enjoying a barbecue on the side.'[3]

At the lecture, he told the same thing in similar words, his speech coming fast and furious in the telling: a small figure in purple on a stage, his dark face passionate. It was the utterance of stark facts, of cruelty endured and cruelty imposed. I wished I had a film camera, or at least a tape recorder. For a moment, in that London lecture theatre, there was a feeling of palpable shock; then the Archbishop continued. He spoke of the transcribers, those whose job it is (as discussed in Chapter 4) to set down 'verbatim' every word spoken. They sat at their keyboards with microphones in their ears, listening to the audio record of those courtroom exchanges. They too, as Tutu reported it, had their own pain to deal with:

> The person heading our transcriptions service told me one day how, as she was typing transcripts of our hearings, she did not know she was crying until she felt and saw the tears on her arms.[4]

Torture and translation
Scribes work with voices in their ears as they type the words onto the screen; often with the voices of absent authors. Those who transcribe

interviews with refugees or victims of torture must listen to pain and be its servant. Translators, by contrast, work from the written page. They do not have the addition of the speaker's voice to deal with; but the experience of taking into themselves the suffering of the author may still be acute. Berhane, a friend who had worked as a translator and transcriber for Amnesty International, told me:

> There were things like reports from prison. It's – sometimes – you get tortured, when you read. You get letters from prison, graphically describing how they were tortured. The last one I was given – about 82 pages – I had to give to some friends, because after a while I could not take it. These friends are also very good translators. And then I would check it myself.

'Do you think it was less painful for them?', I asked.

No, but at least we shared the pain.[5]

Berhane spoke also of the additional work of the translator – the one who must find the means to transpose a text between two languages. Not only was he transcribing the words (originally spoken in Amharic or Tigrinya), he was also having to translate them into English. The choices are subtle; the scribe can shift out of an emotional engagement with the text into an intellectual struggle with language:

> In the process of selecting a word, you get involved. It's like building in our country. Of course, here [in Britain] every brick comes from a factory and therefore they are all the same, so the angle and everything is the same. But buildings in Eritrea or Ethiopia – you are building with stones, and you have to give a little shape – because all the stones are different shapes, you have to adjust the position of the stone… So what do they do? They try to adjust it. If the first stone, or the surrounding stones, are given a certain shape, an empty shape, they will come with a stone that will fill that… So when one translates, you have various synonyms and when you have to select the one that will fit, you get involved… Like, the other day I was thinking about: 'agreement', 'convention', 'pact', 'accord'. Each one has a different shade of meaning.

Berhane is a professional translator and transcriber; those in the TRC's courtroom also were. Having to be the person to type out other people's painful experience is always hard for the person doing the typing. Every reader has their own examples. What he refers us to here, however, is the scribe's own authorship: his own well of language from which he draws. The TRC's transcribers worked fast and skillfully; so fast that they had not even realised it was their own tears that were wetting their arms. Painful though some scribal work must be, there can still be a reward for the scribe in doing justice to the text.

Scorn

Now it may be that you are asked to scribe something for someone and feel the opposite of empathy with their pain. You may feel a kind of contempt for what they have to say, or for the way they say it. You may have had a bad day. Let me offer two very different scornful scribes to keep you company.

Pygmalion

The playwright George Bernard Shaw was a scourge of incorrect pronunciation and a lifelong campaigner for reform of English spelling. In his preface to *Pygmalion*, first published in 1916, he writes something about another spelling reformer called Henry Sweet, on whom, he says he based his character of Professor Higgins. He writes too of shorthand systems – disparaging the more popular Pitman's shorthand in favour of that which Sweet had invented. Suddenly we are at his shoulder, watching him write shorthand and discovering the presence of the secretary who types it out for him in the form we are reading:

> and yet the shorthand in which I am writing these lines [he says] is Pitman's. And the reason is, that my secretary cannot transcribe Sweet, having been perforce taught in the schools of Pitman.[6]

I tried to imagine myself composing my next letter in shorthand (rusty as it is, as I indicated in Chapter 4) and gave up. I could not imagine seeing those 'outlines' on the page as I wrote. It seems a contradiction in terms. Shorthand, to me, is for taking down someone else's words. Well, apparently not.

For the linguist Deborah Cameron, *Pygmalion* is 'one of the great verbal hygiene stories of modern literature'.[7] The story of Henry Higgins and Eliza Doolittle is the story, as she sees it, of a 'verbal hygienist' – by which she means someone who specialises in 'tidying up the language' – boasting of his triumph in transforming a dustman's daughter into a duchess. Shaw was a well-known campaigner for language standards. In his preface to the play, he made clear that this was part of that campaign. 'The English have no respect for their language', he wrote.[8] The play is 'intensely and deliberately didactic'; its message, that a 'scientific' approach to language improvement is the only one that can work:

> Ambitious flower-girls who read this play must not imagine that they can pass themselves off as fine ladies by untutored imitation. They must learn their alphabet over again, and different, from a phonetic expert. Imitation will only make them ridiculous.[9]

The story of Eliza is well known enough, through stage performance and film adaptation; not to mention the musical *My Fair Lady*. Both film and musical altered Shaw's ending to have Eliza and Henry Higgins fall in love. In the play, Eliza's successful suitor is the ineffectual Freddy. Shaw had been clear, Cameron tells us, that for Eliza to marry Higgins would not be a happy ending, since Higgins was too 'godlike' for the relationship to be 'altogether agreeable'.[10] Either way, Eliza's happy ending is to find an eligible man.

What has this got to do with scribing? If you have seen the play or the musical, you may remember the first scene. It is raining. Mother, daughter and Freddy are trying to hail a cab outside Covent Garden. Eliza, known only at this stage in the script as 'the flower girl' is hurrying for shelter with her basket of violets, when Freddy, rushing off into the rain, knocks her down. Under the portico of the church nearby stands a man, referred in the playscript as 'the note taker'. This is the dialogue that Shaw writes next:

THE FLOWER GIRL Nah then, Freddy: look wh'y'gowin, deah.

FREDDY Sorry. [*He rushes off*].

THE FLOWER GIRL [*picking up her scattered flowers and replacing them in the basket*] There's menners f' yer! Te-oo* banches o voylets trod into the mad...

Stage directions follow as to the appearance of the flower girl, ending with:

[*She is no doubt as clean as she can afford to be; but compared to the ladies she is very dirty. Her features are no worse than theirs, but their condition leaves something to be desired; and she needs the services of a dentist.*]

THE MOTHER How do you know that my son's name is Freddy, pray?

THE FLOWER GIRL Ow, eez, ye-ooa* san, is e? Wal, fewd dan y' d-ooty bawmz a mather should, eed now bettern to spawl a pore gel's flahrzn than ran awy athaht pyin. Will ye-oo py me f'them? [*Here, with apologies, this desperate attempt to represent her dialect without a phonetic alphabet must be abandoned as unintelligible outside London.*][11]

This then is Shaw, transcribing 'scientifically' the speech of a working-class girl in early twentieth century London. More specific even than that, through the character of Henry Higgins he pinpoints her as early twentieth century *Hoxton*, East London. For it is Higgins who is leaning against the pillar, taking notes of Eliza and others. He eavesdrops first on this exchange between Eliza, Freddy and Freddy's mother; next, with a 'gentleman' to whom Eliza tries to sell flowers, who turns out to be none other than Colonel Pickering ('the author of *Spoken Sanskrit*'), on his way to meet none other than Professor Higgins ('author of *Higgins's Universal Alphabet*'). Their meeting is the sequel to Eliza's horror at being told by a 'bystander' that 'there's a bloke here behind taking down every blessed word you're saying'. Taken at first to be 'a copper's nark' or informer (who else would be standing in a street and transcribing speech?), Higgins reveals his trade by reading back to Eliza her own words in her exact pronunciation and by accurately naming the birth-places of various onlookers.

Shaw, and his alter ego Higgins, are scribes with no sense of the humanity of their authors. For them, or certainly for Higgins, the speaker is an object of curiosity; what matters is not so much the content of what is said, but the form in which it is spoken. His profession, like Shaw's, is voice production. Both playwright and character are men with an interest in the proper transcription of words; in this case, spoken words – though Shaw himself, of course, was primarily concerned with literature. No worries about their own sense of authorship; both fictional and actual men are entirely confident of their own importance in the world of letters. It is their scorn for the authorship of others that, in the terms I am arguing, make them both bad scribes.

Central Station

From a different language, another street scribe, also (at first sight, at least) with a contempt for her authors. The principal character in the film *Central Station (Central do Brazil)*[12] is a woman called Dora. Every day, she sets up her stall outside the main railway station, charging one buck for a letter, two bucks for the stamp and posting of it. As we first see her, she holds all the power. Her clients depend on her; they dictate, she writes. As she writes their words, her face shows alternately mockery and contempt. Back in her own home in the evening, she sits with her neighbour, Irene, and reads back their letters with scorn. Some of them she throws into her rubbish bin; others into the drawer of her sideboard, to join dozens more, forever unposted. Irene, less heartless than she, half-joins in the amusement and half-resists, asking her more than once to hold back from tearing up another pathetic text.

The film has three sequences showing Dora writing. The first opens the film, with her as scribe writing to the dictation of her clients outside the station. The second, when she and Josue have reached rock bottom, finds her setting up stall at Josue's initiative, to write messages to chosen saints for clients in the site of a pilgrimage where the two of them have found themselves. (The film's references to Christian iconography are several: it seems no coincidence that Josue's father, Jesus, is referred to as a carpenter.) The third and final one is when we see her, on the coach having left Josue reconciled to his brothers, writing her own letter in her own hand to Josue: her farewell.

I want to describe in some detail the first sequence, for within it there are several elements to help us think about the source of Dora's scorn. It occupies the 2 or 3 minutes before the credits roll and is (I believe) a work of art in itself. The quotations in the following account are from the film's subtitles (themselves a scribal text) – transcribed by me after several rewinding and reviewing moves, watching the video version at home.

Without any introduction – not even the preface of the film title – one after another, the faces of five people occupy the whole screen. Film-viewers have no warning, no idea what the first person is doing or to whom she is speaking. Her black hair is tied back and there is an expression of great sadness on her face. The person she is addressing is not only off camera; they seem very far away. 'My darling', she begins, 'My heart belongs to you. No matter what you've done, I still love you. I still love you.'. Her eyes gaze into the distance, left of the viewer, to some out-of-shot person. 'While you're locked up in there all those years', she goes on, 'I'll be locked up out here, waiting for you.'. Tears well up in her eyes as she bites her lip. The camera and sound turn to the rush of train in the station behind her; we see rush-hour people walking fast along platform.

Next comes an old man in hat. This time, the person he is speaking to is evidently near the camera. His first words, spoken boldly, give us a clue, now, as to who it may be: 'I want to send a letter to a guy who cheated me' he says. Then he changes register, and, like the first speaker, seems to be speaking to someone far away: 'Mr Ze Amaro' he says, 'Thank you for what you did to me' (his smile suggests the sarcasm). 'I trusted you', he goes on, 'and you cheated me. You even took the keys to my apartment.'.

Again, the camera turns to the crowds disembarking from the trains in the background.

The voice of the third person is heard before her face is seen. 'Dear Jesus' she says. We see her now, a woman in a cotton dress, with a boy leaning against her shoulder. She goes on speaking, again looking at someone unseen, off-camera, 'You're the worst thing to happen to me'. Then, for the first time, we see a hand writing; a pen is moving on the page. The woman continues: 'I'm only writing because your son Josue asked me to. I told him you're worthless.'.

It is at this point that the viewer sees at last the face of the immediate person each of these people has been addressing: a lived-in face, the hooded eyes looking up sardonically through her spectacles at this woman for whom she writes. She has heard it all before. I said that the others are addressing her, but of course, they are not not. The person whom this woman is addressing is 'Jesus'. 'And yet he still wants to meet you', the woman goes on. For the third time, we see the crowded station behind.

Dora looks up and speaks, for the first time. 'Address?' she asks tersely. Tenderly, the woman replies: 'Jesus de Palva Bom. Jesus do Norte. Pernambuco'. Dora's pen moves across the envelope, the words appear. She (and we) then watch the woman and boy walk away hand in hand, and a different client takes his place. Eagerly he begins: 'Dalva. My hot pussy'. Dora looks up sharply, asks: 'Pussy?'. Nodding happily, he goes on: 'Your body against mine. Rolling around. In the motel bed. Our sweat boiling'(Dora keeps writing, her face closed). 'Me, I still feel...' (he cries, carried away with his recollections) 'I still feel...'. His face beams, his earring glints. Words clearly fail him. Dora, exasperated, suggests: '...infatuated?'. 'Yes', he agrees joyfully 'infatuated!'.

Finally, we see a sequence of people apparently blissfully ignorant as to the need for accurate written destinations for their letters.. 'I don't know the exact address', says a young woman. Pressed to produce something, she says: 'Okay, then write: third house after the bakery Mimoso, Pernambuco.'. A string of four more faces are shown cheerfully offering: 'Casancao, Bahia', 'Carangola, Minas Gerais', 'Town of Relutaba, Ceara', and 'Muzambinh, Minas Gerais'. This is all. We watch Dora packing up for the day (handing the key to a man, saying goodbye to a couple of people, hitching her red bag on to her shoulder as she joins the pack of people on the train), and up come the film title and credits.

The next scene shows Dora and Irene going through the day's letters, Dora choosing whether to bin them or put them in the drawer. The one from Josue's mother is put in the drawer, Dora's contempt for the woman's veiled wish to see her man back, a 'drunk who beat her up' outweighing Irene's sympathy for the woman. Back at the train station the next week, however, Dora finds herself faced by Josue's mother and Josue. The woman asks her: 'The other day I sent a letter. Did you send it?'. Dora cautiously says no, she will be sending it that day. 'Oh good', says the woman: 'Don't send it. Send another. I think I was too hard on him'. She goes on to dictate a different one. As Dora had suspected, she wants to see him herself: 'Dear Jesus, your son really wants to see you. He wants to visit you. He doesn't know you and wants to visit. I'm on vacation next month and can come with him'. At this point she hesitates, and asks her scribe how to end the letter. Thinking aloud, not really listening to the answer, she pauses. 'You know what?' she says to Dora, woman to woman, 'I'm dying to see that bastard again'. Then, to Dora the scribe, she says: 'You're experienced. Tell me, what do I say now?'.

'How should I know?' says Dora, exasperated. 'Help me, please', the woman says. 'You think about it and come back', says Dora. 'The truth is I still like him a lot', she replies. At this point, Dora loses patience and begins to write, shouting out the words as she writes, a parody of a client's dictation: 'Jesus. I miss you so much. It's awful to wake up without you next to me. If I had one strand of black hair left on my head I'd leave it for you to take out'. 'That's great!' cries the woman. 'Wait for me,' continues Dora. 'I'm coming back. Love', looking up at the woman, she asks abruptly: 'What's your name?'. 'Ana', the other replies, her face wreathed in smiles. The transaction ends with her paying Dora again and asking her to put in the envelope a photograph. At this point, the boy, more watchful than his mother, says: 'Mum how do you know she will send the letter? She hasn't even addressed the envelope!'. His mother reproves him: 'Don't be so rude', and Dora says to the person behind them: 'Next?'.

Minutes later, Ana is dead. At the traffic lights, the boy runs to get his wooden top. In her anxiety over him, the mother stands stock still in the path of an oncoming bus and is run over.

In this short sequence between scribe and clients, we see two things that the scribe has to endure. One is the lovingness of her clients towards the unseen recipient of the letter she writes. Not for Dora, we are led to understand, the erotic delights of the young man and his woman. Not for her either, the outburst of passion from Ana for her feckless husband. Yet she has the words that both authors need. To her it comes easy, the word that the young man struggled for and could not find; for her, it was a matter of a few formula phrases to express what Ana wanted to say. Dora has a past that has embittered her: a father who abandoned her as a child and failed to recognise her in the street as an adolescent, and a career as a teacher from which she (like Irene) was made redundant. Having no hope of her own, Dora earns a living as the writer of other people's.

Played superbly by the actress Fernanda Montenegro, the film shows her change from this manipulator of innocent illiterates, to become the accomplice in Josue's passionate search for his father.

After Ana's death, Josue stays on the station, sleeping there at night, waiting in vain for her to return. From an initial hostility towards him, and clearly against her better judgement as a hard-hearted old cynic, Dora becomes sorry for him. He mistrusts her, but finally agrees to go back to her flat for some food and a bed. Next day she takes him to a couple who are quite obviously crooks, but display sufficient charm for her to overcome any qualms she has about the boy's fate to take their money and leave him with them. It is Irene who later, discovering what she has done, persuades Dora to return and, just in time, to sneak into their apartment (now revealed to be the squalid halfway house for child-slaves that Irene had suspected) and escape with Josue. From then on, we follow the two of them on what seems clearly to be a hopeless journey, to search for his father. Travelling enormous distances in the discomfort of two overheated coaches, a long-distance lorry and with a truck-load of evangelists, they eventually lose all their money.

It is in the course of that journey, that a scene takes place in which she is shown for the failure she really is. For Dora (we are told) is that thing which all full-blooded heterosexual viewers are assumed to fear most: she is a spinster, a woman without a man and with no likely prospect of getting one.[13] Briefly attractive to the long-distance driver, who gives the two of them a lift, she is clearly not sufficiently so. In a café break along the journey, she and the man share a drink. She sends the boy off to play at the pinball machine; the thing between her and the man appears to have possibilities; she flirts, goes off to the toilets to apply some lipstick, only to find, on her return, that the man has gone. Through the window of the cafe she sees the dust rising as the lorry turns out of the car park on to the open road.

The portrayal of Dora in this film is the portrayal of a woman who is incomplete because she has no man; a woman whose cleverness with words has condemned her to an occupation where she is merely the messenger of other people's passions. In that sense, however moving, this is a misogynist's film. However, as the portrayal of a world-weary scribe, it is superb. She began with scorn: scorn for the gullibility of her clients, so ignorant that they do not even know the need for a postcode to ensure their message ever arrives. She ends up, in the bus travelling away from the boy in his new family, writing a letter to Josue, the handwriting she has used for so long in the service of others' dreams, for once expressing her own.

Fatigue

A third feeling that a scribe may feel is sheer weariness. The two examples which follow are not fictional; one is from a woman, faithful scribe to her husband; the other, a teacher, confessing to moments of fatigue in the process of negotiating text with a learner.

Consuming yourself like a candle

I have known Inez (not her real name) for some years and knew her to have escaped as a political refugee from Chile and then Argentina in the 1970s. For some years before they left, she and her husband had been political activists in Argentina, for which both were imprisoned, and for which he was interrogated under torture. In the years that followed their arrival in England, Inez acted as his scribe, transcribing to his dictation and translating his Spanish into English. Reading between the lines of what she told me, Inez had often to work at the composition end of the spectrum of scribe work; she would 'change' things he said, because her sense of what would translate into English was better than his. In addition, as she puts it, having been in England for a year longer than he, she had a keener sense of the 'culture'. Perhaps more crucial than both of these was the damage to her husband's powers of expression resulting from the torture he had undergone. He suffered from depression; with this came periods of memory loss. ('He had made such a big effort to forget so as not to denounce anyone. Every time he becomes depressed, this forgetting happens again.')

The transcript below of what she told me speaks both of the compositional process and the effects of this constant scribing work over a long time:

> I was a scribe for my husband for years and years. He was one of the founders of the caneworkers' trade union in Uruguay. We had this wonderful relationship in the middle of the struggle. I was released in 1978, a year before him, and so I got to know the culture here. In the first 10 years we were here, we did a lot of political work. He was an important person for his people in Uruguay. I was his scribe here because I wanted to raise the profile of him and people like him who had a genuine reason for rebelling. I was translating all the time. At some stages, because I was more familiar with the culture, I wasn't saying what he was telling me to say. We were writing a project on using radio as a means of communication for raising

awareness during the dictatorship. We discussed it. I was the scribe, and I realised I was manipulating information. I was changing things. I was doing it because I felt I knew the environment. I felt guilty sometimes. It was my class prejudice. I felt there were some things I had to change when I translated his writing (for magazine articles, trade union information, and so on). He would dictate to me in Spanish. He used the tape-recorder a lot and I transcribed and translated. He would not bother to check what I had written. He trusted me completely.

This was when my own professional training was completely left behind. I dedicated myself to this man for 15 years. I got so tired, mentally. I was not renewing myself. You feel you are consuming yourself like a candle and getting nothing back.

Like Berhane, Inez is combining two layers of work here: translation and transcription. In our interview, she went on to reflect on this, recalling something she remembered reading by Hans Magnus Enzensberger.[14] 'Enzensberger says', she recalled, 'that manipulation is inevitable in communication media. So maybe this changing that I did and do as scribe and translator is inevitable'. Watching and listening to her, I felt admiration. I admired her as someone who had carried her own suffering, as well as her husband's. I also admired her for all that labour of translation from Spanish into English. She was fluent in both: but nevertheless, English was not her first language. What made the work more complicated was the sense she had that her knowledge of English was greater than her husband's,[15] the author; wanting to make sure his meaning would be unequivocal, and that the finished text would do justice to what he wanted to say, she made changes. At the same time, because she did not want to add to his pressures by going through every change in detail, she felt compelled to make these changes without consulting him, and in so doing had to carry the feeling that she had 'manipulated' his words.

There is a view in translation studies of the original being the true and proper text and the translator's job to maintain 'fidelity' to this. The idea, it has been argued, is born of colonialism, where the original (in a European language) would have been assumed to be superior to the translation (into a 'native' language). Some theorists have noticed a connection with gender politics. The translator's task was at one time seen to be, above all, to produce a text that was faithful to the original. Bad translation at that time was unfaithful translation. The original, in this analysis, may be compared to the man, whose own transgressions might be seen as trivial; to whom the translator – as woman – had at all costs to display fidelity (a woman's adultery being met at that period with severe penalties).[16]

Inez was working as both translator and transcriber. At some moments she was co-author, 'discussing' a project and acting as the scribe for both of them. At others, she was working from her husband's dictation: the classic secretary, there to get words on paper in correct formation. Her recollection of the whole is of a weariness; a time when her own authorship was melting away like the wax of a candle: her faithfulness to her husband's text exacting a price in her own expressive life.

The scribe leaves the room

There are times when the scribe needs to leave the work and breathe. Working as a teacher in adult literacy means a lot of time may be spent in the role of a scribe. Chapter 9 looks at several examples of this work, with an emphasis on the process of producing writing. Stella Fitzpatrick, writing about a long experience of working in this way, is the only person I have yet found who has said something about the feelings of the scribe in this process. What she has to say needs to be set in context, for her work in adult literacy education is not typical. As a founder staff member of Gatehouse Project in Manchester, Stella worked for over 20 years with the publication of writing by learners in adult literacy education as her primary purpose. Gatehouse Project, founded in 1977 and later constituted as Gatehouse Publishing Charity and Gatehouse Books, was set up to publish and nationally distribute some of the writing that local groups were already producing, and to give support to the new writers among them. In an analysis of work with four such writers, Stella explains the need for a 'safe space' in which such work may flourish. This sentence alerts us to something more than a familiar reference to the basic skills student's barriers to learning:

> Fatigue, lack of self-esteem, material things *like securing a grant or organising childcare* can be difficult obstacles to overcome on the way.[17] (My italics.)

'Organising childcare' could be the worry of a parent trying to get time to come to a group meeting or class. However, linked to 'securing a grant' it seems more likely to be one of the obstacles of the project coordinators than that of the student participants – who, as I say, are often referred to as suffering from both fatigue and lack of self-esteem. Actually, teachers get tired and low in confidence, too. In short, the obstacles listed here could be common to both teacher and student. So it is not such a surprise as it might be to find this reference later on, to the need for the educator to have a 'safe space' as well as the student:

> There are times, however, when the safe space doesn't provide all that is needed by the participants. Listening to tapes of a series of interactions with one writer, for instance, reminds me of how out of temper that person became about the possibility of change to their writing, and how insistent that person could be, when their expected outcome was threatened or not realised. I remember how on these occasions I invented reasons for absenting myself, albeit briefly, from the talk, in order to give myself some relief, to consider what was happening and to recover my own opinions. Safe space is what educators try to provide and what we need for ourselves.[18]

What I read here is a picture of an author/scribe conflict over matters of style (and perhaps content). The scribe is a literacy teacher and aware of her greater knowledge of the language and culture. She is also a community scribe and publisher, committed to shared work, to negotiation, to the right of previously disempowered authors to hold to their own kinds of self-expression. Much is contained in this short passage; the need to leave the scene and reflect on 'what is happening', the effort needed to 'recover my own opinions'; and all of it possible for her to reflect on as a result of her having tape-recorded these sessions in the first place.

At the end of her chapter about the process of scribing other people's work, Stella turns to her own writing processes:

> As an editor and educator… I work with texts which are not mine and with writers who aren't me. My role is to draw out more from the writer, to plant seeds that might flourish, to discuss and negotiate. Working on my own writing, on the other hand, seems to mean a process of bewilderingly endless selection: discovering the unconscious suppressions as well as finding words to state what clearly has to be said.[19]

What is clever about this is her concept of 'discovering the unconscious suppressions' as we write. By 'suppressions' I understand her to mean not so much ideas or feelings suppressed by an unconscious desire to forget, but undiscovered ones, needing to be discovered through writing. It is a reference to the amount of *unwritten* material from which a writer has to select. The struggle for the scribe to find their own voice is the struggle of containing within ourselves both the scribe beside us, ready to 'draw out more' from us, and the effort to select and edit. This reminder acts as a counterpoint to Stella's earlier note on the effect on the scribe of working in tension with another person as learner/author. It seems important to mention that, while I know this chapter as Stella's editor,[20] I still find these extra layers of meaning on re-reading it some 7 years after I worked with her.

This chapter has looked at some of the ways in which scribes may have their own emotions mixed up in the writing process, as well as those of the clients, partners or students who turn to them for help in achieving authorship. The next chapter looks at how it is as a 'muse' that the scribe enables people to make such discoveries; and as a 'secretary' that she comes to an agreed form in which they may be articulated.

1　Tutu, 1999.
2　Mafani, 2000.
3　Tutu, 1999, p232.
4　*Ibid*.
5　Interview with Berhane Woldegabriel, 18 January 2001.
6　Shaw, 1957, p8.
7　Cameron, 1995, p213.
8　Shaw, 1957, p5.
9　*Ibid*, p9.
10　Cited in Cameron, 1995, p167.
11　This extract appears on p15 of the 1957 edition of the play (Shaw, 1957). It was first produced in London and New York in 1914; the film was first produced in London in 1938.
12　Salles, 1998.
13　One reviewer of the video film is quite clear about this: 'Dora is a spinster without a life who seems to regard the world with the same lack of interest it's always shown to her.' (Lucy Mohl review on www.film.com/ film-review/1998/10361/14/default-review.html – visited on 24 March 2000).
14　Ensenzberger, 1974, p25.
15　For an explanation of the difference between an 'active' and 'passive' knowledge of a language, see website of the Institute for Translators and Interpreters: www.iti.org.uk.
16　Basnett and Trivedi, 1999; and Chamberlain, 1992.

17 Fitzpatrick, 1995, p4.
18 *Ibid*, p6.
19 *Ibid*, p20.
20 If you follow up the reference beside the quotations, you will note that Stella's chapter appeared in a collection for which I was responsible.

CHAPTER EIGHT

Secretary or muse?

Τ he good secretary ensures that her or his boss's letter goes out looking good. No spelling or punctuation mistakes; properly laid out and paragraphed; using the right conventions of greeting and farewell, conforming to what is 'appropriate' (a key concept in the secretary's role). The good muse, on the other hand, is there to help the author produce good music and help the writing sing – particularly if the author's purpose is to captivate the reader. As we have seen, some scribes, asked to perform the function of muse, may resort to the formulae of courtship. Maria, in Chapter 3, 'wrote the same thing for every one' of her clients – as if she was writing the lines for a greeting card manufacturer. Dora, outside Central Station, exasperated with Ana's longing for her 'Jesus', seized the pen and rushed into cliché.

The first section of this chapter, *Love on paper*, introduces two scribal figures from literature in Latin America and France, who cannot help but do the opposite. They can only write the most passionate prose for their authors. Against this, is the figure of the tongue-tied suitor in an Italian village whose scribe (an internationally famous poet) refuses him any help beyond publicly autographing his book. In the second section, *A muse and her poet*, the muse/scribe turns on her poet and speaks with her own voice. Thirdly, there is a brief discussion on the *Inner voice and outer scribe* of the poet: the poet with more than one language to choose from, and the poet who reads aloud or recites their work. Finally, we see how a scribe who is primarily a secretary offers her own way of being a muse in *The scribe joins in*.

Love on paper

Back in Chapter 3, I introduced the street scribes in Mexico City who Judy Kalman had observed. She found them working across a spectrum:

at one end, the scribe takes charge and the client merely provides names; at the other, the scribe acts as 'hired hand' and the client directs the entire thing. Between these two, she found examples of what I call 'give and take', and what she calls 'joint composition'.

One of these examples was that of a young man wanting to write a letter to his girlfriend. The young man was able to say quite a lot of what he wanted to have written; the scribe joined in and offered rephrasings that he found helpful. In this letter he implies a need to regain his lover's faith in him. 'I hope that all will be forgiven this Christmas', he dictates. The scribe proposes an additional sentence, to which the young man agrees: 'I am always thinking of you' (*siempre te tengo en la mente*). There is one point, however, on which scribe and client could not agree. The young man was uncertain as to whether to choose the informal *tu* or the more formal *usted* form of address. His concern (as Kalman observed the discussion) was not only about which form would be correct; he wanted to know which one would sound nicer. For himself, he favoured *tu*. The scribe, however (a 72-year-old man called Pedro) did not agree. To him, it was preferable to use *usted* 'because you must always give a lady her place' (*porque a una dama hay que darle su lugar*). More old-fashioned forms of address, to him, were called for. The more intimate *tu* would be inappropriate. In the end, however, he went along with his client's preference.[1] For letters of feeling a scribe needs to combine the roles of both muse and secretary. Aware of conventions and able to use them, the scribe sometimes has to bow to the wish of an author, whose priority is to produce the language which would 'sound nicer'.

In writing to woo, scribes may be more successful than their clients might have hoped. Harold, one of the scribes cited in Chapter 3, told me:

> There was a problem once when I was writing for a man. The girl I wrote to for him was more interested in the person writing the letter than her boyfriend. She wrote back with a note at the bottom, saying, 'I know it is not you who wrote this, I want to know this person who is writing.' It was embarrassing.

When I asked him how he thought this had come about, Harold said he felt that he had been able to put over what the man wanted to say in a way that connected with 'the flow of letters' between them:

> He had told me the basic things to write but I knew the flow of letters between them and I put my own salt and pepper on it.[2]

Fiction provides other stories like this. The examples here are first, in the character of Florentino Ariza by the Colombian writer Gabriel Garcia Marquez, and second in that of Cyrano de Bergerac by Emile Rostand. Not all scribes agree to write to commission, however, as the third example, a film portrait of the Chilean poet Pablo Neruda, shows.

Love in the time of cholera

Marquez was born in Columbia in 1928. He was awarded the Nobel Prize for Literature in 1982 and lives in Mexico City. This much is known, but what is not known is quite where and when his novel, *Love in the time of cholera*, is set – except by those who know more about Latin American history and geography than I do, who may guess from the references. Let us assume it is somewhere in the Caribbean in the mid-nineteenth century. The three main characters are: the beautiful Fermina Daza, her husband Dr Juvenal Urbino and Florentino Ariza, the man who is her unrequited suitor of 51 years, until Juvenal's death, after which they become lovers. For 30 of those years Florentino Ariza works for his uncle's river-navigation company, starting as a clerk; and there he had a problem. The problem lay in the kind of writing required of him; for Florentino could only write one way and the office letters needed in the job should have been written in another:

> Florentino Ariza wrote everything with so much passion that even official documents seemed to be about love. His bills of lading were rhymed no matter how he tried to avoid it, and routine business letters had a lyrical spirit that diminished their authority.[3]

His uncle urges him to write more appropriately: Florentino tries. As a means to 'unburden his heart of all the words of love that he could not use in customs reports', he spends his free time as a street scribe in the 'Arcade of the Scribes':

> helping unlettered lovers to write their scented love notes... There he would take off his frock coat with his circumspect gestures and hang it over the back of the chair, he would put on the cuffs so he would not dirty his shirt sleeves, he would unbutton his vest so he could think better, and sometimes until very late at night he would encourage the hopeless with letters of mad adoration.[4]

During all that time, he was also writing to Fermina, about whom he thought constantly; but he was getting little back in return. As Marquez put it, Florentino had 'so much love left over inside that he did not know what to do with it'. Looking back as an older man, Florentino recalls a situation in which a boy and a girl had both been his clients, so that on one day he was writing from the boy to the girl, and on the next he was writing back, for the girl. It is, I think, a delightfully told little parable. Here it is in Marquez' words (or rather those of Edith Grossman, his English translator):

> His most pleasant memory of that time was of a very timid young girl, almost a child, who trembled as she asked him to write an answer to an irresistible letter she had just received, and that Florentino recognised as one he had written on the previous afternoon. He answered it in a different style, one that was in tune with the emotions and the age of the girl, and in a hand that also seemed to be hers, for he knew how to create a handwriting for every occasion, according to the character of each person. He wrote, imagining to himself what Fermina Daza would have said to him if she had loved him as much as that helpless child loved her suitor. Two days later, of course, he had to write the boy's reply in the same hand, style, and kind of love that he had attributed to him in the first letter, and so it was that he became involved in a feverish correspondence with himself. Before a month had passed, each came to him separately to thank him for what he himself had proposed in the boy's letter and accepted with devotion in the girl's response: they were going to marry.[5]

This is the tale of a scribe who is truly composing: but the composition is tailor-made, from phrasing to handwriting. He has thrown himself first into the girl's heart and then into her boy's: somehow making sure to keep each one separate and consistent with itself, and writing each with such sincerity and passion that the recipient could not but be won over. What he had failed to do with Fermina, he succeeded twice over in doing here.

After half a century's worship of Fermina, however, her husband dies and Florentino renews his suit. Here Marquez has him suddenly writing in a different style – choosing, after all these years of careful calligraphy, to type it. He goes to work that day. The office is full of the sound of typewriters. He decides to risk writing a letter to Fermina on one. He takes 15 days to teach himself to type adequately and then does so:

It was a six-page letter, unlike any he had ever written before. It did not have the tone, or the style, or the rhetorical air of his early years of love, and his argument was so rational and measured that the scent of a gardenia would have been out of place. In a certain sense it was his closest approximation to the business letters he had never been able to write.

Fermina replies and allows him to visit. She also begs his pardon for any problems he may have had in reading her handwriting, explaining that she had nothing more advanced to write with than her steel pen.[6]

The idea is wonderful. Florentino is such a passionate writer that he cannot write business letters and must perforce use up his lyrical gifts in scribing for others. When it finally becomes possible to meet the one true love of his life, he can only write in the measured prose of a business letter. Marquez' attention to the *tools* of writing in this character are particularly appealing: the carefully chosen and cultivated handwriting styles for each client; the studied choice of the new writing machine to write at last to Fermina; and her apology for the use of a mere pen with which to reply to this.

Cyrano de Bergerac

Writing nearly a century earlier, Edmond Rostand set his play in the year 1640. Its hero, Cyrano, has the nose of a clown and the soul of a poet; never at a loss for words, he is portrayed as bold and witty, a gallant with a following. Inside, however, his heart yearns hopelessly for the beautiful Roxanne. It is hopeless because Roxanne is already besotted with Christian, a soldier in Cyrano's company. She confides in Cyrano (who is, after all, her cousin, they have grown up together). Now, Cyrano knows that while Christian is handsome, he is also dumb. Not only can he not write a decent love letter, he cannot properly talk either – or at least, not to a woman. So Christian turns to Cyrano for help, who lets him have and post, as if from him, a letter that he had already written to Roxanne without any hope of success (for who could love a man with a long nose?). Overcome with gratitude, Christian sends the letter in no time. Roxanne lets Cyrano know that she wants to meet Christian. Christian, in turn, is terrified. How will he speak to her? And so follows the famous scene in which Cyrano speaks to her on his behalf, hidden among the shrubs beneath Roxanne's window, wooing her with poetry. Roxanne falls for it.

The drama hinges on the conviction that Roxanne could not – or not at first sight, at least – fall in love with a man who is seen to be ugly and disfigured. What she falls for first is Christian *before he speaks*. The letters and the words of adoration entrance her; it is only well on in the piece that she says to Christian that she would love him even if he were ugly. It is then that Christian wants to reveal all, for he is at the end of his tether with the attempt to keep up the pretence. 'I want her love for the poor fool that I am – or not at all!' he cries to Cyrano. Yet it is too late; in the heat of battle, in the next scene, Christian is killed. Cyrano heroically maintains the pretence of his authorship of the letters and Roxanne enters a nunnery, distraught with grief. Fifteen years later, Cyrano (who has been visiting regularly, as a cousin, each Saturday) reveals the true authorship as he manages to read by heart in the gathering dusk the last letter that (as she had thought) Christian had written her. So Roxanne finally discovers him, just as he breathes his last.

The play has been translated more than once and adapted into a film, starring Steve Martin and Darryl Hannah, set in small-town America.[7] The adaptation is clever. Charlie (Cyrano) is the chief of the local fire brigade. Just like Rostand's Roxanne, who – apart from a weakness for muscular men in uniforms – is clever, as well as beautiful, this one is an astronomer. Chris (the hunk of her dreams) is new to the fire brigade. Unlike Christian in the play, Chris in the film makes an attempt to write the letter first on his own. He spends all afternoon at his desk, strewn with pencil shavings, pencil sharpener and scrunched-up paper. (Word processors cannot show the desperation of writing like this. The delete button does not have the same theatrical effect as the scrumpled balls of hopeless text.) At last he rings Charlie and begs him to help. Charlie agrees and Chris goes round to his flat. By this time, Charlie is only too aware that Roxanne has fallen for Chris, rather than him. This has not stopped him calling in to the local chemist's shop to buy some panstick make-up in an attempt to reduce the effect of his nose, he hastily rubs this off just before Chris arrives at his door.

The scene that follows is a very funny picture of scribe and author switching places. Chris asks Charlie to read his letter. Charlie reads it, controls the horror that is about to spread across his face and tactfully suggests something more might be needed. Chris does not know what to say. Charlie asks him to tell him about his feelings for Roxanne. Chris's vocabulary, Charlie plainly feels, is not up to the job. Charlie winces and offers him alternative phrases. Chris is delighted, tries to write these down as Charlie suggests; then pleads with Charlie to write it for him. Here is how it goes. First, Charlie reads Chris's letter aloud:

> Charlie: Dear Roxanne. How's it going? Want to have a drink some time? If so, check this box.[8]

It took some time and replaying of this scene for me to realise, as Steve Martin turns over the page looking for more writing, that it was not a box he expected to see – as I did; as in 'check out this box' – but *more writing*. Chris was asking Roxanne just to reply with a tick. For Charlie, knowing Roxanne as he did as an educated woman in love with words, this is the ultimate in 'inappropriate' wooing-language.

> Chris: Well?
> Charlie: How long did you work on this?
> Chris: Well, today. You know, since noon.
> Charlie: It's a very long time.

Charlie gets up, walks away from the table, looks round and suggests (tactfully) to Chris that the letter has got to be 'more interesting', and in due course, that's what he manages to make it. Asking for the words from Chris is clearly no use, however:

> Charlie: How do you feel about her?
> Chris: Me? About her?
> Charlie: Yes. How did you feel when you first saw her?
> Chris: Horny.
> Charlie: Okay, okay. But you can't say: 'I felt horny'. You've got to say – 'I felt moved. Alive. Er – on fire!'
> Chris: That's beautiful.
> Charlie: Okay. How did you feel when you first spoke to her?
> Chris: (pause) Like a dickhead.
> Charlie: No, no, no. You can't write: 'I felt like a dickhead'. You have to say, 'I felt like a child standing the sun for the first time, feeling only your radiance.'
> Chris: Radiance! I like that. I'm going to underline that.

This goes on for a while: Charlie producing inspired words that Chris eagerly takes down, Chris beseeching him to take on the writing himself. Eventually, Charlie relents (not before making sure that Chris will check the supper in the oven) and picking out his best pen and paper, sets to work.

As Cyrano does for Christian, Charlie becomes Chris's 'soul'. Both find the words to tell Roxanne what she wants to hear, going beyond mere carnal words of lust to the language of metaphor and simile. 'You see, I am and always have been the one who loves you without limits', Charlie calls up from the darkness beneath her balcony. 'Why should we sip from a teacup when we could drink from the river?'. The question is a direct lift from Rostand's own text – in Brian Hooker's translation rendered as:

> Come away,
> And breathe fresh air! Must we keep on and on
> Sipping stale honey out of tiny cups
> Decorated with golden tracery,
> Drop by drop, all day long? We are alive;
> We thirst – come away, plunge, and drink, and drown
> In the great river flowing to the sea![9]

In Marquez' novel, Florentino Ariza's work for the young couple in the square was based at first on what he *imagined* each of them would want to read; a kind of inspired guess, which proved right. Cyrano and Charlie are weaving language around a woman they already know. 'Cooking up' phrases seems the right phrase for it, given that Charlie – when Chris comes to his apartment – is in the middle of preparing what looks like a gourmet meal in his kitchen. (He may be ugly, the scene suggests, but he sure knows what to do with the herbs.)

In neither the play nor this film adaptation do we ever see or hear of Roxanne herself writing letters. She may be an academic and a scientist; but in matters of the heart she is the adored, the courted, the reader, the recipient, the object of desire. This observation leads us on to the third example of a scribe with a tongue-tied suitor.

Il Postino

'Le donne vanno pazze per le sue poesie' says the newscaster in the village cinema. Women go crazy for his poems. Women are susceptible. For the man writes love poetry, and love poetry *(si sa, e l'argomento preferito dal sensibile anima femminile)* everyone knows, is the kind of thing the delicate feminine nature most wants to hear.

Our third scribe for tongue-tied love is the Chilean poet Pablo Neruda – or at least, a fictional version of him in exile on an Italian island – the hero of Mario, the village postman, who (in the darkness of the cinema) longs to have his way with words, so that he too might have women jostling to meet him off a train and planting lipsticked kisses on his manly cheeks. The film in which these characters appear is called *Il Postino*: the postman.[10]

Mario lives with his father, a fisherman. The village population is presumed to be almost totally illiterate, such that this has to be the first question asked of Mario when he applies for the job of postman: Are you illiterate? (*Sei analfabeto?*) No, says Mario. I can read and write – not fast, but I'm okay. (*Io so leggere a scrivere – senza correre, pero.*) Giorgio, the postmaster, explains to him that his job will be to deliver the mail to the new resident in the village, Neruda; that there will be no-one else to deliver to as, of course, they are all illiterate round there. Mario gets the job, and we see him, peak-capped, riding his bike up the steep cliff path beside the brilliant blue of the Mediterranean, to the house where Neruda is staying with his mistress, Matilda.

The yearning Mario feels for Neruda is all in this. He sees in him the man he wants to be: living a life of the mind, perhaps; but most of all living with a beautiful woman who loves you. What else is literacy good for? His own has not yet succeeded in rescuing him from the poverty of his father's life; although getting the postman's job is clearly shown as one step out of this. Being the poet, he sees, means being free to write about the sea, rather than having to go out in it every day in cold fishing boats. Despite Giorgio's disapproval back in the post office, Mario remains fascinated by the names on the back of the letters that Neruda receives each day. All women! Or almost, they seem to him. 'Look!' he says, and Giorgio scolds him. Women are interested in politics too, you know. Mario is not convinced. He wants to know how to become a poet, and he begins to have conversations with Neruda about this after delivering his mail. He buys a copy of one of Neruda's collections and asks him to sign it, disappointed that he has not also written in his own name. He tries to read and understand the poems. Then one day, everything changes. Mario falls in love. The object of his longing is called Beatrice (pronounced, in Italian, Bayatrichay, every vowel at full stretch). She works in her aunt's bar in the village-square. We see him see her for the first time and see, too, how ravishing she is: sulky yet innocent, full-bodied yet slender, playing alone at the pinball machine. Later, breathless and desperate, Mario knocks on Neruda's door and tells him of his desperate plight.

Beatrice, as Neruda quickly points out to him, is a name resonant in Italian literature as the lifelong passion of Dante Alighieri, the father of all poets. This, if anything, redoubles Mario's passion and he begs Neruda to help him. 'How?' says Neruda. 'You must write for me, you must write a poem', says Mario. 'But this is ridiculous!' says Neruda. 'I have not even met her. Have you spoken to her yet?' Mario's reply is the same that Christian (or Chris) gives, struck dumb by a beautiful woman: I looked at her and I was unable to utter a word (*'La guardava e non mi usciva neanche una parola'*).

Dumbstruck by beauty, overcome by a kind of terror, is exactly how the young Dante Alighieri described himself on his first sighting of his Beatrice.[11] Neruda remains impatient with him and says, of course he cannot write for him. The reason he gives is a very practical one, rather than any moral scruple. It is not that it would be wrong for him to write for Mario a poem to Beatrice, but that he had not yet met her and 'I cannot make something up out of nothing' (*non posso inventare qualcosa da nulla*).

As things turn out, Mario copies one of Neruda's existing poems and reads this to Beatrice later, giving her the copy. Beatrice's aunt, a stout peasant figure called Donna Rosa, who has dark suspicions about men in general and their intentions towards women, accosts her in her room on her return from a romantic walk by the sea with Mario. She questions her, 'What did he do to you?'. 'He talked to me of metaphors', says Beatrice, dreamily. 'He said my smile was a butterfly'. Her aunt persists, 'But what did he *do* to you?'. 'Nothing', Beatrice replies, 'He just talked.' Far from finding comfort in this, her aunt is even more convinced of Mario's evil intentions: 'Listen to me, my girl. When a man touches you with words, his hands are never far off', she warns; and later, as a confirmation of her suspicions, finding her niece stuffing a paper down the front of her dress, she fishes it out and takes it off to the priest to read. The first word of each line in the poem is *'nuda'* (naked: female gender). The priest agrees reluctantly to read, but gets no further than this first word. Donna Ana, beside herself, storms out. In the next scene we see her on the poet's veranda, demanding that he tells Mario to keep away from her niece.

Mario, then, is another in what begins to look like a long line of tongue-tied male suitors: Beatrice the object of his desire, and Neruda, the one who is clever with words, who can capture the woman he wants in a net of words. Neruda refuses to write for him; but is caught up in the affair despite himself, for it is his poem found down the front of Beatrice's dress, and it is this that enrages the aunt into trying to impose a ban on their meeting. As things turn out, she fails and the couple are married with Neruda as chief witness. Later Neruda and Matilda return to Chile; reading press reports of his travels, the villagers (especially Mario) become more and more disappointed at his failure to keep his promise to return and visit them. Mario and Beatrice have a child, whom they name Pablito, in memory of Neruda. Mario becomes politicised, as well as poeticised; and we see him killed in the crush of the crowd, while attending an anti-fascist demonstration in Rome at which he has been asked to read out one of his own poems. When Neruda and Matilda finally make their return to the village, Beatrice and her son (Pablito) greet him and tell him the news.

Neruda then was more than a muse for Mario and something less than a scribe. The clinching scene in Mario's courtship of Beatrice, however, is not in the reading out of a poem. It is in the café, before that. Neruda has agreed to join him there to see this love of his life. As she stands at their table taking their order, Neruda asks for a pencil. Turning to Mario, he asks him to lend him the notebook that he had given him as a gift. Slowly and deliberately, making sure that Beatrice and nearby onlookers can all see, he writes in Mario's book: to my intimate friend and comrade Mario Ruppolo, from Pablo Neruda.

From then on, Beatrice (we are led to believe) is won over. Or maybe, from then on, Mario becomes the lover he aspires to become. The writing, for him, had been merely a means to that end. Later, after his death, Beatrice is left to bring up their son on her own, and when Neruda eventually makes his return visit to the village, she greets him with reproachful eyes.

A muse and her poet

Have you had enough of love-sick men? Carol Ann Duffy has. You may remember the legend of Orpheus and Eurydice. Orpheus was the great musician whose music was so exquisite that he bewitched all who heard it. Savage beasts would stop to listen; even the trees would follow him. He lulled dragons to sleep with his songs and overcame the deadly Sirens in their fearful seductions of the Argonauts. Eurydice was his great love and he married her. Mortally bitten by a snake, Eurydice dies. Orpheus is distraught and begs to be allowed to go down into the Underworld. Only his music persuades the gods to relent in their refusal. You may go and get her, they said, but on one condition: on the way back up to the world again, do not look back. Not once. If you do, she will be forever returned to bowels of the earth. Almost returned to the gates of Hades, with Eurydice behind him, Orpheus cannot resist; he turns to look at his beloved wife, and in so doing, condemns both of them to eternal separation.

It is a tragic tale, the subject of much creative work. One such is a poem by Carol Ann Duffy in which the voice who tells the story this time is Eurydice's. She is telling it to a bunch of women friends and, after first telling them of her death, she goes on:

> So imagine me there,
> unavailable,
> out of this world,
> then picture my face in that place
> of Eternal Repose,
> in the one place you'd think a girl would be safe
> from the kind of a man
> who follows her round
> writing poems,
> hovers about
> while she reads them,
> calls her His Muse,
> and once sulked for a night and a day
> because she remarked on his weakness for abstract nouns.

Free at last, in a place that is *supposed* to be safe, what should I discover (she tells us) but that this man, my husband, has come to get me back; the man who I put up with, trailing around after me calling me 'His Muse' and 'hovers about' waiting for my uncritical admiration of his poems. When he had first courted her, she goes on,

> Big O was the boy. Legendary.
> The blurb on the back of his books claimed
> that animals,
> aardvark to zebra,
> flocked to his side when he sang,
> fish leapt in their shoals
> at the sound of his voice,
> even the mute, sullen stones at his feet
> wept wee, silver tears.
> Bollocks. (I'd done all the typing myself, I should know.)
> And given my time all over again,
> rest assured that I'd rather speak for myself
> than be Dearest, Beloved, Dark Lady, White Goddess, etc., etc.[12]

The accumulation of creatures, flocking around Orpheus and dancing and weeping at the sound of his voice suggests a child's picture book (you can imagine the clever illustrations that could go with it). Then, like the bang of a rolling pin on the table, comes Eurydice's down-to-earth 'Bollocks'. It was all (to coin a phrase) a myth. After all, who better to know the reality than the woman who had done all the typing?

According to the legend, Orpheus could not resist looking back because his longing for his beloved is so great that he has to turn to make sure she is still behind him on the long journey back from the underworld. Duffy's Eurydice has a different story. 'I did everything in my power/to make him look back', she says, and nothing worked, until 'inspiration finally struck'. She thought of the one thing that would make him turn around:

> He was a yard in front.
> My voice shook when I spoke –
> *Orpheus, your poem's a masterpiece.*
> *I'd love to hear it again...*
> He was smiling modestly
> when he turned,
> when he turned and he looked at me.
>
> What else?
> I noticed he hadn't shaved.
> I waved once and was gone.[13]

What am I to say to you that you have not already found in these lines? Just this. At one level this could be read as the woman scribe's revenge: the final answer to a whole history of unpublished women putting up with the vanity of their published male partners. Eurydice had done it all. She had flattered his ego, put herself in the shade while he took the limelight of a legend, been his inspiration and his home and, to cap it all, she had copy-typed for him every one of the poems he had written. I think this is a good reading of a clever poem. However, I also think that, to leave it at that is to miss something else that Duffy achieves. The revenge is bitter-sweet. Despite her triumph at no longer having to deal with a husband's sulks and vanity, there is a breath between those lines:

when he turned,
when he turned and he looked at me

that holds an enormous poignancy. All that wooing, once upon a time, had touched her. Along with Beatrice and Roxanne, Eurydice is a lover of good music and poetry and when it is directed at her, who is she to refuse it? Along with them, she had been the object of a poet's desire and, for a while, she too had fallen under its spell. Unlike them, however, Carol Ann Duffy's Eurydice speaks of the mixed pleasure of having been the secretary, as well as the muse.

Inner voice and outer scribe

If the male poet's muse is a woman, who is the muse for a woman poet? The Welsh poet Menna Eflyn says this:

> People are sometimes surprised (she writes) when I talk of the roles of a poet and a mother as necessitating similar responses. One cannot allow the wailing of a poem inside the head to go unheeded any more than one can ignore a child's cries.[14]

It is an image of writing – of being the scribe to her own voice. The mother cannot ignore the cry of the child; the poet cannot go deaf to the sound of her own poem. As Menna Eflyn goes on to say, for her there were two extra pressures to deal with in listening to this call. First, she is a mother, and like other writing mothers, she has had to learn to combine or 'dovetail' writing with motherhood, having to muffle the poem's wail in the interests of the child's cries. Second, she has a memory of her own mother's voice being regarded as unwanted, undesirable and wrong:

> Whenever I returned to school, after a period of illness, my mother's notes of explanation in Welsh would always enrage the teachers. I was told countless times to inform her not to write again in 'that language'.
>
> Needless to say I never carried the messages home, as I knew my mother would courteously yield to their demand.[15]

For the bilingual person, as Menna Eflyn is, there is an inner translation at work; as a poet, she is in any case always 'renaming words and experiences as she tries to voice herself'.[16] For someone who translates her own work, this must be a complex process.

Nicole Ward Jouve, a writer in both French and English, has grappled with it. 'I live and write in two languages', she says. The first 20 or so years of her life she lived in France. The same number of years, subsequently, saw her living in England. She has three bilingual children. She has published fiction in French and then published the same work, with herself as translator, in English. Like Eflyn, Jouve sees the work of writing itself as a kind of translation. The writer translates experience into language. The experience on which she draws has to be translated to become literature. That experience is, of necessity, grounded in a particular linguistic culture:

> Translating made me feel sick. What had happened was that, in some of the stories at least, I had already 'translated' mostly 'English' experiences into (a) fiction, (b) French, (c) layers of significance that had to do with those other translations.[17]

In order to be her own scribe, she had to hold on to a separation between two selves, 'two writers: one French, the other English'.[18] To do this meant a kind of nausea. To overcome the sickness, she had to see the task as one of rewriting; then she is able to relish the specific patterns offered by each language:

> Make it into a different object. Let the grain of whatever language I'm moving in impose its pattern... I love the way English can rely upon prepositions, short words, imperative or telegraphic modes. By contrast, I've found that I often get on to something interesting, or simply get to wherever I feel that I must be, by doing, with French, what Philippe Sollers calls 'flocculation: abundant flowering, thick as the petals of a carnation, hovering like a humming-bird, whose multiple spiralling wing-beats maintain it in the air long enough for it to get at a flower'[19]

Then there is the heard voice of the poem, its music. Listening to poets read their own work: in pub rooms, classrooms, concert halls and cafes, each person present loses the sense of being a solitary reader; we are in the company of many others, also listening to a writer we may have never met before – or only on the page. For that evening, we all give our ear at the same time. Of course, poets are not always the best readers of their own work, and sitting through a poetry reading can sometimes be boring. They may give too long an introduction to each poem, or read in low, monotonous voices, or rush without pause from one poem to the next. 'Regular readers on the poetry circuit' may be fine writers, but have little skill in breathing out the music of their poems. So there are plenty of people who dislike poetry readings, and there are enough occasions when the reader does not do justice to their own work to make this understandable. However the speaking voice of the writer who *is* capable of doing this justice gives another meaning to their writing. For Liz Lochhead, listening to another poet read his work, she found a different understanding of the rhythms than she had found in reading it in silence:

> When I first heard Adrian Mitchell reading – way back in 1972 – I understood properly for the first time why 'ballad' came from a word for a dance. His voice danced jazz and his feet beat out the rhythm. I thought: I want to do that.[20]

What of the poet themselves, up there behind the mike, reading to us? What is their experience, translating the written word into out-loud voice? How does the private writer accomplish the transition to being the public performer? Michelene Wandor, like Lochhead, both poet and playwright, describes how the same poem, on two different occasions, can come out of her mouth in a different spirit. On one occasion (she writes) she feels a loss of belief in the words she is reading. She feels sure no-one else is finding them interesting. She finds herself thinking 'God, that's boring. I'll read another one'. On another, the same poem seems to take off:

> I have a very strong sense of the whole of me speaking through the sounds my voice is making.

She describes 'a kind of intimacy' that occurs between audience and poet, as if there were 'no distance between us at all, except the sound of my voice and the silence of theirs'.[21]

The experience is given as preface to a discussion about Wandor's own voice, and the sense she has of her poems as being both hers and not hers. It is a discussion, too, of the changes of direction in her work, of periods when journalism took precedence over poetry and when fiction-writing 'took a back seat'. It is an interesting account of her move between several voices, between what she calls her 'thinking voice' ('that kept worrying away at me with questions like "what am I writing about?"')[22] and her poetic voice, between 'the conscious, political voice' and 'the subconscious, poetical' one.[23] She refers also to the tension between academic writing and other kinds. For her, however (unlike many others), this is not a tension between an imposed form and a self-chosen one (for she describes herself as someone who relishes the 'play of logic and argument in good and exciting theoretical writing'),[24] but a battle between one side of herself and another.

Poetry itself is a mix of technical skill and mystery, the poet is a scribe for experience itself. As one poet has put it:

> I feel like the secretary to the morning whose only
> Responsibility is to take down its bright, airy dictation
> Until it's time to go to lunch with the other girls,
> All of us ordering the cottage cheese with half a pear.[25]

Poetry's origins are always in the oral; its purpose (among other things) to evoke rhythms and to make music. By way of illustration for this remark, here is an anecdote recalled by Bob Mole in his introduction to a collection by the rap poet Benjamin Zephaniah:

> The first time I heard his 'Green Poem', I asked him for a copy of it. Haven't written it down yet, he said. A rapid, romping performance piece with some intricate rhythms and tricky rhyme, composed entirely in his head. He dictated it (and told me off for spelling 'dis' with a 'th'). He couldn't sit down and dictate it, either; he had to keep moving as he spoke.[26]

After reading this, I found some of Zephaniah's own reflections on poetry in a film made for Channel 4. The film opens with him seated in front of a candle, his long rasta locks falling either side of his dark, meditative face. Slowly he raises his head and speaks a poem direct to the viewer. The rest of the film is a mix of interview extracts and his voice-over commentary to clips of his poetry performances. I found it illuminating.

> People usually read poems from books, with lots of hidden meanings and things and my poetry is not like that. It's about rhythm. It's performance, really... Unlike most of the poets who

read a lot of poetry and like poetry, I started writing poetry because I didn't like poetry. I thought it was quite boring. And I couldn't read and write. That was a nothing thing. So it wasn't something that I was kind of attracted to. But like, when, later, I did understand poems, I thought, well, I can do this... I used to look at a piece of poetry and say: I can do better than this. I can write words that you can dance to and you can clap your hands to.

The next thing he did was to speak one of his poems. It took me ages to transcribe this accurately. Like Bob Mole, I had to follow him moving and speaking at a certain pace, and my ears and pen had to work hard to catch the exactness of his wording:

Dis poetry is not the kind dat is written in a book.
No, dis poetry needs ears to hear and eyes to have a look.
Dis poetry is verbal reading, no big words involved...[27]

I made the effort to catch the words on paper because I wanted to quote them here. Yet I also enjoyed listening and watching the film, first, without writing at all. As Zephaniah said, 'I can write words that you can dance to and you can clap your hands to'.

The scribe joins in

In this final section, we see how a scribe, working primarily as secretary, also played a role as muse for those she scribed for. Sitting alone, she works from the tapes of three people's animated conversation. We will see how they, and she, made a connection with each other across time so that she too has a presence in the finished transcription she made of their conversation.

Academic researchers commonly record voices on tape with the intention, later, of transcribing the tape and using the transcript as source material or 'evidence' for their research. A collaborative research approach to this might be when several people do such recorded activity together. To think about the experiential learning they organised as part of their teaching in an arts course, three academics met weekly over a period of some 4 years to talk over the group sessions that each of them led.[28] The person who under-took the transcription of these tapes was Joyce, the mother of Alex, one of the three. Living alone and having an interest in the professional life of her daughter, she volunteered to do this, working at it a few hours each week at her sitting-room table. Several times she spoke of enjoying the work and would ask Alex when the next tape was coming. For preference, Alex recalled, she wrote on plain paper, not lined, and, unless she had run out, she hand-wrote the transcripts in green ink. She would play the tape on her personal stereo, with the earphones in her ears. Her handwriting, as I saw when I was invited to read the transcripts, had a clear, even, looped, cursive style.

In all, Joyce transcribed around 20 of these tapes. Alex would make copies of the transcripts she had made; she and her two colleagues, Sarah and Janet, would read them; they would then meet to discuss the themes they had found in them. Some time during all this work, the three of them co-wrote and published two chapters for academic books that drew on their discussions.

Reading some of these transcripts, there were moments when I had to remember that these three women and Joyce were not in the same room. Here is one:

> We're finishing, mother, for this Tuesday. We'll see you next Tuesday.
> J & S. Bye. (24th October 1995)

These two lines come at the end of several pages in which the three speakers are talking about their own work; so they came as a surprise. As reader, I had to remember that I was reading speech; I also had to realise that the person doing the transcription of that speech was the person whom the speakers were addressing – and that *she* was writing down their greeting to *her*. (I tried to think what this made me think of: and then I remembered Margery Kempe and her scribe, writing about himself in the third person coming to believe in her experiences, in the middle of the account in which she is relating these.) At other points in the transcript, I found similar moments, when Joyce was both being addressed as if present by someone whose words were originally spoken, and at the same time is being the writer of those words, giving them back to the speakers. While Joyce was Alex's mother, Janet would be the one in the recordings who would use the term 'mother' or 'mum', as in the end of a recording, where several times I found:

> J Goodbye mother. (23rd March 1993)

What was particularly enjoyable, however, was Joyce's way of writing in her own responses to greetings of this kind. I found three examples of this. The first was simply a quick reply to a greeting from Janet at the start of a recording session:

Hello Mum
Mum. Hello Janet.

In the second, Jane plays with the idea of her being with them a bit further, and Joyce, in transcribing, is playful in response:

J. Hello mother.
A. This is Tuesday 31st October and Janet is not to mention tea.
I promise, but God, I'd like one. I've got my cig, though. You have
a cigarette.
Mother: Ta. (31 October 1995)

The third example shows Janet reminding Alex that Joyce 'is listening to this' – which is both true and untrue. Joyce, as they are talking, is not there. Joyce, in producing the transcript for them to read later, is. The moment occurs when the three of them had just been talking about the 'mother' role they had sometimes found their students expected from them in convening their groups. Sarah had just told how she had met one of her students in the park near her home. As it happened, she had just had an argument with her partner. At the tail end of her account, Alex offers her a joking response, Janet comes in with her reminder, and Joyce herself offers a written comment:

Talk about bad mothers!
Yes, your mother's listening to this.
Mum. With sympathy and a broad grin (17 June 1997)

Transcribers of other people's voices are invisible to the speakers. Often the interviewer does her own transcription. Often, too, however, the transcriber is a skilled outsider, listening to people they have never met. In this case, Joyce was writing down the working conversations of three people she knew and who knew her; a skilled insider who, from time to time, was remembered as being a part of the process – and who wrote herself into it, as well.

1 Kalman, 1999, p71–8.
2 From an interview, 12 April 2000.
3 Marquez, 1989, p167.
4 *Ibid*, p170.
5 *Ibid*, pp170–1.
6 *Ibid*, pp292–3.
7 Schepisi, 1987.
8 American English uses 'check' where UK English uses 'tick'.
9 Rostand, 1981, p109.
10 Radford, 1994.
11 Dante's prose poem *Vita Nova* (1292) has been seen, alternately, as autobiography, religious allegory and a meditation on poetry itself. Mark Musa's translation (Alighieri, 1999) includes a useful introduction.
12 Duffy, 1999, pp58–9.
13 *Ibid*, pp61–2.
14 Elfyn, 1994, p283.
15 *Ibid*, p280.
16 *Ibid*, p282.
17 Jouve, 1986, p46.
18 *Ibid*, p47.
19 *Ibid*.
20 Lochhead, 2000.
21 Wandor, 1986, p72.
22 *Ibid*, pp79–80.
23 *Ibid*, p83.
24 *Ibid*, p78.
25 A particularly good find, for me, this poem by Billy Collins (2000) from a collection I bought after enjoying him read from this and other works of his.
26 Zephaniah,1992, p9.
27 Goulds, 1987.
28 Alex, Sarah and Janet are pseudonyms. I am grateful to them for permission to quote from their research material on these terms.

CHAPTER NINE

Scribes and authors in adult literacy

I n adult literacy education, 'language experience' describes the situation where the teacher acts as scribe for the learner. To anyone outside the business, I suspect it is a bit mystifying. In this chapter I hope to remove some of that mystery, by describing language experience at work, and assembling some of the justifications for its persistent use in teaching practice. For there is no doubt about it, language experience is an approach that, for some 30 years at least, has been a central feature of adult literacy education in a number of countries, at least where English is the medium of instruction. From my own observation over that period, I have had discussions about its use in New Zealand, Australia, Canada and America, and seen the process in action in many parts of Britain. I have also seen it promoted, in the interests of participatory approaches to literacy education, in the training of literacy instructors in Uganda, Sudan and Nepal. Yet, as I said in the Introduction, there has not been much published about it and it seems that more needs to be said.

When adult literacy teachers use language experience to make texts with learners, there is a debate about whether to transcribe oral speech 'verbatim' (where 'verbatim' means 'every word heard' – for these purposes, I don't think of 'um' and 'er' as words). When someone speaks, they use language idiomatically, with dialect features that differ from standard English. As we saw in Chapter 6, in some circumstances such features and idioms get ironed out: the scribe in a courtroom tidies up any 'incorrect' forms of speech that a judge may happen to use. To produce a written text that is in idiomatic, non-standard English in a literacy classroom might be a faithful transcription: but there is a worry that it encourages 'incorrect' writing, or writing that might be harder for the literacy learner to read.

In this chapter I first consider *Issues of accuracy* that this practice raises, by looking back at some of the sources used in this book. From there, we move to some of the *Origins of language experience* in educational practice. With the help of examples offered by current literacy practitioners of their use of this approach, we then see how this *Language experience is alive and kicking* and what strategies can be used to deal with three problems it can raise:

- putting words in the mouth;
- slow-motion dictation;
- intrusion.

Issues of accuracy

Scattered throughout this book are examples of texts for which I have been scribe. They have been of two kinds. The first has been transcribed as exactly as possible, from speech to text, usually with the help of a tape recorder.[1] The second is a selected version of the spoken words, scribbled down at the time and copied up neatly later.[2] I learned both these techniques first as an adult literacy teacher and trainer in the 1970s. In both cases, my hope was that what *did* get written down would be as near word-for-word as possible. With the taped interviews, I used the usual technique of an audio-typist: that is, I listened, stopped and typed, over and over again. There were times when I had to replay and listen to the same passage two or three times before I could be sure what to type. I always meant to type only those parts that I knew would be most likely to be relevant; but I never quite managed it, and would find myself transcribing the interview in its entirety. I think there are three reasons for this. First, I wanted to be able to see the whole of the exchange, as far as possible, to read it from the page as a whole, and discern the process of composition at work.

The second reason I found it good to transcribe these interviews in full was that checking for the exact wording can reveal turns of phrase, or unexpected twists in language, that were not always fully appreciated at the time. (In the transcript with Walter Hemingway [Chapter 6], for example, I noticed how the word 'proficient' recurred in what he said – as in: 'When I had been there a little while and was proficient, and not nervous, I went into the boss and took dictation from the boss'; and 'after a while [as a court shorthand writer] I became proficient enough to go into my own courts'. Noticing this on the page helped me understand how I had got a feeling of calm confidence from his interview.)

There is a third argument for verbatim transcripts of at least *part* of an interview, and that is for the value they may have to the interviewees themselves. We will shortly glimpse some of the ways in which receiving back spoken words on paper can be a potential gift for learning for the learner/author. Here, I propose some reasons why it may also help the learning of the teacher/scribe, as well. For this is labour-intensive work, and when resources are limited, such labour needs to be justified. I believe the value of verbatim transcription from speech to writing is that it preserves the rhythm of the author's words and ensures that their meaning is fully expressed. Two examples from sources quoted in this book may help me to convince you.

Accuracy and rhythm

The first comes from the transcription I made from the video film about the poet Benjamin Zephaniah, quoted in the previous chapter. Here is part of that quotation, with the words that he actually said.

> People usually read poems from books, with lots of hidden meanings and things and my poetry is not like that. It's about rhythm. It's performance, really. I usually say it's a cross between normal poetry and rapping and toasting in Jamaica or America.

In the film, Zephaniah spoke rapidly; his voice tinged with what sounded like a moderate Birmingham accent, the words tumbling out. In order to transcribe them accurately, I had to replay that section of the videotape three times, stopping to check and catch words I had missed and scribble them down, later copy-typing this onto disk. One more check of text against tape revealed one more error. Where I had written *'Usually I say'*, Zephaniah had actually said *'I usually say'*, as in:

> I usually say it's a cross between normal poetry and rapping and toasting in Jamaica or America.

What difference does it make? Maybe very little: in fact, I'm not sure it matters at all. Except in this respect. If you listen – that is, if you try saying these words aloud, first in the version I had written and then in the version he had actually said, you hear a different rhythm: *'Usually I say* it's a cross between…' carries the beat on the vowel 'u' – rhyming with 'you'; *'I usually say* it's a cross between…' stresses that it is he who is offering the answer.

Later on in the tape, Zephaniah recites one of his poems straight to camera. This is what I got down:

Dis poetry is not the kind that is written in a book.
No, dis poetry is the kind that needs ears to hear and eyes to have a
look.

But, replaying the tape just to be sure, I found I had again made a mistake. When I heard what he actually said, I thought: 'Of course! The version I have down is not his style at all!' This is what he had said:

Dis poetry is not the kind that is written in a book.
No, dis poetry needs ears to hear and eyes to have a look.

Again, as in the first case, the difference is about sound and rhythm: matters that are central to what Zephaniah was talking about. My earlier version had packed into the line four more beats than he had intended ('is the kind that') and overcrowded it. Given that I was transcribing the conversation of a poet, and one who lays a lot of store on music, this mistake was more serious than my first one. This is a poem he was reading to us, and I had put in words that were not his, words that altered the rhythm (and for the worse). In short, I was in danger of misquoting him. Zephaniah may move around freely as he recites or dictates his poems, but scribes like Bob Mole and myself need be all ears, or we risk misrepresenting his work.

Accuracy and meaning

The second example of my own struggles with accuracy comes from the interview with Sandra, quoted in Chapter 3. Sandra spoke to me in her home with energy and eloquence. I am English, and Southern English at that, and an Edinburgh accent is not familiar to me. I had taped our conversation – and later, when I came to transcribe it, I found some parts of the tape, when Sandra was speaking, almost impossible to make sense of. Anyone used to doing this kind of research will advise you (as I would) to transcribe as soon as possible after an interview, and I had left it a few days. During the interview itself Sandra and I had understood each other fine. When we were sitting together, I had understood what she was saying quite clearly. A week later, having only the tape to help me, I found I had to replay the passage several times before I could produce the text that follows. Later I made a calculation. It had taken probably 30 seconds for Sandra to say these words. For you to read it on this page now may take you much the same. Yet for me to transcribe them so that what she said has become what you see took me nearly 20 minutes:

> When I'm writing on a piece of paper, I feel more relaxed. I feel more secure. It's my world. But when I've got to do it on the computer, no matter what I've got to do and people are around me, I don't like it. Well, it's happened, one time. What I do, I don't think about the word, I don't think about the sentence, I just type away what I've got to do. Then at the end, go over, spell check first. But this woman came behind me. 'Sandra, you don't know how to – !' I had the letters the wrong way around. And then she picked something else up and then she picked something else up. I just got up, went to toilet and I sat there and cried. Then came back, and I was right off for the whole day.

Now that I have it down, I recall the flow of Sandra's speech and see on the page the shape of her meaning. There is something about the three main clauses that follow her opening which gives a depth to her utterance. Again we might ask, what does it matter? If, for example, I had left out the second and third sentences, might that not 'improve' it, make it more concise? It would read:

> When I'm writing on a piece of paper, I feel more relaxed. But when I've got to do it on the computer, and people are around me. I don't like it.

I've taken out: 'I feel more secure' and 'It's my world'. I've also, in the interest of keeping the text 'concise', taken out the phrase 'no matter what I've got to do'. You could argue (and I would agree) that the meaning is still there and these three phrases could be cut without any loss to it. My reason for keeping them in, for struggling with the tape-recorder to ensure that I had heard all the words that Sandra said, is that I was trying to convey the feeling as well as the thought. In these extra phrases, Sandra gives a fuller sense of the contrast she feels – between the ease and safety of writing on paper and the feeling of being on view and exposed to correction that she gets when she is writing on screen. If we are to get the full extent of this contrast, we must hear her say:

> I feel more secure. It's my world.

Origins of language experience

Writing the exact spoken words can be crucial in language experience work. Teacher-scribes may think their amendments would make a text that it is easier for their student to read, but as Julia Clarke suggests, such worthy motives may actually make matters worse:

> When a student dictated the sentence 'I took my motorbike to pieces', I suggested we write 'I took my motorbike to bits' (thinking 'bits' would be more useful for later phonic teaching). This confused the student, who continued to read 'pieces', where I had written 'bits'. So, I eventually changed the written sentence to 'I took my motorbike to pieces', whereupon he read 'I took my motorbike to bits'. We finished by tearing the paper it was written on to bits (or pieces).[5]

The idea of language experience is that a student in an adult literacy class works with their tutor/scribe to co-produce a text of their own composition. The student/author, for that time, has their teacher as a secretary. Very little is published about the theory behind this approach. 'Anecdotal evidence' suggests that it was a widespread practice in the 1970s. It was certainly a common ingredient in tutor training courses; and the short piece I wrote myself on the matter derived from using the approach and training others to do so over some years.[4] The clearest accounts of its value and purpose that I have found are those by Irene Schwab and Jud Stone (1985) and more recently by Wendy Moss (1995) from her research into the use of language experience in practice. The earlier account set out the argument like this:

> The use of a scribe or tape recorder as an intermediary between thought and writing allows the handling of concepts more advanced than the level of reading skills. Students can feel very frustrated when they cannot write down what is in their minds. They feel obliged to write using only those words which they know they can spell and the resulting text may bear little relation to the original idea. By using their own language to express their own thoughts, they are working entirely within their own terms of reference.
>
> This concept of student control is a central one. We consider that even with beginners, from the very start, writing is important

and that writing skills go hand-in-hand with reading skills. It is integral to the learning process that students see themselves as producers and not just consumers of ideas.[5]

According to this account, language experience is founded, first and foremost, as a means to ensure student control. It also assumes that students know more than they can read and write, and it enables them to bring closer together the effort of learning to read with that of becoming more proficient writers.

There were, I think, a number of tributaries flowing in the early 1970s that fed into what I would call the 'language experience movement'. In listing them here, I am not assigning any particular priority to one or the other. The idea of 'student control' certainly was important; it harmonised with that of the learner being a creator of knowledge, not merely a recipient of it, for which, as Wendy Moss suggests, the Brazilian educator Paulo Freire should be credited as a key inspiration.[6] Language experience also offered the advantage for a beginner reader of having a text to read that is written in their own words: it was an approach which could encourage reading, as well as writing.[7] This idea was almost certainly influenced by materials developed as part of the Programme in Linguistics and English Teaching (1964–70) directed by the eminent linguist M.A.K. Halliday. 'Breakthrough to Literacy', as it was called, deliberately set out to show children that *reading and writing could be part of the same thing*.[8]

Thirdly, there was an idea, which Irene Schwab and Jud Stone's work made clear, about *authorship*: enabling students to become their own authors, to be found interesting and read, and to be published – which, in the mid-1970s, linked *Write First Time*[9] with the just-starting national network, the Federation of Worker Writers and Community Publishing.[10] Finally, there was a great deal of work beginning to happen at the time to liberate language variety from the straightjackets of standardisation. The Afro-Caribbean Language and Literacy Project based in London, which had stimulated the work reported by Schwab and Stone, was an important beacon of this work. It encouraged classroom teachers to undertake their own research. The values of this movement were explicit:

We feel that in literacy teaching the use of a student's own language is central. For many students, particularly those from the Caribbean, the stigma attached to their language was an important factor in their alienation from previous education at school.[11]

This is more than an academic or pedagogic argument; it is a political one, in which language experience is seen to be a matter of social justice.

In the stories I have listened to about this from literacy teachers over the years, what I always listen for is the moment when they tell me how good questions elicit new thinking: how the move between asking and answering enabled the hesitant writer to realise '*this* is what I wanted to say', or 'yes, *that* would make my meaning clearer to a reader'. These are the moves of editors working with composers. The questioner is not always the teacher. The best questioning can happen from an equal – that is, in a literacy classroom, another student. However, the position of the equal who is both encouraging and critical takes practice. It requires teaching, and it gives recognition to the point made by Schwab and Stone: namely, that the intellectual abilities of literacy students are often out of balance with their reading and writing skills; and that what is needed is a means by which they can express concepts that their present level of literacy skills does not permit.

Earlier, I showed how my own inaccuracies in transcribing the speech of Benjamin Zephaniah and Sandra affected a reader's experience of their meaning. In her analysis of four language-experience partnerships at work, Wendy Moss discusses the importance of keeping to the student/author's own language. What she found was a tendency by teacher/scribes to want to 'improve' or 'correct' the idioms of their student/authors, with resulting 'disfluencies' between what the student-author actually said and what the scribe wrote. Moss does not argue, however, that the teacher/scribe should abandon all her own experience of conventions and style – give up entirely being a teacher, as it were, and become merely the 'hired hand' kind of scribe. As she points out, there are many kinds of oral forms to choose between, and students can be offered choices. In some cases, as she found, learner/writers may say something informally in conversation and then, when they know it is being written down, 'formalise' the same statement. She gives the example of a student called Carol, recalling Sundays in her childhood and changing phrases used in her original version when she repeated the story for Wendy to write: from '*me mum*' to '*my mum*' and from '*Here you are, put those on*', to '*Wear those*'.[12] Working with someone who is a beginner to reading and writing, Moss argues, it is important to produce text that is as close to their words as possible. Nevertheless the teacher/scribe is still able to offer, for example, words that might turn an oral utterance into a recognisable sentence. The message of her study is: if corrections need to be made, these need to be discussed, not imposed; teacher/scribes should aim to be facilitators, not correctors; and critical awareness of how oral and written language differ can usefully be part of the whole activity.[13]

Language experience means relieving the author/student, for the time being, from the worry about transcribing, in order to give all their attention to the work of composition. You may remember this distinction in the discussion about letter-writing scribes in Chapter 3. In order to simplify the processes entailed in writing, Frank Smith portrays two separate people at work: an author and a secretary, the first dictating to the second. The author attends to composition; the secretary's job is to attend to matters of spelling, punctuation, grammar and handwriting or typewriting. Both these people could equally claim to be the writer of the text that emerges and both are essential to its production.[14] The problem for many people, says Smith, is that (certainly in educational institutions) they are expected to manage both these roles at once, being both composer and transcriber. These two different roles are in tension with each other, with the anxiety about *transcription* entirely eclipsing any capacity to compose. Smith's conclusion for teachers is to keep composition and transcription separate, 'transcription must come last'.[15]

Language experience is alive and kicking

For too many people, the worry that their writing will *look* wrong puts all hope of composition to flight. The fear of exposing themselves to ridicule silences them; they have something to say, but cannot say it. So that is what language experience offers: a chance to learn what it feels like to be a writer – someone capable of achieving a synthesis between composition and transcription – in circumstances where they can be free from anxieties about all those things that make them feel most vulnerable.

Language experience is a wonderful means to create text, but there are two things about it that teachers have to consider. One is that, as a method of teaching, it seems to be highly labour-intensive. One teacher works with one student, sometimes for up to 20 minutes at a time. While this is going on, what is the rest of the class doing?

In times of scarce resources (which means any time), we have to justify this kind of attention. This can be answered by recognising the potential for showing others in the class the way that scribing works. Allowing others in the class to watch language experience in action is one way to help them see the process of composition at work, and to watch how two people can collaborate in writing. The other issue is that of how to balance the role of scribe and that of teacher. As we saw earlier, the legal scribe may be a guide to their author; the religious scribe may be transcriber or servant. The educational scribe is a mix of all these. There are, inevitably, temptations to take over the authorship of the text, or to hurry it up; and there is a danger in imposing a topic for writing, or even insisting on one that is actually a private matter for the student. The following accounts describe how three literacy teachers and their author/scribes dealt with each of these problems.

The problem of putting words in the mouth

Teachers have to persuade students to become authors, partly by example (reading other authors), and partly by encouraging them to talk and see how they could use that talk for writing. This is fine, but some students are not sure what to say.

> Jeff has been in the class for four months. Every lesson he'd want me to write a letter to his girlfriend. 'I'm going to write to Tracy', he'd say. I'd have a pen in my hand and I'd wait. 'What do you want me to write?'. 'Oh, you know', he'd say. There would be a long pause. 'Shall I put: "Can't wait to see you?"'. 'Oh yeah', he'd say; 'that's all right'.

Cath (who told this story) sits waiting for the text; the text does not come; she offers a possible wording, which is accepted; she writes it down. This is slow work. The hope is that for Jeff the process will gradually help him see how he might choose his own words.[16] Meanwhile, for want of any other, they must both resort to something second best.

Freda Berridge's description of a language experience process with a student in a beginners' literacy class in a Community Centre in Poole shows a development from the exchange between Cath and Jeff:

> Christine is a woman in her mid-20s. Her outward appearance is immaculate. She suffers from agoraphobia, has an eating disorder

and associated health problems. She has four children and she cannot walk them to school. It was her social worker, from the local community health team, who would bring her to the class.

With Christine, I would begin with a friendly chat. I would say, 'What have you been doing?' and tell her a bit about what I had been up to. I would then scribe some of what she told me. It would be three or four sentences. I would read it to her and sometimes she would add or change something. I encouraged her to talk about her children, as she could not spell their names. (Georgina and Jacqueline. Pity she had not chosen easier ones – like Bob or Pat!) It would be very factual, at first. I would read it again and get her to join in with the words she could read, and let her take over if she sounded confident. I would make a note of the difficult words to work on later. Much depended on the words she had used. This activity could take up to half an hour.

Christine would then copy-write the text while I worked with someone else. She liked to use an exercise book for this writing. It retained the flavour of a diary. We could go back and read different weeks and she could see how her handwriting was improving.

I felt it was important that the work should belong to Christine and in the early stages I did not suggest changes of vocabulary or grammar. These came later as I could see her confidence increase.

I would then tape the diary entry with the idea that Christine could listen to it and read the text back alongside it at home. (In reality, I don't think she did this very often. She would say she hadn't had time.)[17]

In this account, we see how the roles of scribe and author are adopted in the interests of creating the text, and how the roles of teacher and student are then resumed in the interests of promoting the student's learning. As teacher and student, they engage in a 'warm-up' conversation. Then, for a short time the teacher puts the student in the lead, writing to her words. Back as teacher again, she reads the text back to the student (knowing that, independently, Christine could not do this). As scribe, she then makes the amendments Christine wants. Reverting to teacher, she reads it back again and gets her to 'join in with the words she could read'. Once the 'three or four sentences' are written to the student's satisfaction, the teacher notes words that could be worked on later. The tricky part is for the teacher to stand back at the point when the text is being produced ('I did not in the early stages suggest changes of vocabulary or grammar').

The problem of slow-motion dictating

Even if the student has something they know they want to talk about, consideration for the scribe may make her or him anxious about saying it in their normal pace of talk. Worried at what they see to be an evident effort to keep up, they slow down what they are saying and dictate, one word at a time. The flow of what they were saying is gone; the student seems to feel as if they are 'on show' and begins to sound stilted. A solution proposed by one teacher is to have an ordinary conversation for a few minutes. She then recaps what the student has said, as exactly as she can, and checks it with them: as in 'So what you said to me was 'I hate getting up...' etc.[18] Language experience means the scribe has to be a good scribbler, able to read their own scribble back and to make a fair copy of the finished, agreed version.

In the following account by Kate Tomlinson, we see how she and Jenny, the author, worked from a picture Jenny had drawn to bring out a text between them, piece by piece. We then learn of how, after a response-and-question session with another tutor, and then a third, the text evolved: so that Jenny's 'flow' is both encouraged and channelled with her scribes' collaboration.

> Jenny is a student with a learning disability who was educated at primary level in a special school. She has always resented the fact that she was not taught to read and write until she took matters into her own hands as an adult – many years ago – and joined an ABE group. After a period of one-to-one tuition she has been coming on a regular basis to groups. Despite suffering from severe epilepsy, she is immensely motivated and determined. She is married to Martin, who is also epileptic and has learning difficulties, and they live in their own home with some supervision from a care support team. Jenny's interests mainly lie within her home and garden. She works at a charity shop in Stroud and is an active member of our local learners' organisation.[19]
>
> The success of her efforts varies enormously from week to week both in reading and writing. She has quite a lot of experience of using a scribe, though on most occasions she likes to have a go herself. She will sit at home and write letters which she brings in to be checked.

The writing I discuss here came about as part of a course which we had been asked to do at the College called 'Planning the Future'. For Jenny this was particularly bad timing as she had just been told that her eyesight, which was failing, might go altogether. As she says herself in the text, this was all she could think about.

During the first session, we asked students to fantasise about 'a perfect day in five years' time' and – if they wanted to – to draw a picture to illustrate this. Jenny drew a picture of herself, blind, and being carried off to hospital. We discussed the picture and the difficulty she was experiencing in getting beyond this thought. I scribed the sentences to go with the picture.

That's a bed – all right? And I'm laying on the bed and them taking me to hospital. That's all I'm thinking.

We then talked about things she would probably still be able to do. Being a naturally cheerful and optimistic person, she began to describe what she would like to do with her house and garden – extending it into the space at present occupied by her neighbours. The last piece we wrote was fantasy, as, in fact, Martin's parents are already dead. I tried to write down what she said as closely as I could to the way she said it, and I asked some questions to prompt her or clarify some points.

I just like to achieve my work – my writing.

I thinking I might change doing the house – like wall papering and a lot of new stuff in the house.

A lot of things in the garden – I know it's not our fence – I'd like to move it into the nextdoor neighbour's. I'd like to plant all the flowers: like roses, daffodils, red rose and all that. And we want new windows.

If I be tired I not bothered to do nothing for work. And I still come to my reading and writing class.

And the holidays – we like to have a car – and we go on a nice long holiday with my Mum and Dad and Martin's Mum and Dad to Butlins.

The first draft took about an hour and since it was in my handwriting which would have been hard for her to decipher, I read it back to her. Once she seemed satisfied with it, I typed it out for her. At the following week's session, she read aloud from this script. As a result of discussion with the volunteer tutor, Dorothy, with whom she usually works, a few amendments were made, notably:

> *I'd like to move it into the next door neighbour's, <u>then I would</u>*
> <u>*have more space*</u>*; and*
>   *If I <u>am</u> tired I not bothered to do nothing for work.*

More work and more re-reading with another tutor meant that other changes were made too; for example, in order to explain the origin of the picture more clearly, Jenny agreed to a new introductory sentence:

> *I had a dream that I was in bed.*

and, still in the interests of being clear for her readers, she and Dorothy amended other wording, such as:

> *And I'm laying on the bed and <u>they are</u> taking me to hospital...*
> *If I <u>am</u> tired I will not be bothered to do <u>anything</u> for work.*[20]

To begin writing by drawing a picture gave Jenny the freedom to get past words and their limitations. She had a huge life-change facing her; the topic of 'planning the future' could not have been more challenging. Kate's strategy to then write her summary of the picture enabled her to begin to produce an utterance about where she was then and there ('laying on the bed...thinking'). The fact that Jenny had not one, but three tutors in all giving her a response to her writing meant that the issue of what she might or might not be able to 'dictate' just went away.

In all this work, several choices are being made. Jenny chooses what to draw in her picture. She chooses what to say to Kate about it. Kate chooses what to write of all that she says, and chooses to write it in Jenny's idiom. Dorothy chooses to ask more about something that is not clear to her. She chooses which bits to encourage Jenny to amend. Jenny chooses to accept the amendments, and so on. All this is writing in action; the text being read, amended, re-read, commented on, amended and read again. The work of language experience is about writing: but its value is also in giving the learner/author experience of being an active, critical reader, listening to the questions and uncertainties of readers who are present to her and in so doing learning that lesson which all authors must learn: to imagine our unseen readers.

The problem of intrusion

'Tell me about something you know about'; or 'what about your childhood'? and any number of other openings by a scribe/teacher could be taken as an intrusion into private life The choice of topic needs to be mutually agreed. The growth of the text into one that others may read must also mean a growth in the author's consent to it being more than a private exercise. Language experience, like any other kind of scribing, is an approach that can be used to generate all kinds of texts: critical as much as autobiographical, persuasive as much as reflective.

This account, by Amy Burgess, stresses the importance she felt in clarifying the purpose of the activity. What began as a conversation on the topic that was most on the student's mind at the time did indeed become a piece of draft writing. Her later concern as to the 'suitability' of the resulting text for his work as a learner led her to offer him the chance to work with her on another topic.

> I used this approach quite recently with a new student, who I'd been told was at Entry level. After chatting to him for a while, I explained that I wanted him to tell me a few things about himself for me to write down and explained why I was doing this. He asked if he could tell me about the break-up of his marriage, and proceeded to do so in intimate detail. Surprisingly (since I don't think he'd ever tried language experience before), he had no difficulty in speaking in a way that made it easy for me to write down his words. He spoke pretty much at normal speed, so several times I had to ask him to wait while I caught up. When I re-read and reflected on what he'd dictated, I felt that actually it was so personal and so emotionally charged that it would be unsuitable for language experience work. I explained this to him in the next session as tactfully as I could and he very obligingly agreed to work with a volunteer on another piece of language experience work – this time about his friend's rottweilers!
>
> When Ray produced the text about the break-up of his marriage he had only just joined my class and I was concerned not to ask him to do anything which might make him feel awkward or upset. I was worried that he would find re-reading his piece and then using it for language work painful. Also it seemed to me that turning the text into a cloze exercise or whatever would be disrespectful. I had explained at the outset that I would like to use his text to help him with his reading and writing, but because he was new to the class he obviously didn't know exactly what this would involve. I know him better now and he knows the other students, so if he were to suggest working on this or another sensitive topic I wouldn't have the same concerns.
>
> The rottweiler text, which he produced with my volunteer, was about five sentences. He did some language work on this text and

either he or I (I can't remember who, I'm afraid) read it aloud to the group.

It was later published in a little collection I made of students' writing and Ray was quite proud of that. The group consists of six students (all men, as it happens) who were all beginners needing lots of one-to-one support. They really enjoy discussing issues in the news and this often leads on to language experience work. The students' writing is always read aloud to the group. Mostly they like to read their own writing out, but sometimes they ask me to do so instead. They also read and talk about each other's writing.[21]

The more neutral topic of his friend's dogs seemed to come easily to Ray. Amy's role shifted from scribe to reflective editor, conscious of the effect the first choice of text might have on him once made more public in the collection of students' writing. The publication of Ray's writing created material for him and others in the group to read and discuss.

Drafting and re-drafting is a notion that is new to many literacy students, but an important one if the writing is to become valid, both for them and for other readers. Julie Brailey wrote to me about a student in his early twenties called John. He had come to ABE classes for help at the age of 17 when he decided he wanted to learn to drive and needed to be able to read the highway-code. He worked in a local factory making ring binders, played rugby in his spare time, and lived at home with his father and stepmother. He got little help from them, and did not practise his reading and writing, so his progress was slow between the weekly class he attended. With Julie, he had written several times using the language experience approach. Early in 2001 they began work on a description of a place, which had to be completed for the Freewriting module for which he was working.[22] He chose to write a guide to the town where he lives (Stroud) for people who did not know the area. On the first evening they began, he read the text back for himself. He also copied it on the computer. As they completed each section, they also did some redrafting. She prompted him with questions; he suggested what to add or subtract. The work went on for several weeks. The booklet that was eventually produced enabled him to gain the credit for Freewriting; he was proud of it and, at his suggestion, it was put in the teaching room for other students to read. The whole exercise, in Julie's view:

boosted his confidence enormously: he has good ideas for stories, or for describing events in his life, and finds using language experience a way of relieving the frustration of being unable to write it down himself – not least because John had a purpose and an intended readership for the writing.

Learners may share their own thoughts on working with language experience, and teachers like Julie can report them to us; but there is little published that puts these thoughts in learners' own words. A rare resource, then, is this exchange, which Kate later transcribed from a conversation she had with Jenny about the process of doing the writing we saw just now. She asked her, first, to say what the writing meant to her.

> J: This is a rough copy – it come out of my own head. That's a draft and then I brought it in and I show Dorothy and then after that Sue looked at it and then she helped me out.'
> *K: What did you think about the changes?*
> J: I was a bit rushed doing it, see. All right. Then Dorothy's taked over. Dorothy helped me out.
> *K: How did you feel about this way of working?*
> J: Calm. And I listen to you and I listen to Dorothy the same. It helps see spelling and proper words in the proper places. I think what I'm doing myself is rushing things – writing and all that. If I calm down a bit and take it steady I might do things properly – a bit better. I feel it's my own writing but someone's helped me out – put me straight and all that… Sometimes I like to write it myself… private things I like to write myself. You and me sit down and talked about it and after that you said, 'It's all right Jenny, you might change something'. Asking questions helped me spell and write about it.

The first thing to notice about what Jenny said is the sense of ownership of the writing that she conveys. She saw the first draft which Kate had scribed as her own ('it come out of my own head'). As she says later, 'I feel it's my own writing', reminding Kate how she had encouraged her by saying it was all right to 'change something' and by asking questions that helped her remember how she might be able to spell and write about it herself. What is striking, too, is the first word she uses, in answer to Kate's question. How did she feel about this way of working? 'Calm'. The process had succeeded in pushing away her panic – that old enemy of many adult basic education students. The experience reminded her of what she is capable of, when she manages to keep the calm feeling. Being 'allowed' to re-think how she had said something, watching someone else add her amendments to her text, meant she could be a witness to the routines of re-drafting familiar to more experienced writers.

Language experience means providing an opportunity for an unskilled writer to see the skilfulness they are working for being acted out. Kate's experience, she told me, is that the approach is particularly useful for 'someone facing a subject which is complex for them'. In Jenny's case, the subject must have felt complex, indeed. She had recently been told she was going to lose her sight. Soon after this interview, she rang Kate to ask for help in working out how to use the 'Talking Book' materials she had been provided with. She was having to contemplate a future when spectacles would no longer help her. To be asked to imagine what her sightless future might be like, for a classroom exercise, was to dip into what must have been a whirlpool of feelings. Using a scribe allowed her to clarify some of her thoughts on these and to choose which of them she was prepared to put in writing for others to see.

I began this chapter with some arguments for verbatim scribing. The other proponents of language experience have argued for its importance, too. These examples have shown us how, in practice, there is a dialogue at every stage between scribe and author. A cardinal principle of the approach is that the choice of topic and expression must be in the student/author's hands. However, as I have also shown, the teacher is there to enable the writer to be conscious of these choices: to be aware of their effect on others, to have the opportunity to re-state and re-formulate what was not clear. Like all scribal activity, language experience work is a creative endeavour.

What the skilled adult literacy teacher does is to see how the creativity in this kind of collaboration may be applied to what may sometimes feel like the tiresome routines of learning, such as record-keeping. At regular intervals (ideally at every class meeting) they ask students to note their own evaluation of the work that they have been doing. What did we do? How did it go? What shall I work on next time? It is tempting for both student and teacher to leave a one-word response to the middle question: 'OK', or 'alright'. It is only when we articulate *what* was alright and *how*, that any one of us are exercising our powers of reflection. As experienced adult literacy teachers know only too well, the best way to foster this kind of reflectivity is in dialogue.

1 Such as the interview with Walter Hemingway (Chapter 6) or excerpts from the videotape of *Central Station* (Chapter 7).
2 All the interviews in Chapters 3 and 4 were done like this.
3 Schwab and Stone, 1985, p8.
4 Mace, 1979, pp92–7.
5 *Ibid*, p89.
6 It was in the early 1970s that Freire, 1972 and 1974 first appeared in English translation. In those days, translators' names were not even noticed, let alone mentioned.
7 Moss, 1995, p146.
8 The 'Breakthrough to Literacy' programme. See: Mackay, Thompson and Schaub, 1981. Together with this was the writing of James Britton, 1970, who – like Frank Smith – helped some of us recognise that writing is not a matter of putting down ready-made thought, but is itself a generator of thinking. Incidentally, even though they do not use the phrase 'language experience' anywhere, I notice with hindsight that the two words 'language' and 'experience' recur near each other throughout both these publications.
9 *Write First Time*, a quarterly broadsheet originating in an idea about producing reading materials of relevance to adult learners, was first published in 1974, and until March 1985 circulated a print run of some 6,000 copies to adult literacy centres in the UK. All the 20–25 pieces published in each issue were written by literacy students, except the regular column 'You and the Law' written by a lawyer and the editorial (written by the group of tutors and students editing that particular issue). When the funding ran out in 1985 a group of us put together copies of every back issue and all the records of the process into an archive, which has been housed ever since in the library of Ruskin College Oxford.
10 The Federation of Worker Writers and Community Publishers can be visited on their website: www.fwwcp.mcmail.com.
11 *Ibid*, p9.
12 Moss, 1995, pp157–8.
13 *Ibid*, pp166–8.
14 Smith, 1982, p19.
15 *Ibid*, pp24.
16 From an interview with Cath de Veuve, November 1999.
17 Reproduced, with permission, from correspondence with the author, July/August 2001.
18 This note was contributed by Gwynneth Shiers in a letter to me, written 26 June 2001.
19 GOALS or the Gloucestershire Organisation for Adult Literacy (Stroud) was founded in the 1980s, primarily as a pressure group for students at a time when classes were threatened with closure. At the time of writing it continues to publicise and organise social activities; it has also become increasingly independent of tutor support. GOALS has raised money to support ABE students with fees to move on to mainstream college courses and buy extra equipment, such as lap-tops for out-centres. Kate's account of the group's trip to Germany to meet and work with ABE students there was reported in *RaPAL Bulletin* no. 19, Autumn 1992, pp8–10, 'More ripples in the European Pool'.
20 Reproduced, with permission, from correspondence with the author, July/August 2001.

21 Reproduced, with permission, from correspondence with the author, July/August 2001.

22 The OCN (Open College Network) provides certificates for students wanting to follow accredited courses in all kinds of subjects including ABE. Units are written and submitted for approval giving outcomes and assessment criteria for all kinds of specific skills, such as spelling at particular levels. Contexts chosen can be student-centred, so Jenny could work on grammar, reading, or spelling, for example, using her Language Experience texts. John's 'Free Writing' unit gave evidence of his ability to write for a number of specified purposes and audiences.

Postscripts

There is always something to add when a letter has been written. Convention provides us with the postscript ('p.s.'). The following are the persistent afterthoughts, which for me have emerged from all this thinking about scribes.

Individual and group

In the middle section of this book, we considered the clerk in a Quaker business meeting. As I suggested there, there seems some useful material here for adult education – not so much in further courses teaching people 'how to write minutes', but rather in promoting more equitable models of meetings as democratic processes, in which the work of the minutes secretary (the group's scribe) is recognised as one to be supported. To be the sole recorder for a whole group is an even more complex task than being the secretary to an individual. Yet it is a common activity, not only in meetings, but in other education and training settings. Conference workshops appoint 'rapporteurs' to make a note of a group's discussion to 'feed back' to a plenary session; one or two brave people volunteer (or get conscripted) to produce this feedback in the form of key words or phrases on a large piece of flipchart paper which has to be produced when the whole group reconvenes. In another situation, it is the teacher or trainer who scribes; typically, asking a whole group for definitions or associations with an idea and writing her version of these up in front of them on the flipchart stand or whiteboard. In both these situations, someone is taking, or being given, the task of being the scribe for a group. This is both easier and harder than the near-verbatim transcribing of one person's speech. The task is to synthesise and select; missing out in the process whole slices of talk and skipping all sorts of nuances; the aim being to distil, to summarise and to give back to the group a draft as a collective script.

This same principle of 'giving back' is at work in another account of language experience I was given: this time not with an individual, but with a group. The added extra in this case is that group was multi-lingual: an ESOL (English for Speakers of Other Languages) class of women in East London, described to me by its teacher, Monica Lucero.[1] In this session her purpose, she told me, was only partly to generate some writing that they could use as reading material; it was also to help (as she put it) in providing them with a 'space where they could open up and talk about their problems'. This, then, was more than an exercise in improving their literacy; it was an opportunity for them to attend to their development as women. As Monica saw it, the second could only properly be achieved if the first happened:

> What they say to me I have to guess, because I don't speak Somali or Bengali. I try to interpret what they say, transform it into teaching materials and give it back to them. But it is very manipulated, with a lot of my own thoughts. I wish I could keep it pure, in their own words.
>
> When they come in in the morning they usually bring lots of problems: the children are ill, the husband has brought guests again and they have extra cooking to do and beds to make. Or the husband has been telling them how stupid they are because they don't learn English fast enough to be efficient in their domestic work – shopping, dealing with the doctor, etc. They are absolutely overwhelmed; they often haven't slept properly, and they have all the symptoms of depression: headaches, migraines, pains in the joints. These are young women. They shouldn't feel so poorly; but it is their lives.
>
> There's usually this little moan at the start of the morning, and this gives a feeling of communality, that we all have the same problems. So I make a brainstorm out of it. For instance, I might make a circle with the words 'women like us' at the centre, and branches out for them to offer their words to complete – such as 'get headaches', 'sleep little', 'don't have time for ourselves'. This then can make reading material that they remember. Because the problem is that they have very poor memory skills and after a year they are supposed to take Pitman's exams. Their English literacy is very limited. They

want to write, but they don't care about grammar. They just want to express themselves. Whenever I ask them to do the kind of exercises they need to do for the exam – like 'describe a friend' or 'describe a journey' to show they can write the simple past or simple future, they make mistakes.

What often worries me, when I am trying to use their words for our materials, use language experience and write up for them what they say, is that I can't get to the essence of what they are telling me, because they are having to tell it all in English, and this is difficult for them. It means that I can't understand it in the way that they want me to understand it. That is the frustration.

I write little stories about them – Husna does this, or Rhuksana goes there. If they are about issues that have to do with them, they will remember and it does help them progress with their English. But I am also interested in their women's development. This is the only place they can open up and talk about their problems. For a couple of women this is a lifeline.

I have a Catholic background myself. We talk about spiritual things. The long words they remember – like 'origins', or 'eternity', or 'creation'.

The women in Monica's class were attending a course for 15 hours a week from September to the following June; conditions which make it easier to encourage the feeling of 'communality' than would apply if they had been attending for just 2 or 4 hours a week. Monica sketches a scene of their arrival in the morning as one of talk and unloading – the 'little moan' at this stage enables a feeling of relief from all the pressures they have each brought with them and of common ground to stand on. From her invitation to them to 'brainstorm' the things they have begun to talk about, she produced a kind of diagram, a picture as well as a text.

Monica expressed some satisfaction to me in the value of this work for the women, but she also felt frustrated that she had not kept the writing 'pure', 'in their own words.' The purpose of the exercise had been to enable the women to talk about the important things in their life. The difficulty she faced was in reconciling this with the official purpose of the class (to prepare them for assessment of their English) and also in matching this oral work with her role as the group's scribe: making a single text out of many voices; struggling to find expression for strong feelings in a language not yet their own.

This account, exceptional in the level of scribing skills evident in it, provides a dramatic example of the process that we routinely expect from an individual scribing for a group.

Issues of authorship

The community scribe in a mainly non-literate community is a person who takes interviewing one step further: she or he captures the spoken word of interviewees; they also check back what they have written with the person they have interviewed. In my introduction, I referred to a discussion with community development workers in Nepal about this. Yagya Bahadur Limbu, the editor of a village wall newspaper published in Danda Bazaar, near Dankhuta, up in the hills of Eastern Nepal, now sees himself as such a scribe. In the village, barely a handful of schoolchildren can read and write; Yagya's work (handwriting the stories of local people and publishing them on the walls) is now negotiated with the people he interviews. A blacksmith, for example, despite being unlettered himself, was very clear with him as to how he wanted the text of his story presented:

> Not only did he order me to write [it] in bigger letters, he also told me that he would come to check my work.

What is interesting, too, is that the man was in no doubt who the written work belonged to:

> Once the story was up, the man was very proud to see his life story published.[2]

Yagya and any other community scribe could be said to be not unlike a ghostwriter, whose job is to hide their own identity and who writes in the first person of their subjects. They are different because while the former is a role, the latter is a job. (Ghostwriters, like other scribes, surrender their own authorship to that of another. Working, as they usually do, with celebrities however, they tend to be in a different economic relationship with their authors than community literacy scribes with theirs.) In both cases, however, the publicly-named author is the person originating the story. This only gets difficult when two people might want to stake equal claim in its composition – as in the performing arts, where there is money as well as glory at stake. In the history of improvised jazz music for instance, who is to say who wrote what? Bill Evans, the pianist, composed and performed many pieces in the 1950s with the trumpeter Miles Davis. In his view, one of their most famous compositions should have been attributed to himself alone:

> Actually it's my tune, even though Miles is credited as co-writer for reasons only he understands. One day at Miles' apartment, he wrote on some manuscript paper the symbols for G minor and A augmented, and he said, 'What would you do with that?' I didn't really know, but I went home and wrote 'Blue in Green'.[3]

The finished work, in truth, was probably a mix of both men's inspiration; for Bill Evans, it seemed to irk him that he only got half the credit for its composition.

There are, of course, other situations in life when the last thing a scribe might want to do is claim to have been the author of a text. We do not expect to see anybody's name at the bottom of public notices of warning or prohibition. Similarly, when forgery is involved (as Amy Shuman found in her study of adolescent students' forged notes to school authorities), 'the main goal [is] to avoid the charge that "you wrote this yourself"'.[4] When it comes to scribes who are publicly and officially there to support disabled students in their examinations, it becomes vital that the scribe takes on no authorial role whatever. An Australian handbook on the matter sets out a useful set of notes on this. The scribe 'must not reword, restructure, fill out or in any way augment what is dictated'. They must 'gain the confidence of the student quickly, otherwise the pressure of exams can mar the performance of both'. There should be no 'possibility of collusion or perception of collusion' and 'each answer sheet should be headed "Written by Scribe" to ensure that the person marking the paper knows'. Most interestingly, this guide also advocates that the student who uses the scribe should take practice in dictating.[5]

From thought to utterance

Scribing, whether for groups or individuals, is so often a matter of transitions from oral to written. The spoken word itself only ever partly expresses the thought behind it; so that writing must always be selective, freezing what otherwise is a very fluid matter. Many stories in this book have shown the give and take that occurs between author and scribe and between composition and transcription. The ebb and flow between thought and utterance, and utterance and script, is another kind of giving and taking. A last example says something about how it has contributed to this book.

When an individual in a conference or seminar is asked to give a presentation of their 'work-in-progress' to a group, it seems to me always a good idea to have a couple of volunteers to support them: one, to act as their time-keeper (alerting the speaker to their when they have 2 minutes to go), the other to act as their scribe – not to make notes from what they say, but to keep a note of the comments and questions made by others when they have finished their presentation. This gives the speaker the freedom to think and listen and interact with ideas at the time, with the confidence that later, there will be a record of the thinking that the presentation provoked. Without this scribal support, a speaker may leave the session having no memory whatsoever of what it was that people had asked or said. Yet it is from the questions we are asked that we learn what it is we still have to make clear. In my own case, I gained much food for thought from colleagues at a conference where I gave a seminar on scribes and letter writing. These were among the questions and points noted for me by the person in the group who volunteered to be my scribe in the discussion:[6]

- Do we count emails as letters? Or the number of messages sent by young people in one day?
- Is there anything about the effect on the scribe of scribing?
- Coping with illiteracy: scribe in the home has power, loses it once the scribed-for gains confidence – cause of tension.
- Does the content of letters that scribes write shift from period to period?
- Difficult issues at work – letter often written by several people before it is sent out in another's name.
- Some (prison) inmates will turn to different scribes for different kinds of writing. The scribe knows things about the other person.

- Language experience: scribing which enables students to move from basic skills into creative writing.

In the landscape of this book, there are places where those comments and questions certainly influenced the shape or direction of different passages. Though not credited by name, the people in the discussion that day are as much a part of it as any one of those others whose conversations and interviews are more directly quoted in the text.

Scribing at moments like this helps to create the numerous bridges necessary to move from thought to utterance. In that sense, a friend or colleague acting as a scribe is a chronicler: the recorder of a question or an idea until then unuttered. Like Jenny, the literacy student in the last chapter, any one of us may experience a sense of calm when someone performs this service for us: taking down our message, coaxing out our words, turning unuttered thoughts into marks on paper. When it is our turn to do it for someone else, we can recognise it as part of a balance. Scribing provides us with a lens through which to understand the literacy practices of everyday life. It is commonplace. Its use as a tool for literacy education is liberating. Like any other human activity, there can be good or bad experiences of it; but when people take on the roles of scribe and author, in the spirit of trust and creativity, there is truly a sense of mutual benefit. The key to successful scribing lies here and any one of us can learn it. From one day to the next, we may find ourselves being first an author, then a scribe.

1   I scribed this account from a conversation with Monica in a café in June 2000.
2   de Vries, 2001, p7.
3   Cited in Carr, 1999, p151.
4   Shuman, 1997, p248.
5   Edwards, 1999 (this is a website).
6   Taken at 'Travellers Tales' the annual conference of SCUTREA (the Standing Conference for University Teaching and Research in the Education of Adults, July 2001).

Bibliography

Where translators have been named in publications, these have been named after the author. This is not a common bibliographic practice. In a book about scribes, it felt important to do this.

ALBSU/Gallup (1993), *The Cost to British Industry: Basic skills and the workforce*, Adult Literacy and Basic Skills Unit.

Alighieri, D. (1999) *Vita Nova (New Life)* (trans by Musa, M.), Oxford University Press.

Auerbach, A. (1999), 'The Power of Writing, the Writing of Power: Approaches to ESOL writing', *Focus on Basics*, Vol. 3, Issue D, pp1–6.

Bambara, T.C. (1992), 'What is it I Think I'm Doing Anyhow', in: Sternburg, J., *The Writer and Her Work*, Virago, pp64–9.

Barton, D. (1994), *Literacy: An introduction to the ecology of written language*, Routledge.

Barton, D. and Hamilton, M. (1998), *Local Literacies: Reading and writing in one community*, Routledge.

Barton, D. and Ivanic, R. (eds), (1991), *Writing in the Community*, Sage.

Basic Skills Agency (2001), *Adult Literacy Core Curriculum: Including spoken communication*, Basic Skills Agency.

Basnett, S. and Trivedi, H. (1999), *Post-Colonial Translation*, Routledge.

Baynham, M. (1988), 'Literate, Biliterate, Multiliterate? Some issues for literacy research', in: McCaffery, J. and Street, B. (eds), *Literacy Research in the UK: Adult and school perspectives*, Research and Practice in Adult Literacy (RaPAL).

Benet, M.K. (1972), *Secretary: An inquiry into the female ghetto*, Sidgwick and Jackson.

Brice Heath, S. (1983), *Ways with Words*, Cambridge University Press.

Britton, J. (1970), *Language and Learning*, Penguin Books.

Brunvard, J. (1993), *The Baby Train*, WW Norton.

Cameron, D. (1995), *Verbal Hygiene*, Routledge.

Carr, I. (1999), *Miles Davis: The definitive biography*, Harper Collins.

Chamberlain, L. (1992), 'Gender and the Metaphorics of Translation', in: Venuti, L. (ed) *Rethinking Translation – Discourse, subjectivity, ideology*, Routledge: 57–74.

Citron, J. (1989), *The Citizens' Advice Bureaux: For the community, by the community*, Pluto Press.

Clanchy, M. (1979), *From Memory to Written Record: England 1066–1307*, Edward Arnold.

Collins, B. (2000), 'Tuesday, June 4, 1991', in: Collins, B. *Taking off Emily Dickinson's Clothes: Selected poems*, Picador.

Crompton, R. and Jones, G. (1984), *White Collar Proletariat – Deskilling and gender in clerical work*, Macmillan.

Davies, M.W. (1982), *Woman's Place is at the Typewriter: Office work and office workers 1870–1930*, Temple University Press.

de Vries, L. (2001), 'One Does Not Have to Beliterate to Write a Story', in: *Community Literacies: Newsletter of community literacy project Nepal,* August, Issue 4, pp4–8. www.eddev.org/Hosted/clpn.

DfEE (2000), *Skills for Life*, Department for Education and Employment, para 129.

Dickens, C. (1994 edn), *Bleak House*, Wordsworth Editions.

Duffy, C.A. (1999), 'Eurydice' in: *The World's Wife*, Macmillan, pp58–62.

Eco, U. (1983), *The Name of the Rose*, Martin Secker & Warburg, translated from the Italian by William Weaver in 1983.

Edwards, M. (1999), *The Scribing Manual: Guidelines and procedures for using a scribe in written examinations*, University of Western Australia. www.studentservices.uwa.edu.au/disability/scribingmanual/whole_scribing.html.

Elfyn, M. (1994), 'Writing is a Bird in Hand', in: Aaron, J. *et al.*, *Our Sisters' Land: The changing identities of women in Wales*, University of Wales Press.

English, J. and Card, R. (1996), *Butterworth's Police Law* (5th edn), Butterworths.

Ensenzberger, H.M. (1974), *Elementos Para una Teoria de los Medios de Comunicacion*. 2nd edn, Mayo, Cuadernos Anagrama, p25.

Enzensberger, H.M. (1987), 'In praise of the illiterate', *Adult Education and Development*, No. 28, pp96–106.

Enzensberger, H.M. (1997), *Kiosk*, translated by Michael Hamburger and Hans Magnus Enzensberger, Bloodaxe Books.

Fingeret, A. (1983), 'Social Network: A new perspective on independence and illiterate adults', *Adult Education Quarterly*, Vol. 33, No. 3, pp133–46.

Fingeret, H.A. and Drennon, C. (1997), *Literacy for Life: Adult learners, new practices*, Teachers College Press.

Fitzpatrick, S. (1995), 'Sailing Out from Safe Harbours: Writing for publishing in adult basic education', in *Mace (op.cit.)*, p1–22.

Flanagan, S. (1989), *Hildegard of Bingen: A visionary life*, Routledge.

Freire, P. (1972), *Cultural Action for Freedom*, Penguin (no translator mentioned).

Freire, P. (translator) (1974), *Myra Bergman Ramos, Pedagogy of the Oppressed*, Penguin.

Gardener, S. (2001), 'Adult Literacy in the 21st Century: How programmes relate to policies', *Adults Learning*, Vol. 12, No. 10, pp21–6.

Gaur, A. (2000), *Literacy and the Politics of Writing*, Intellect Books.

Gee, J. (1990), *Social Linguistics and Literacies: Ideology in discourses*, Falmer Press.

Gee, J. (2000), 'The New Literacy Studies: From 'socially situated' to the work of the social', in: Barton, D., Hamilton, M. and Ivanic, R., *Situated Literacies: Reading and writing in context*, Routledge, pp180–197.

Giere, U. (1992), *Die Welten der Worter: Plakate zur alphabetisierung* (Worlds of Words: Literacy posters), Hamburg, UNESCO Institute for Education.

Goulds, S. (producer) (1987), *Off the Page: Benjamin Zephaniah – A Channel 4 Learning Video*, produced for Pearson Television International Ltd, London, Channel 4 Productions.

Graff, H. (1979), *The Literacy Myth: Literacy and social structure in the 19th-century city*, Academic Press.

Grant, L. (2000), *When I Lived in Modern Times*, Granta Books.

Gregory, K. (ed) (1976), *The First Cuckoo*, Times Books.

Hall, R. (1984), *Just Relations*, Penguin.

Hattenstone, S. (2001), *The Guardian*, 12 February.

Henley, J. (2001), *The Guardian*, 8 September.

Heath, S.B. (1983), *Ways With Words*, Cambridge University Press.

Hill, S. (ed) (2000), *Jumping over Trees: Poems from the Poetry Library*, The Poetry Library.

Houston, R.A. (1988), *Literacy in Early Modern Europe: Culture and education*, Longman.

Howard, U. (1991), 'Self, Education and Writing in 19th-century English Communities', in: Barton, D. and Ivanic, R. (1991), *Writing in the Community*, Sage Publications, pp78–109.

Indian Express, 1 June 1997a.

Indian Express, 21 December 1997b.

Johnson, S. and Finlay, F. (2001), '(Il)literacy and (Im)morality in Bernhard Schlink's *The Reader*', *Written Language and Literacy*, Vol. 4, No.2, pp195–214.

Jouve, N.W. (1986), '"Her legs bestrid the Channel": Writing in two languages' in: Monteith, M. (ed), *Women's Writing: A challenge to theory*, Harvester Press, pp34–53.

Kalman, J. (1999), *Writing on the Plaza: Mediated literacy practices among scribes and clients in Mexico City*, Hampton Press, Inc.

Knight, S. (1983), 'Does the Scribe THINK?', *The Scribe: Newsletter of the Society of Scribes and Illuminators*, Autumn, No. 29, p9.

Lesirge, R. and Mace J. (1991), 'Read This and Pass It On: Writers, academics and managers', *Adults Learning*, Vol.2, No.8, April 1991, pp236–7.

Lochhead, L. (2000), 'Verse burst', *South Bank Magazine,* 1st issue.

Loewenstein, A. (1983), 'Teaching Writing in Prison', in: Bunch, D. and Pollack, S. (eds), *Learning Our Way: Essays in feminist education*, Crossing Press, pp34–48.

Mace, J. (1979), *Working with Words: Literacy beyond school*, Writers and Readers.

Mace, J. (1980), 'Hello Writers of Collective Prose', *History Workshop Federation Bulletin*, No.1, September 1980, p15.

Mace, J. (1992), *Talking About Literacy: Principles and practice of adult literacy education*, Routledge.

Mace, J. (ed) (1995), *Literacy, Language and Community Publishing: Essays in adult education*, Multilingual Matters.

Mace, J. (1998), *Playing With Time: Mothers and the meaning of literacy*, Taylor and Francis.

Mace, J. and Wolfe, M. (1994), 'That Old Story: Illiterates and fiction', in: Savitsky, F. *et al.*, *Living Literacies*, London Language and Literacy Unit.

Mackay, D., Thompson, B. and Schaub, P. (1981), *Breakthrough to Literacy: Teacher's manual* (2nd edn), Longman Publishing.

Mafani, P. (2000), 'Victims' Understandings of Forgiveness and How They Relate to Reconciliation (South Africa): Cultures of political transition: memory, identity and voice – International Conference', Institute of Commonwealth Studies (unpublished paper).

Marquez, G.M. (1989), *Love in the Time of Cholera*, translated from Spanish by Edith Grossman, Penguin.

Maugham S. (1951), 'The Verger', in: *The Complete Short Stories*, Vol. 2, Heinemann, pp938–44.

Meek, M. (1991), *On Being Literate*, The Bodley Head.

Millard, R. (2000), *The Guardian*, 14 June.

Milne, J. (ed) (1992), *W. Somerset Maugham: The Verger and other stories retold by John Milne*, Heinemann.

Mitchenall, P. (2000), 'I Just Can't Ignore the Print' in: Mace, J. (ed), *Reading and Everyday Life: A collection of experience*, Lewisham Library Service, p8.

Moore, T.G. (1999), *Anthony and Berryman's Magistrates' Court Guides 1999*, Butterworths.

Moser, C. (1999), *A Fresh Start: Improving literacy and numeracy, The report of the working group chaired by Sir Claus Moser*, Department for Education and Employment.

Moss, W. (1995), 'Controlling or Empowering? Writing through a scribe in adult basic education', in: Mace, J., *op. cit.*, p145–71.

NACAB (2001), *Social Policy Bulletin*, June 2001, NACAB.

O'Kane, M. (2000), *The Guardian*, 28 November.

Ong, W. (1982), *Orality and Literacy: The technologizing of the word*, Routledge.

Paretsky, S. (1999), *Hard Time: A V.I. Warshawski novel*, Random House.

Peters, L. (1992), 'Why Dorothy Wordsworth is Not as Famous as Her Brother' in: Dawson, J (ed), *op. cit.*, pp19–20.

Politkovskaya, A. (2001), *The Guardian*, 12 February.

Pringle, R. (1989), *Secretaries Talk: Sexuality, power and work*, Verso.

Radford, M. (Director) (1994), *Il Postino*, Miramax Film (Touchstone Home Video).

Ramdas, L. (1990), 'Women and Literacy: A quest for justice', *Convergence*, Vol. XXIII, No.1, pp37–8.

Redfern, K. (1994), *Before the Meeting: A handbook for clerks*, Quaker Home Service.

Religious Society of Friends (Quakers) Committee on Truth and Integrity in Public Affairs (1988), *Decisions, Decisions – A Quaker view on the process*, Religious Society of Friends in Britain, p6.

Religious Society of Friends (1995), *Quaker Faith and Practice: The book of Christian discipline of the yearly meeting of the Religious Society of Friends (Quakers) in Britain*, Religious Society of Friends in Britain.

Rendell, R. (1978), *Judgement in Stone*, Arrow Edition.

Ritt, M. (Director) (1989), *Stanley and Iris*, MGM.

Rock, F. (2000), *Silent Witness? The Relationship Between the Process of Witness Statement-Taking and the Product*, University of Birmingham (unpublished).

Rostand, E. (1st published 1898, this edition 1981), *Cyrano de Bergerac*, translated into English verse by Brian Hooker, Bantam Books.

Saldarini, A.J. (1988), *Pharisees, Scribes and Sadducees in Palestinian Society*, T & T Clark.

Salles, W. (1998), *Central do Brasil (Central Station)*, Sony Pictures Classics.

Sassoon, R. (1995), 'Handwriting: The forgotten facet of literacy', *Basic Skills*, Spring (pp14–18) and Summer (pp10–12).

Saunders, B. (2000), *The Guardian*, 18 September.

Schepisi, F. (Director) (1987), *Roxanne*.

Schlink, B. (1998), *The Reader*, translated by Carol Brown Janeway, Phoenix.

Schwab, I. and Stone, J. (1985), *Language, Writing and Publishing: Work with Afro-Caribbean students*, Hackney Reading Centre, City & East London College.

Scragg, D. (1974), *A History of English Spelling*, Manchester University Press.

Sharman, C. (1983), *Servant of the Meeting: Quaker business meetings and their clerks,* Quaker Home Service.

Shaw, G. (1957 ed, first pub 1916), *Pygmalion: A romance in five acts*, Penguin.

Shuman, A. (1993), 'Collaborative Writing: Appropriating power or reproducing authority?', in: Street, *op. cit.*, pp247–72.

Skage, S. (1994), *Literacy Scribe Service Manual Red Deer College*, Alberta, Canada, p1.

Skinner, J. (1998), *The Book of Margery Kempe: A new translation*, Image Books.

Smith, F. (1982), *Writing and the Writer*, Heinemann.

Spiegel, M. and Sunderland, H. (1999), *Writing Works: Using a genre approach for teaching writing to adults and young people in ESOL and basic education classes*, London Language and Literacy Unit (LLLU@sbu.ac.uk).

Street, B. (1984), *Literacy in Theory and Practice*, Cambridge University Press.

Street, B. (1991), 'Putting Literacies on the Political Agenda, Open Letter' *Australian Journal for Adult Literacy Research and Practice*, Vol.1, No.1, pp5–16.

Street, B. (ed) (1993), *Cross-Cultural Approaches to Literacy*, Cambridge University Press.

Sutherland, J. (1999), *The Guardian*, 6 December 1999.

Tomlinson, K. (1992) 'More Ripples in the European Pool' in *RaPAL Bulletin*, No. 19, pp8–10.

Toynbee, P. (2001), *The Guardian*, 19 January.

Tutu, D. (1999), *No Future Without Forgiveness*, Rider.

Viau, J. (1959), 'Eyptian Mythology', in: Graves, R Larousse, *Encyclopedia of Mythology*, Paul Hamlyn, pp8–49.

Vincent, D. (1993), *Literacy and Popular Culture: England 1750–1914*, Polity Press.

Vincent, D. (2000), *The Rise of Mass Literacy: Reading and writing in modern Europe*, Polity Press.

Wandor, M. (1986), 'Voices Are Wild', in: Monteith, M. (ed), *Women's Writing: A challenge to theory*, Harvester Press, pp72–89.

West, M. (1996: first pub. 1959), *Goodness Had Nothing to do With it: The autobiography of Mae West*, Virago, pp142–3.

Wilson, A. (2000), 'There's No Escape from Third-Space Theory: Borderland discourse and the "in-between" literacies of prisons', in: Barton, D., Hamilton, M. and Ivanic, R., *Situated Literacies: Reading and writing in context*, Routledge, pp54–70.

Windeatt, B.A. (1985), *The Book of Margery Kempe*, Penguin.

Wolfe, M. (1996), Reading Gender: An exploration of illiteracy and gender in Ritt's Stanley and Iris, (unpublished paper).

Works Progress Administration (WPA) (1998), American Slave Narratives: An online anthology, http://xroads.virginia.edu/~hyper/wpa/wpahome.html (visited: 22 February 2001).

Zephaniah, B. (1992), *City Psalms*, Bloodaxe.

Zimmeck, M. (1995), 'The Mysteries of the Typewriter: Technology and gender in the British Civil Service, 1870–1914', in: de Groot, G. and Schrover, M. (eds), *Women Workers and Technological Change in Europe in the Nineteenth and Twentieth Centuries*, Taylor and Francis.

Index